VOICES OF THE DEAD.

BY THE

REV. JOHN CUMMING, D.D.,

MINISTER OF THE SCOTTISH NATIONAL CHURCH, CROWN COURT, COVENT GARDEN;
AUTHOR OF "VOICES OF THE NIGHT," "VOICES OF THE DAY,"
"SCRIPTURE READINGS," ETC. ETC.

BOSTON:
PUBLISHED BY JOHN P. JEWETT & COMPANY.
CLEVELAND, OHIO:
JEWETT, PROCTOR & WORTHINGTON.
1854.

PREFACE.

This volume consists mainly of Voices from ancient days, and from the lives of faithful and sainted men—especially those recorded in the eleventh chapter of the Epistle to the Hebrews. They overcame through faith, and entered into their rest. The records of their biographies remain for our study and profit. Their acts, and sufferings, and words of consolation, are still reverberating in the church of Christ.

It is written of a celebrated French regiment, that they so loved their commanding officer while at their head, and so venerated his memory after he had fallen in battle, that they required his name to be retained on the regimental roll, and called with the names of the living every day;—on the name of the dead warrior being called, a living soldier answered for him, "Dead upon the field." The eleventh chapter of the Epistle to the Hebrews is the roll-call of the illustrious and the sainted dead, and each of their names, as it is enunciated, should stir our hearts as a trumpet sound.

I wish I could have dwelt on every heroic martyr and patient saint whose name is inscribed in this holy calendar. But, perhaps, by the blessing of God, the few I have considered may

. . . . "remind us
We can make our lives sublime,
And, departing, leave behind us
Footprints on the sands of time."

The study of such records is the real communion of saints. The sacred page is the only pure picture gallery—apostolic portraits are alone admissible into our churches.

CONTENTS.

CHAPTER I.

CHAPTER II.

CHAPTER III.

CHAPTER IV.

CHAPTER V.

CHAPTER VI.

CHAPTER VII.

CHAPTER VIII.

CHAPTER IX.

CHAPTER X.

CHAPTER XI.

CHAPTER XII.

CHAPTER XIII.

CHAPTER XIV.

CHAPTER XV.

CHAPTER XVI.

CHAPTER XVII.

CHAPTER I.

THE SPEAKING DEAD.

"Thus though oft depressed and lonely,
All my fears are laid aside,
If I but remember only
Such as these have lived and died."

"Abel being dead yet speaketh."—Hebrews 11: 4.

Abel "being dead yet speaketh;" that is, Abel, removed in his bodily presence, yet through several channels, or in some family or society, speaks and acts, and influences those who now live. The common and the popular notion is, that death is the end of man as far as this world is concerned; that the grave which conceals the bulk of man's form covers and keeps within its chambers all man's influence; and that the instant he has ceased to breathe on earth, he has ceased to act. It is not so; this is a popular mistake.

It is true of Cain, and of Abel, and of every man, that being dead they yet speak. We die, but leave an influence behind us that survives; the echoes of our words are evermore repeated, and reflected along the ages. A man has two immortalities. One immortality he leaves behind him, and it walks the earth and still represents him. Another immortality he carries with him to a loftier sphere, the presence and the glory of God.

If this be so, it may be asked, what are the media through which man thus acts upon those that come after him? It is not by the epitaph written upon his tombstone by weeping affection, frequently the least true expression of his character. Nor is it by the newspaper paragraph, which has been put in as it has been penned by relatives, and is, therefore, not a severe and faithful rescript of what he was. It is what man was that lives and acts after him. What he said sounds along the years like voices amid the mountain gorges; and what he did is repeated after him in ever-multiplying and never-ceasing reverberations. It is true of every man that he "being dead yet speaketh;" assuredly he has left behind him influences for good or for evil that will never exhaust themselves. The sphere in which he acts may be small, or it may be great. That is not the real question. It may be his fireside, or it may be a kingdom; a village, or a great nation; it may be a parish, or broad Europe; a race, or all mankind: but act he does, ceaselessly and forever. Whether the sphere he fills with posthumous influence be narrow or large, it continues. His friends, his family, his successors in office, his relatives, are all receptive of an influence, a moral influence, which he has transmitted and bequeathed to mankind; either a blessing which will repeat itself in showers of benedictions, or a curse which will multiply itself in crashes of ever-accumulating evils. Let us feel most deeply this great fact, that we can neither live nor die neutral.

There are two great defects in the practical conception of this truth among mankind. One thinks, I am so insignificant that it does not matter what I do; and another thinks, I am so important that the whole world is beholding me. Both of these make equally great mistakes; every man should feel that, however small, or however great, neutral, uninfluential upon mankind, it is impossible that he can be. Every man is a missionary, now and forever, for good or for evil, whether he intends and designs it or not. He may be a blot radiating his dark influence outward to the very circumference of society, or he may be a blessing spreading benedictions over the length and the breadth of the world; but a blank he cannot be. There are no moral blanks, there are no neutral characters; we are either the leaven that sours and corrupts, or the light that splendidly illuminates, and the salt that silently operates; but being dead, as being alive, every man speaks.

> "Tongues of the dead not lost,
> But speaking still from death's frost,
> Like fiery tongues at Pentecost."

If this be true, let the candidate and aspirant for posthumous influence ponder this very solemn fact. We know how fondly authors and poets long to be remembered after they are gone. *Non omnis peream.* Posthumous reputation is the thirst of thousands. Yet, after all, a passion perhaps in itself, and without reference to ulterior things, more worthless, it is scarcely possible to conceive. The utterance of our names, after we are dead, will not probably be heard by us; and to desire posthumous renown for its own sake is therefore just as if one should desire that loaves of bread should be laid upon his tombstone, while he sleeps quietly and insensibly below. But while posthumous fame in itself is thus worthless as an aspiration, yet let him who seeks it take care to remember that he is craving posthumous power, and that wherever there is posthumous renown — that is, reputation after death — there there is, for good or evil, a posthumous and an enduring influence. The seed sown in life will then spring up in harvests of blessing, or harvests of sorrow. A holy heart alone should desire to be remembered in the world after death. Not merely great men, but good men alone should pray that they may be recollected by the generations that succeed them. To wish to be remembered as great, but to be forgotten as good, is a desire unworthy of a Christian. To pant to be remembered only as evil, is a thirst peculiar to demons. To desire that we may be remembered as good after we are gone, is an aspiration worthy of saints and martyrs; a desire that holy hearts and enlightened minds will delight to cherish and seek after. Cain spoke after he was dead, as well as Abel. The words of wrath that he uttered, the stroke of fratricide he dealt, the character and the remorse that he exhibited, all still live in the sacred page, and are remembered and made use of, and exert an influence on successive generations of mankind.

It may be that the saved in glory feel it an accession to their joy, that something that they were when alive upon earth is distributing beneficent influence behind them. And it may be that the lost in misery feel their agony aggravated a thousand-fold, because they learn that something they did is dealing destruction upon thousands of families they never saw, and yet ever corrupt. Thus, whether our influence be great or small, whether it be good or evil, it lasts, it lives somewhere, within some limits, and is operative wherever it is. Death, instead of annihilating that influence, only makes it more obvious. Death clears up the lineaments of the moral character of man. It takes the body, but it leaves behind the real likeness of the real because inner man. The grave buries the dead dust, but the character walks the world, and distributes itself, as a benediction or a curse, among the families of mankind.

Now, to a Christian, this must be a most consolatory thing, that what he was below still endures and acts. It must be a very joyful thought to a saint in heaven, that whilst he is busy chanting God's praise in glory, he is not less busy doing God's work upon the earth; that neither in the earth he has left behind him, nor in the heaven he now occupies, is he one moment idle. In the former he is a missionary still; in the latter, he is a saint rejoicing ever. The sun sets beyond the western hills, but the trail of light he leaves behind him guides the pilgrim to his distant home. The tree falls in the forest; but in the lapse of ages it is turned into coal, and our fires burn now the brighter because it grew and fell. The coral insect dies, but the reef it raised breaks the surge on the shores of great continents, or has formed an isle in the bosom of the ocean, to wave now with harvests for the good of man, and to be a gem hereafter for the diadem of the great Redeemer. We live and we die; but the good or evil that we do lives after us, and is not "buried with our bones."

This great fact of the speaking dead is a solemn, a grave responsibility, yet at the same time a very refreshing and joyous thought. It assures us that those who have preceded us to glory have left us visibly, but not really; that those who once mingled with us, being dead, yet speak to us. The babe which perished in the bosom of its mother, like a flower that bowed its head and drooped amid the death-frosts of time, has left behind it the lesson, "The wages of sin is death:" for, though it had not sinned after Adam, yet it was a participant in the effects of Adam's fall; and, being dead, that babe, not only in its image, but in its influence, still lives and speaks in the chambers of the mother's heart, and in the sanctuary of God's people. The friend with whom we took sweet counsel, and in whose company we walked to the house of God, is removed visibly from the outward eye; but the lessons that he taught, the grand sentiments that he uttered, the holy deeds of generosity by which he was characterized, the moral lineaments and likeness of the man, still survive, and appear in the silence of eventide, and on the tablets of memory, and in the light of morn, and noon, and dewy eve; and, being dead, he yet speaks eloquently, and in the midst of us. In the words of a beautiful poet, whom I have before quoted:

" When the hours of day are numbered,
And the voices of the night
Wake the better soul that slumbered,
To a holy, calm delight ;

" Ere the evening lamps are lighted,
And, like phantoms grim and tall,
Shadows from the fitful fire-light
Dance upon the parlor wall ;

" Then the forms of the departed
Enter at the open door ;
The beloved, the true-hearted,
Come to visit me once more ;

" He, the young and strong, who cherished
Noble longings for the strife,
By the road-side fell and perished,
Weary with the march of life !

" They, the holy ones and weakly,
Who the cross of suffering bore,
Folded their pale hands so meekly,
Speak with us on earth no more !

" And with them the Being beauteous,
Who unto my youth was given,
More than all things else to love me,
And is now a saint in heaven.

" With a slow and noiseless footstep
Comes that messenger divine,
Takes the vacant chair beside me,
Lays her gentle hand in mine.

" And she sits and gazes at me
With those deep and tender eyes,
Like the stars so still and saint-like,
Looking downward from the skies.

" Uttered not, yet comprehended,
Is the spirit's voiceless prayer ;
Soft rebukes, in blessings ended,
Breathing from her lips of air.

"O, though oft depressed and lonely,
All my fears are laid aside,
If I but remember only
Such as these have lived and died!"

Mahomet still lives in his practical and disastrous influence in the East. Napoleon still is France, and France is still almost Napoleon. Martin Luther's dead dust sleeps at Wittenberg, but Martin Luther's accents still ring through the churches of Christendom. Shakspeare, Byron and Milton. all live in their influence, for good or for evil. The apostle from his chair, the minister from his pulpit, the martyr from his flame-shroud, the statesman from his cabinet, the soldier in the field, the sailor on the deck, who all have passed away to their graves, still live in the practical deeds that they did, in the lives they lived, and in the powerful lessons that they left behind them. In fact, the earth is a vast whispering gallery, and the centuries are but telegraphic wires which convey the thoughts of one age to another. The nineteenth century sits at one end of the electric telegraph, and the first century at the other, and the former hears transmitted to it lessons from the latter that mould and shape it for heaven, for happiness, or woe. A very able writer makes the remark, which I think is perfectly true, that nothing that is said is ever extinguished, that nothing that is done ever ceases its influence. It goes out from us, and is never arrested or put an end to. Every schoolboy knows that matter is infinitely divisible; that is, if I divide a thing in half, those halves can still be divided into other halves, and each of these again into other halves, and each of these into other halves, — one-half divided into one-fourth, and one-fourth into one-eighth, and one-eighth into one-sixteenth, and one-sixteenth into one-thirty-second, &c. &c.; and thus we may go on dividing infinitely, since what remains after the last division never can be so small that we cannot conceive it divisible still. What is true of visible nature is no less true of the audible voice. The sound we utter, and the deed we do, are equally infinitely divisible, and neither cease. In the language of Professor Babbage, who has written most ably on this subject, "The air is one vast library, on whose pages are forever written all that man has ever said, or woman whispered." In other words, when I utter a word, its echo goes round and round the world, growing less *ad infinitum*, and will do so ceaselessly till the structure and constitution of the world has been altered and disorganized for ever and ever. The pebble that I drop into the sea will send out its undulations for ever and ever. The blow that I strike upon the earth will transmit its vibrations for ever and ever. The act I thought no eye followed, that deed which I fancied was done and annihilated forever, is each still sounding in successive vibrations and repetitions in the atmosphere, and throughout the earth; and at the judgment-seat God has but to make man's ear more sensitive, and his eye more susceptible, and all he said and did will come back to him, the good in sweet music, the evil in crashes and reverberations of woe and agony, that shall never, never cease. It is, surely, a very solemn fact, that everything we do never terminates. It is quite true, it terminates to us with our present organization at a certain point, because we can only hear a sound up to that point at which it becomes too faint for us to hear it; but it has not ceased, and may not be too faint for others to hear it; and, if our senses were more acute, we should be able to trace it still. But science can demonstrate with absolute precision that a blow once struck carries on its vibrations to the end; that a word once said is repeating itself in the air till the judgment-day; and Scripture leads us to infer that it will at that day meet us again, a memorial of the good or the evil we have done.

A similar law occurs in light. Everybody knows that, before I can see an object, a ray of light must leave that object and fall upon my eye, and that the ray of light is simply a missionary from the object revealing it clearly to me. We well know that light travels two hundred thousand miles in a second. But, great as this velocity is, it is evident that light takes time to travel. In other words, the missionary beam from the distant star takes time to reach my eye. A ray of light takes four minutes in reaching me from the sun, so that we cannot see the sun till four minutes after he is actually above the horizon. And, if this be true, it is no less so of light reflected from this world to distant orbs. In other words, a ray of light must leave this world and reach the distant orbs before they can see the object from which it came. Now some stars are so distant that the rays of light from them take a thousand, four thousand, or even six thousand years in reaching us; and there is no doubt that there are some stars so distant that, though light travels two hundred thousand miles in a second, still the rays from them have not yet reached our world. Thus, light taking time to travel, we can conceive that the ray of light reflected from Adam and Eve in the midst of Paradise is now travelling upward into the infinite space of the universe, and that the inhabitants of some distant orb are at this moment, if their senses be acute enough, as we can conceive them to be, beholding Adam and Eve in the midst of Paradise. In a star, again, of the twelfth magnitude, which we can see with our telescopes, the inhabitants, if their senses be acute enough, may now see the cross erected on Calvary, and Jesus uttering the words, "It is finished." And, in nearer stars, the inhabitants may see Martin Luther at this moment burning the Pope's bull in Germany. If, then, we can conceive the senses of the inhabitants of distant worlds to be sufficiently acute, all that has transpired on earth from the beginning is seen by them, as the rays reflected from them travel upward and onward to their distant abodes. And if we can conceive that a glorified being has the power to travel from star to star, we may imagine that he might go to one star and see Martin Luther just revealed, then to another and see Abraham, to another and see Paradise. Thus, the universe becomes a vast picture-gallery, successively showing its scenes to successive orbs; and what is done is thus never annihilated, but ever revealed to more and more distant lands, travelling through the universe, and representing itself to the minds that fill the orbs which God has created.

What a tremendous interest does this give to every act that we do! What a solemn thought, that everything now transacted upon earth is passing from the earth, and is visible to others; and that, when we are dead and gone, it will be still transmitted from orb to orb, till the whole universe knows what I was and what I did!

The same writer introduces another very striking thought illustrative of the same idea, derived from electricity. He says, what indeed is very likely, that there is never a thought in the mind, nor an action in the body, that does not throw out currents of electricity. Nothing, therefore, seems more probable than that one man may yet know what another man's thoughts are. There is to me nothing more improbable in this than that one person at Dover and another in London should be able to converse together by means of electricity, or that houses and trees should be their own pictorial painters. Moreover, it is not at all impossible that our thoughts may be transmitted through electric currents by the medium of the nervous system, and record themselves to distant tenantry as our real and inmost thoughts, and thus all the universe may know not only what man is and what he is doing, but also what he thinks. The darkness hideth not from God; the night is as light about us. What we do is transacted on a stage of which all in the universe are spectators. What we say is transmitted in echoes that will never cease. What we are is influencing and acting on the rest of mankind. Neutral we cannot be. Living we act, and dead we speak; and the whole universe is the mighty company forever looking, forever listening, and all nature the tablets forever recording the words, the deeds, the thoughts, the passions, of mankind.

Still, I admit that the main practical truth contained in the assertion of St. Paul is, that the influence we exert is conveyed to others that succeed us, that what we are will shape the character of those we leave behind. We cannot refuse to transmit an influence; this is not left in our power; but we may determine whether that influence shall be beneficial or the reverse. It is a thought worth remembering, "None of us liveth to himself;" others are affected by that life; "or dieth to himself;" others are interested in that death. Hearts will bleed, or hearts will bound, fifty years after this, from something we now say, or do, or are. What we now are is preparing victims for woe, or, through the grace of God, heirs for glory. What we now are and say and do is either communicating demon joy to the fiends, or angelic ecstasy to angels that are about the throne. Our queen's crown may moulder, but she who wore it will act upon the ages which are yet to come. That noble's coronet may be reft in pieces, but the wearer of it is now doing what will be reflected by thousands who will be made and moulded by him. Dignity, and rank, and riches, are all corruptible and worthless; but moral character has an immortality that no sword-point can destroy, that ever walks the world and leaves lasting influences behind.

Some men not only speak to audiences of thousands, but have the power of writing, and conveying their sentiments to tens of thousands. And if it be true that from what we live, and speak, and are, succeeding generations will be influenced, it is still more applicable to those who avail themselves of the power which printing gives them; for they influence not only cotemporaneous generations, but the remotest living generations still to follow. However limited may be the influence of any book that I may write, — and it must be very limited, — I speak by it to many who have never seen me; for my sentiments thus reach India, Australia, and the continent. In fact, I have two congregations, however small, — one within walls, and another outside; and this very pleasant thought also, that the loaf of bread that feeds seventeen hundred within may feed seventeen thousand outside. I have two pulpits; one is in the sanctuary, and the other is the publisher who commits my writing to the press; and from both my pulpits I speak; and when the pulpit I speak from shall be occupied by a stranger, and I shall be a stranger to it, the other will still remain; its influence I cannot recall, its lessons I cannot hush. Thus, if it be important to watch what men speak, it is infinitely more important to weigh well what men print. And to be able to say there is not one line that dying one would wish to blot, — what a blessed retrospect! what a glad, refreshing, and desirable occurrence!

What is true of printing is true of every other art. For instance, the paintings which are the masterpieces of the artist hung up in our galleries are at this moment either encouraging the licentious inclinations of the heart, or are ministering in their place to whatsoever things are just and honest and of good report. The statues that are cut out by the chisel from the cold marble are either suggestive to succeeding generations of what is pure, or of what is unholy and bad. Monuments and columns and statues, erected to heroes, poets, orators, statesmen, are all influences that extend into the future ages. "The blind old man of Scio's rocky isle" still speaks. The Mantuan bard still sings in every school. Shakspeare, the bard of Avon, is still translated into every tongue. The philosophy of the Stagyrite is still felt in every academy. Whether these influences are beneficent or the reverse, I do not now pronounce; but that they are influences fraught with power, is what every one must, without qualification, admit. How blest must be the recollection to a Howe, a John Bunyan, a Baxter, a Butler, and many others who might be named, that, though now they surround the throne, and are worshipping within the vail, like setting suns they have left a trail of light and glory behind them, by which others can see a way to the rest that remaineth to the people of God! How refreshing to them to feel that, though their lips are sealed in death, the echoes they have left behind them still break forth in sweet music on cottage thresholds, and are the joy and the gladness of many a country congregation!

Knowing well that what we do, or say, or print, or paint, or build, will act permanently behind us, how fervent should be our prayer that we may be so sustained by the Holy Spirit of God that the least influence we leave after us may be a missionary of great beneficence, a teacher of souls, a motive to live holy, and a help to die happy!

Now, the first prescription I would give the reader, in closing my remarks upon this part of my subject, is, Be Christian, and your influence will be so; be good, and you will do good. It is not what men try to play that will influence the ages, but what men actually are. It is not what a man does or says that tells most after him, but it is what a man is. We forget the rash word, we can forgive the incidental and hurried and sinful act, because we see behind both a character whose tone and temperament is moulded and inspired by the principles of the Gospel of Jesus. It was not what Jesus said and did that struck mankind, so much as what Jesus was. "Never man spake like this man," just because never man lived like this man. The unconscious influence of a Christian man is the power that shapes society most rapidly, and tells most powerfully, and leaves behind it the most enduring, beneficent impressions.

And, in order to be Christian, study, first, God's holy word. The great original is there, of which we are designed to be copies. The motives, the hopes are there, which we are to study, and seek to be inspired with. Looking into that perfect law of liberty, we are informed as by the Spirit of the Lord.

And the next, and perhaps the most important prescription is, Seek to have your hearts inspired by the Spirit of God. It is only the pure fountain that brings forth pure water. You may arrange your outward actions as beautifully as you like, you may adjust your attire as you please, but all these will be faults and failures, and on the whole will have little influence. Whereas, if the heart be right, we need not think of any external adjustment to catch man's eye. The good tree will produce the good fruit; the pure fountain will bring forth pure streams. If the centre from which all proceeds is holy, the radii of influence that start from it will be holy also. Therefore, pray that the Holy Spirit will give you a new heart, and, having that new heart, go forth into the spheres that you occupy, — the employments, the trades, the professions of social life; go forth into the high places or into the lowly places of the land; mix with the roaring cataracts of social convulsion, or mingle amid the eddies and streamlets of quiet and of domestic life; for, whatever sphere you fill, you will carry into it a holy heart; and, having regenerated hearts, — that is, being Christians, — you will radiate around you life and power, that will reflect themselves upon you again in happiness, and you will leave behind you a holy and a beneficent influence, that will meet you again at the judgment-seat of Christ, concentrated in these beautiful and musical accents, "Come, ye blessed of my Father, inherit the kingdom prepared for you from the foundation of the world."

CHAPTER II.

VOICES FROM GLORY.

From the eternal shadow rounding
  All our sun and starlight here,
Voices of our lost ones sounding
  Bid us be of heart and cheer,
Through the silence, down the space, falling on the inward ear.

Know we not our dead are looking
  Downward with a sad surprise,
All our strifes of words rebuking
  With their mild and loving eyes ?
Shall we grieve these holy angels, shall we cloud these blessed skies ?

Let us draw their mantles o'er us,
  Which have fallen in our way ;
Let us do the work before us,
  Cheerly, bravely, while we may,
Ere the long night-silence cometh, and with us it is not day.

" Abel being dead yet speaketh." — HEBREWS 11 : 4.

IN the former chapter, I have spoken of the fact that every man leaves behind him, to be transmitted to successive generations, influence either for good or for evil; that the common notion, that when our bodies are buried the good and the evil die with us, is not correct; but, on the contrary, that the moral lineaments of man are only cleared up, not obscured, by the touch of death, and that whilst one immortality has passed into the skies, another immortality walks the world, and executes its mission of blessing or of bane to those who are left behind. I showed that it is not in our choice to determine whether we shall leave an influence or not, but that it does rest with us to determine whether that influence shall be a blessing or shall be a curse. I endeavored to demonstrate that not a life has been spent, not a work has been written, not a sculpture has been chiselled, not a painting has been finished, that has not left behind an enduring influence, and become creative of good or pernicious impressions. I showed that whoever speaks, or whoever uses that extraordinary — but, because common, it has ceased to be extraordinary — power, the press, in making his sentiments known, touches a lever the sweep of which no arithmetic of ours can calculate. I preach a sermon. It is heard by some fifteen, sixteen, or seventeen hundred people. If I print it, it may, peradventure, be read by fifteen, sixteen, or seventeen thousand people. The loaf that I break among my people feeds not merely a thousand; but, by the touch of printers, may be distributed among and feed twenty or thirty thousand. And thus there is an influence going out from every one who speaks or writes, more or less extensive; and that influence, in virtue of the press, survives the speaker. Whilst the glorified soul is praising God beside the throne, he is still living, acting, speaking, as a missionary upon the earth below; neither idle in the midst of his joys, nor inactive in the world he has left behind; but being dead he yet speaks. We endeavored to show that recent discoveries of science, which we have brought to illustrate the successive chapters of Genesis, all confirm the same position. It is surely one of the most solemn facts, that a word once spoken — not only every bad word, but every idle word — never can be extinguished. I showed there was a law called the law of infinite division of matter. If I divide anything in half, I can divide that half, and I have a fourth; that fourth, and I have an eighth; that eighth, and I have a sixteenth; that sixteenth, and I have a thirty-second; in short, I cannot conceive any matter to become so small, by division, that it can be incapable of yet further division. If I utter a sound, that sound agitates the air, and it will go on agitating the air round and round the globe, till the day of judgment. It will not cease to act by the law of dynamics, by the law of acoustics, by the law of division of matter. Now, what a solemn thought should this be, that the words which were spoken to-day may be reheard by us at the judgment-seat of Christ! that the expressions we have used to-day may rise at that moment, either in the symphonies of the sweetest music, or in the crashes and reverberations of a righteous and terrible retribution! I showed, too, that what we do is no less lasting than what we say. I explained to you that, in order to see an object, a ray of light must come from that object, and touch my eye. We know that light travels at the rate of two hundred thousand miles a second, and that it takes four minutes in reaching us from the sun. I showed you that, in order that an object may be seen, a ray of light must go from it to the distant beholder. Now, the telescope brings stars within our view from which light has been travelling, I believe, six thousand years. And, if light comes from other orbs to us, and rays proceed from us to them, it may be that a ray of light may have started from the face of Adam when he was in paradise, and it will be now touching some distant orb, and may present to them a picture of our earth as it was then; so that this world will present to different orbs different scenes in its history, if their senses be sufficiently acute. Thus, they are seeing in one Martin Luther burning the Pope's bull; and in another they are regarding the Crusades, and Peter the Hermit, and Walter the Penniless. And so the whole universe may become translators of the events consummated in this world; and the things done upon the bosom of the earth will never cease being seen, but spread and extend through the realms of infinitude, to be witnessed by world after world, till the magnificent idea comes to be realized by us, that we are surrounded not only by clouds of witnesses upon earth, but by groups of witnessing worlds, regarding what is done, and pronouncing, it may be, verdicts upon what we are. If it be so, surely it strengthens the idea that we endeavored to illustrate, — that being dead we yet speak; that an influence proceeds from every man that never ceases. After this *résumé*, suggested by the interest of the subject, we will record some of the specific lessons that Abel, and others of the sainted dead, being dead yet speak.

The first truth that Abel speaks to us is, that "sin entered into the world, and death by sin." Abel being dead tells us that sin was seen in Cain, and its fruit, death, was illustrated in himself. In the case of both, there was evidence of their relationship lost to God, and, therefore, of their relationship disturbed to each other. I doubt not, when the weeping parents saw death for the first time, — and it was the first time it ever occurred since Adam and Eve were created, — that they started in perfect horror from the ghastly spectacle; and that whilst Adam, as a parent, wept, as a sinner he felt bitter remorse, while he recalled to memory his first sin, and saw it rebound in Abel. "That dead body is because I sinned. The fathers have eaten sour grapes; and the children's teeth are set on edge. We fell, and we have dragged all humanity with us. Sin entered, and death by sin. All have sinned, and all, therefore, are sufferers."

Another lesson that Abel being dead yet speaks to us, is a more consolatory one. He says, "The wages of sin is death;" but he adds also, "The gift of God is eternal life, through Jesus Christ." If Cain's death had happened first, what an awful spectacle of the full effects of the curse it would have been! — exhibiting death temporal, death spiritual, death eternal, as the very first fruits of Adam's sin.

But we see mercy mingling with judgment, in the fact that the first who died was the sainted and the pious Abel. He was a sinner, for he died; but he was a believer, for he triumphed over death. In one respect he was death's victim; but in another he was redemption's trophy. Abel being dead cries from the grave where his ashes are, or, rather, speaks from the choirs of seraphim and cherubim, which his soul has entered, "Mercy and truth are met together, righteousness and peace have kissed each other" in my death. A martyr's death was an unexpected dismissal, but also unexpected and lasting glory.

Abel being dead tells us now that "without shedding of blood there is no remission of sins." If Abel's voice were now audible, he would say what now being dead he silently says, "Cain made the experiment of bringing a beauteous offering selected from the loveliest spots of the blighted earth, and he laid it upon the altar, and presented it to God as an offering expressive of his obedience and his adoration; but the flowers withered as they touched the altar, and the offerer and the offering were blasted and sent away together. But I," says Abel, "taught by grace, offered to God the firstling of my flock. I shed the blood of the inoffensive lamb. I did so, not because I believed that that lamb's blood could expiate my sins, but because in that lamb's blood I saw the foreshadow and the pledge and the type of the blood of the Lamb slain from the foundation of the world; and through him and in him I have made the experiment, and I have found," says Abel, "forgiveness of sin." And what Abel detected in the shadow we now see clearly in the substance; for we know in whom we have believed. Jesus died, not a martyr, but an atonement; not an example of patient suffering, but an expiatory and atoning victim; and through that blood alone, shed once for all for the remission of sins, Abel cries from his starry throne, There is now justification, and pardon and acceptance before God for the chiefest of sinners. Abel speaks, being dead, "For our light affliction, which is but for a moment, worketh for us a far more exceeding and eternal weight of glory." He says, "I traversed the rough and the flinty road, but it ended in a glorious close. I passed through a dark and a mysterious porch, but it was the vestibule of a majestic and a glorious temple. Mine, indeed, was a martyr's death; but it is forgotten in the weight of glory that is now around my brow. I have found that the cross leads to the crown. Afflictions come from the same fountain as the morning dews, and are equally saturating and refreshing, too. Your worst trials are but the April showers that precede the bright summer. Your afflictions, light even when heaviest, work out for you an exceeding, even an eternal weight of glory. Be patient, therefore," says the voice of him being dead. "Those clouds will either break in benedictions, or they will be scattered. Those billows will soon be laid; and the rainbow will span the one, and be reflected from the other; and you will say each from the heights of heaven, as I now say, It was good for me that I have been afflicted."

But, while noticing these as the special voices of Abel, every departing Christian leaving a specific influence behind him speaks also being dead to those who are still in the flesh. And what lessons do the sainted dead now teach? "What God does you know not now, but you shall know hereafter." Some departed one whom you knew, and took sweet counsel with upon earth, if he could now be audible, or could become vocal in the midst of us, would say, "Once I was perplexed; once I could not understand how that bad man prospered, and that good man suffered. Once I could not divine how all seemed to go against me, and nothing seemed to prosper in my hands. My feet stumbled; I was almost overwhelmed; I was tempted to believe that God had forsaken the world. But now, if I have grief at all, it is because I should ever have sinfully thought so. The whole past is now luminous. I see there was a reason for every trial; I now know that there was a 'needs be' in every pang. I am satisfied a mission of benevolence was in all that befell me, and that all things, from the least to the loftiest, the pleasant and the painful, have worked together for good to me; and therefore, I implore you, let not your hearts be troubled; all events are working for good to you also."

Another voice from heaven would be, "Absent from the body, we are present with the Lord." Some one who reads these pages has lost a father, another a mother, a third a friend. If these lost ones could be heard, they would say, and what they substantially though not audibly teach, "Weep not for us. When your tears fell fastest upon us, our joys were deepest and nearest to our hearts. When I closed my eye upon all bright and beautiful things below, it was only to open it upon brighter and still more beautiful things above. When I could no more see you, — the lost I left behind me,— I found I was introduced into the midst of the lost that had gone before me. I found that I was merely translated from a portion of my family — pilgrims upon earth — to another portion of my household, who had some time preceded me to glory. And therefore weep not for me, but weep for yourselves. I am unspeakably and perfectly happy."

What a blessed truth is this, that the instant a departed Christian has ceased to be interested in the things that are around him, that moment his more glorious sympathies are all settling upon brighter things, even on familiar things that are above him! What a glorious and consolatory thought is this, that the dead body which he has left behind is but the cold and the worn-out house that could no longer serve the purposes of the grand inhabitant within; and that he has now entered on a land of eternal sunshine, and left the body for the grave to do its work upon, in the hope that Christ will still touch and transform it, and make it one day a fit house for so holy an inhabitant, a suitable fane for so grand and sublime a worshipper! Thus, every believer in glory speaks being dead, "Absent from the body, I am present with the Lord. I passed through no purgatorial torment; I was detained in no intermediate state; the instant that I left the world below, I was ushered into the splendor and joys of the world above. Purgatory is a fable, a dream, a delusion; a mine dug by priests, and drawn on by priests, and kept open for the priests' profit, not for man's consolation or God's honor. Absent from the body is present with the Lord, with not an interval between."

Another voice that the dead convey to us is, "Blessed are the dead that die in the Lord; for they rest from their labors, and their works do follow them. This," some dead saint says, "is my joyful experience. I have rested from labors, but I do not rest from service; for I am amid that bright and shining throng who stand before the throne of God and the Lamb, and we rest not day and night, but serve him continually, and without ceasing. The air I breathe is all balm; the light I bask in is all sunshine; our fears are gone, our infirmities are removed, our tears are all wiped away. Work is not weariness, but refreshment, now. I am among those who have come out of great tribulation, and I have washed my robes and made them white in the blood of the Lamb; therefore am I before the throne of God, and serve him day and night in his temple; and he that sitteth upon the throne dwells among us, and we hunger no more, neither do we thirst any more, neither does the sun light upon us, nor any heat; for the Lamb who is in the midst of the throne feeds us, and leads us to fountains of living waters, and God has wiped away all tears from all eyes."

Recur to the tables of memory, where the images of the dear dead are enshrined; and think of some one very near and very dear to you, as self can be to self, and hear that one being dead yet speaking. Is it a mother that has left you? That mother being dead still speaks to you, and she says from her happy abode, "I find here a new home, under whose glorious roof-tree are your brothers and sisters that left us, a fireside that is never darkened, a family circle that never can be interrupted; and the babe that withered in my bosom, like a frost-stricken flower in winter, I find now no more a sufferer, but clad in redemption-robes, and lifted into a sublimer temple, a worshipper within the vail in a house not made with hands, a participant of joys unutterable and full of glory, which shall never fade away. I recognize the links that I lost on earth now restored, and I sit down with Abraham, and Isaac, and Jacob, and those with whom I took sweet counsel, and with babes that lived on earth only to weep. Here all lost relationships are restored, all ties snapt asunder are re-knit; and I see those I knew upon the earth, and they see me and know me, and we know each other just as we are known of God himself. The glass through which I saw darkly is broken, and in the clear light of that transparent land, from which all shadow has fled, and all darkness is a stranger, I see and know even as I am known. I long for the day of your death, that you, too, may join this joyous group. Our true life is here. Come speedily, Lord Jesus, re-consecrate the earth, that we may descend as a bride adorned for the bridegroom, or bring mine on earth to me in glory! Do not grieve, dear children, below for us. We are lifted to a loftier spot; you are to be pitied, not we." Strange it is, when a Christian dies, we weep; but if any one should weep, he should for us, not we for him; for, if he dies in mid-age, he is spared the last half of his journey, and, instead of having to eat the bitter bread of this world's inn, he is lifted unexpectedly to the presence of his God, and the hidden manna and living water. And, therefore, to those that weep for such, he now says, "The thunders and the lightnings that you see we hear, — the one in their unspent echoes, and the other far down below. The trials and the sorrows that you feel we are now strangers to for ever and ever. Ages roll on, but our joys are ever new. You have night and day, but there is no night with us; all here is unfading brightness, perennial bliss: and, if sorrow should be felt by any, it is by us, that you have twenty or thirty years more to spend in the valley of tears below." Thus it should be joy on your part, that those you have lost have gone and anticipated all, and are now in the presence of God and of the Lamb, unspeakably and unchangeably happy.

The speaking dead say to us, "Come up hither; come now by faith, come upon the wings of prayer. The nearer you draw to Jesus, the nearer you approach to us. The more Christ-like you become, the nearer, the clearer, and more luminous, you shine to us. Anticipate in faith and hope that blessed day when you shall be with us, and we shall altogether be forever happy with the Lord. Did you know the full pitch of our joy, the rich glory into which we have entered, — did you see one glimpse of the bright Sun we see, or hear one note of the grand harmonies that roll around us, — you would say, 'O that I had the wings of a dove, that I might flee away and be at rest forever!'"

Another fact that the dead would tell us is, that things which agitate the world scarcely reach the realms of the happy; that many an event which the world sees not, or, if it sees, undervalues and despises, has its echo in heaven, and sweeps like the breath of God over the harps of the blessed. For instance, when thrones are tottering, and empires are falling, and presidential chairs are rocking on previous ruins, such facts are scarcely seen above; they certainly do not interest the company of the blessed. But when the soul of some poor beggar by the wayside, or of some poor orphan in the great congregation, is touched by the grace and transformed by the Spirit of God, then there is joy in the presence of angels that such an event has happened; and the whole company of the redeemed thrill with new ecstasy at the spectacle of a new accession being made to their happy and their blessed band. In heaven, things on earth are looked at only in the light of heaven. We estimate events by their influence upon us; the blessed measure events on earth by their relation to eternity. Great events on earth are pressed into little bulk there; and what the world thinks insignificant occurrences are there the grand facts and impressive phenomena. Those who are there can distinguish substance from shadow, and facts from dreams.

The dead, too, speak to those who neglect the great salvation, as well as to those who have loved it, and rejoice in the knowledge of it. They say, "How can you escape, if you neglect so great a salvation?" If the dead could be heard by the thoughtless sinner who is living without God, and without Christ, and without hope in the world, those departed ones who have preceded you to glory, — the father, the mother, the sister, the brother, who found their way to heaven through Christ, and showed they had gone there by the trail of beauty and of moral glory that they left behind them, — if they could be audible by you, they would say, "How long will you sport with eternity? how long treasure up wrath against the day of wrath? What shall it profit you, if you gain the whole world and lose your own soul? Turn ye, turn ye; why will ye die? Come to Jesus, weary and heavy-laden, and he will give you rest. 'The Spirit and the bride say, Come. And let him that heareth say, Come. And let him that is athirst come. And whosoever will, let him take the water of life freely.'"

Even the lost in hell in this matter send up an awful and a piercing voice. "Send Lazarus to my brethren that I left behind me, lest they also come into this place of torment." They, too, would lead you from a course that ends in perdition; the saved in glory would attract you to a career that will end in happiness. Two eternities address us; one eternity urging sinners not to come here, another eternity opening its bright bosom to receive them. Do not hesitate. Turn your back upon the one; lift your face and your heart to the other, and determine that, as for you and yours, you will henceforth serve the Lord Christ. And the sainted and happy dead speak to you and say, "If you will come to heaven, if you will escape its antipodes, there is but one way, and that way unequivocally proclaimed in Palestine, 'I am the way, the truth, and the life. No man cometh unto the Father but by me.' Abel took that way. It is the way in which Abraham walked, that prophets trod; it is no strange one. It is beaten smooth by the feet of multitudes who have traversed it. It is so broad, that the greatest sinner may walk in it and find room; and yet it is so holy, that that sinner must leave his sins on the threshold, and continue his career alone, and seek to be saved and sanctified alone."

"My mother, my father, my son, my daughter, my sister, my brother, except you be born again you can never come here, — you cannot see the kingdom of God." This is most true: we need not only a righteousness which is our title, but we need a fitness which is our only, but indispensable, preparation. Our eyes need to be anointed, that they may see heaven's glad scenes. Our hearts need to be sanctified, that they may beat in unison with the happy hearts that are there. Our tastes need to be repaired, in order that heaven may be heaven to us. All analogies, all experience, all induction, prove one great fact, — that every man needs, not only a title which he forfeited in Adam, which is restored in Christ, but that he needs also a fitness for that happy abode which the Holy Spirit alone can give him. If I were lifted just as I am, and with my existing physical organization, and placed in Saturn, Jupiter or Mars, I could not live there. Their gravity, their density, their whole structure, as astronomers can calculate, would render it absolutely impossible that, with my present physical organization, I could live at all, or, at all events, that I could live happily there. Every inhabitant must be fitted for the orb in which he dwells; and any one who knows this world, and what man is, notwithstanding the terrible degeneracy that has fallen upon both, can yet see that, physically, man was made for this earth, and that this earth was made for man. Now, the great law that we find in our experience extends into the better land: it is made for the holy, and the holy are made for it. There needs not only an adaptation of the place to the inhabitant, but an adaptation of the inhabitant to the place. And thus, without a complete revolution of nature, not a reformation only, — without a complete transformation of intellect, and head, and heart, and taste, and sympathy, and preference, — if we were placed in heaven, it would be agony, not joy; and to be projected from it and cast into the depths of ruin would be our inevitable desire, though it would be our certain and terrible destruction. It is, therefore, the immutable and everlasting law which God's word proclaims upon the earth, which the saints in glory echo from their happy mansions, that except a man be born again by the Spirit of God, he never can be fit to enter there.

All these the texts of the Bible, written on the sacred page, are not more obligatory or forcible because I have supposed them to be enunciated by the blessed in heaven being dead yet speaking. This only we may ask, that if a saved one were allowed to descend from the realms of glory, and to occupy the place where the minister of Christ stands, with what thrilling eloquence, with what earnest persuasion, with what force of argument, with what weight of appeal, with what solemnity of tone, would he speak to the vast multitude who are journeying onward and onward, either to a woe that never can be exhausted, or to a blessedness that has no measure, no suspension and no end! But I forget, "If they hear not Moses and the prophets, neither will they be persuaded, though one rise from the dead."

Let us regard these truths as being as fresh as if an angel now spoke them. Let us hear the testimonies, remonstrances and eloquent persuasions, just as if the most loved one that has preceded us to heaven were to come down and speak them in unearthly tones, and with unearthly eloquence. It is God's own word, ever fresh, ever applicable, ever true. Its obligations rest upon us with a weight and pressure, at this moment, which we can no more fling from us than we can fling from us our own immortality. Whilst we are saved by grace, we are not saved in indolence. It is not true that we are borne to heaven without knowing it. It is not God's law, in any department of human life, that a man should get on without toil. If one wish to prosper in trade, he must be up early and go late to bed. If he wish to make progress in learning, he must read very hard. If one wish to get on in commercial matters, one must study the markets, the ears ever listening, the eyes ever open. If one wish to be a first-rate poet, labor is essential. It is a great mistake to suppose that ministers preach by inspiration, or that poets write by instinct. It is all very pretty to say so; but the best sermons are always the result of the hardest toil, and no poet ever wrote what will be remembered except by labor as well as thought. And my strong conviction is, that in the world of mind the difference of intellect is comparatively little; it rests much more on the difference of application. And if this be true in God's natural world, why should it be dispensed with in God's higher world? It is not; for every expression in this Book denotes energy, labor, toil. "Strive," (ἀγωνιζετε) literally, "Agonize to enter in at the strait gate." "Lay aside every weight," like the racer in the Olympian games, "and run the race set before you, looking unto Jesus, the author and the finisher of your faith." And those who now occupy the starry heights of glory are there by grace most truly, most surely; but they did not reach their repose without toiling, running, striving. We see the crown, but we see not the path that has led to it. We see the glory that is entered, but we are ignorant of the toils which must have preceded it.

"The mighty pyramids of stone,
That wedge-like cleave the desert airs,
When nearer seen and better known,
Are but gigantic flights of stairs.

"The distant mountains, that uprear
Their frowning foreheads to the skies,
Are crossed by pathways, that appear
As we to higher levels rise.

"So heights by good men reached and kept
Were not attained by sudden flight;
But they, while their companions slept,
Were toiling upwards in the night."

CHAPTER III.

THE TRANSLATED ONE.

And after he was dead and gone,
And e'en his memory dim,
Earth seemed more sweet to live upon,
More full of love, because of him.

"By faith, Enoch was translated that he should not see death; and was not found, because God had translated him: for before his translation he had this testimony, that he pleased God." — HEBREWS 11 : 5.

THE simple historical fact to which this passage relates is told in very few words in Genesis. It is said in the fifth chapter, at the twenty-fourth verse, "And Enoch walked with God: and he was not; for God took him;" which is translated by the apostle, "By faith Enoch was translated that he should not see death; and was not found, because God had translated him: for before his translation he had this testimony, that he pleased," or, as it is in the original passage in Genesis, "that he walked with God."

Now, there seems to be something exceedingly appropriate in bringing in the record of the translation of a saint amid the melancholy statement of the effects of sin that then began to develop themselves in the fallen world. Perhaps God meant also by this statement to foreshadow him who, indeed, according to the prophecy, should die; but who, according to the promise that is in the prophecy, should rise again. Probably Abel, the first martyr, was to be the symbol and the figure of Jesus Christ, the great Propitiation for our sins, whose "blood speaketh better things than the blood of Abel;" and so Enoch's translation may have been meant to be a type of the resurrection and ascension of him who has entered within the vail, and ever liveth in the true holy place to make intercession for us. In these we see the promise, "The woman's seed shall bruise the serpent's head," more and more unfolding itself; and in the death of the martyr Abel, as in a mirror, the death of Jesus reflected backwards on the world; and in the ascension and the translation into glory of the sainted Enoch, a dim foreshadow of that great resurrection in which, and by which, we, too, shall rise from the dead.

Abel and Enoch's different circumstances may be meant to teach us another lesson. In Abel's martyrdom by Cain the murderer, we have an illustration of the reception that true and living religion may expect in this world. In the translation of Enoch, the sainted follower of God, we have an illustration of what religion, true religion, may expect in the world to come. And, lest men should be discouraged by seeing a truly pious man made a martyr, God adds the other fact, that a truly pious man is sometimes, and in this case certainly was, translated, that he should not only escape the pangs of martyrdom, but should not even see death. Hence, let us not be depressed by seeing real religion persecuted in this world; for we know that it is only for a season, and that it shall be consummated by a translation, lasting, glorious and blessed.

This incident of the translation of Enoch occurred, as we can easily see from the history, about the time of Adam's death. Jude calls him, "The seventh from Adam." In Adam's death men read this terrible lesson, "The wages of sin is death." In Enoch's translation they read that glorious sentiment, "The gift of God is eternal life." In the one case they beheld what sin can do; in the other, what grace can achieve. In the one case, they saw how deep, how dark, how terrible a grave sin could dig. In the other, they saw how bright, how glorious a temple the grace of God could construct. In the death of the one, they saw Eden in all its beauty set like a fading sun in the tomb. In the translation of the other, they saw the second paradise in yet more transcendent glory emerge from below, and dawn upon a longing and a weeping world.

It is remarkable that the two most distinguished saints of the Old Testament scriptures, who were translated and did not see death, were men who protested alone in the midst of all but universal corruption. They were what would be called, in modern language, great controversialists. Enoch and Elijah were sound protestants; men that could not see spreading superstition without entering their protest against it, and contending, as became them, earnestly for the faith once delivered to the saints. How remarkable is this, that the only two men who were translated that they should not see death, in the Old Testament, were not only distinguished by great spirituality, but were marked also by the severest and most determined personal struggle against all that dishonored God and ruined the souls of men! Enoch walked with God when the whole world was rushing from God. He breasted the torrent — pursued the upward, whilst all beside him took the downward course. Read Elijah's biography in the Book of Kings; read his conflict with those who were worshipping Baal; read his eloquent and impressive appeal, "If the Lord be God, follow him; if Baal be God, follow him;" and see what stern stuff he was made of. And yet these two men, who took so prominent a part in stormy times, who pursued their path in conflict and struggle, God signally honored by translating them that they should not see death. Both were transferred from suffering to joy, from conflict to peace, from mortality to immortality, from this corruptible to that incorruptible.

But I must study the picture before us. It is that of Enoch, and not of Elijah. In the language of the apostle, "he pleased God." In the language of Moses, on which the apostle's is a commentary, "he walked with God." What means this expression, "He walked with God," which is declared by the apostle to be so pleasing to God? The word "walk," I may notice, denotes and implies essentially "progress." When a person makes no progress, he stands still. When he walks, he makes progress in some one direction. There are but two walks in the world: the one is to God, with God, before God, or after God, which are all departments of the same walk; and the other is from God; and every man, it matters not who he is, pursues at this moment either of these two courses: walking from God further and further every day, or walking with God, and to, after, or before God, nearer and nearer to him continually. There is no standing still. There is no neutrality. There are two great currents in the life of humanity,— one rushing from God into the depths of ruin; the other rising and swelling to the source from which it came, there to be lost and merged in that ocean of joy which is at God's right hand, and in those waves of pleasure which are for ever and ever. It need not be stated that everlasting heaven is just everlasting approximation to God; that everlasting hell is just everlasting recession or departure from God. In heaven, we shall constantly grow in knowledge, in light, in happiness, in joy, new problems being solved every day, new disclosures made every minute, the capacities of the soul enlarging with the objects that fill them, our never-ending years being never-ending additional joys, and our daily pleasures marked, like the days and hours on the sun-dial, only by the bright sunshine. But, in the realms of the lost, there will be everlasting departure from God, the recollection of lost opportunities deepening as we depart, our capacities of woe increasing as that woe accumulates, and, from the very nature of the thing, there exists in the future no possibility of return; for the same gate that shuts in all the happy that are in the realms of the blessed shuts out all the lost that are in the regions of woe. Departure from God commences when man is born. Walking towards God begins when man is born again. Departure from God begins the instant that a man is born into the world. We are born children of wrath, even as others. All have sinned, and all are born in the eclipse. All are by nature strangers to and wanderers from God; and only when we undergo that change which is surely something different from being sprinkled with or being plunged into water, — when we undergo that change which is not sacramental. which is not ecclesiastical, which is not ritual, but inward, spiritual, real, called being "born again," — do we change our course; we are then converted, the word "conversion" coming from the Latin word *convertere*, to turn round. We are then turned right round. Instead of moving with our faces hitherward, we are turned round, and proceed with our faces thitherward. This is the difference. There are two grand processions. A great body of men who have been born again walking towards God, before him, after him, into heaven; and another great body walking from God, under an evil heart of unbelief, by which they depart from the living God.

We thus see two great classes. Nothing should make us forget that it is possible to be found in the midst of the Church of Rome, and yet to be walking towards God, in spite of surrounding darkness and deadly superstition; and that it is perfectly possible, and not uncommon, to be found in the Protestant church, and yet to be walking from God. God says that he has, in the midst of the Church of Rome, a people: "Come out of her, my people;" and who can doubt that there have been some of his saints in that apostasy? God tells us that, in the purest church upon earth, there are tares to be burned, bad fishes to be cast away, goats to be separated from the sheep, men that are not walking with God, but contrary to God. All we do, when we try to enlighten the victim of Roman Catholic superstition, is mainly to break the screen that keeps from him the light of truth, and to break open the padlock that shuts from him God's word. Let us try to enlighten him by putting the priest aside, that he may see the Sun of righteousness far above and beyond him; by depressing the church, that he may see the light of him who is the Lord, and the Creator, and the Sanctifier of the church. But, for Protestant and Romanist, there is but one way to God. Conversion is a thing that we cannot create; that is God's prerogative; but, whenever and wherever it is asked in humility and faith, God has promised richly to bestow it.

Let us mark well the way in which Enoch walked of old, and was conducted to happiness. The way in which Enoch walked to God and with God is that in which the Christian still walks. It was proclaimed upon the banks of the Jordan, and, though known, needs to be more clearly pointed out and more distinctly revealed in every church. "I am the way, the truth, and the life; no man cometh to the Father," and, I may add, "walketh with the Father, but by me." The way to heaven is not through a church, but by Christ. There is no more possibility of getting to heaven by the stairs of St. Paul's, in London, than by the penitential stairs of St. Peter's, at Rome. You may climb the stairs of the one, or the steps of the other, but you will not have reached heaven when you have got to the top of them. The way to heaven is not through a church, nor a chapel, nor a meeting-house, nor a cathedral; but through him who says,

"No man cometh to the Father but by me." Here is at once the exclusiveness of Christianity, and here is its catholicity also. It states that no name, no party, no sect, is the way to heaven. He only is who may be found in all sects, and by all parties, — for whom we have not to ascend to heaven, or to descend into the depths of the earth — but who is nigh to every one of us. We see, at once, that the Christian religion is no novelty; that our reformed religion is no upstart device. It was known in the days of Enoch; it was preached in the times of Elijah; it was predicted in the days of Isaiah, and in the sermons of John the Baptist, just as it is known now. There never was, since the fall, but one way to heaven, and there never will be any other. This way is so accessible to all, so broad, so holy, so complete, that it can be superseded by none. The greatest sinner needs no other, and the holiest saint cannot get to heaven by any other.

In order to walk in this way, like Enoch and the patriarchs of old, with God, it has been remarked by every commentary on this passage, there must be unity of sentiment and judgment between two parties before they can walk together. In order that we may walk with God, we must be of one mind with him as to all that is around us; or, if not of one mind, we must ask him to make us so. It implies that, to walk in the same direction, towards the same blessed end, our opinion must be the echo of his, our character the reproduction and the reflection of his. And, unless there be this coincidence of judgment between God and us, it is impossible that we can walk or keep company with him in the same way; for often we must feel it our duty to walk aside, and to leave God and those that are with him in order to pursue our own way.

There must be, in the next place, before we and God can walk together, perfect reconciliation. Not only must we be of one mind with God, but we must be of one heart with

God. Is it possible to be otherwise? Who that has learned the elements of theology, or the simplest lessons of his Bible, does not know that the natural heart is enmity to God? The Bible does not tell us that we are born enemies to God; we might be so accidentally, but it tells us that the essence, the concentrated essence of enmity to God, is lodged in every man's heart, and that all the explosions of war, of envy, jealousy, malice, hatred, are but the buddings of the fruits, and the developments of the seminal enmity that is latent, dear reader, in your and in my human heart. If our hearts be enmity to God, then it is quite plain that we cannot walk with him, and rise upwards to one to whom we are not only enemies, but enmity. One asks of God, "How can two walk together except they be agreed?" Two friends can walk together, or two relatives, who are at one: but if they are not at one with each other, not merely in conviction, but in heart, — if the one hates the other, or totally differs from the other, — they cannot walk together; their attempt would only add to their common misery. Before we can walk with God this heart that is enmity must be made love; the elements of hostility to God must be extracted from it by him who can change it. We may know whether we are walking with God, by introspection, if I may use the word; that is, by looking into our own hearts, and seeing and feeling what is there. If we cannot do this, we may judge by our outward life whether the inner life be an inspiration from God. In order to reconciliation with its Maker, the heart must not be merely patched up, but altogether changed. A Christian is not a man improved by civilization, learning, courtesy, refinement; but a new creature, — the creation of God, and not the manufacture of priest or pope. This is not a doubtful disputation, a conjecture of man, a problematical inference of a rash interpreter, but the clear and oft-repeated declaration of God's holy word. He says, "Except a man be born again, he cannot see the kingdom of God;" "Uncircumcision availeth nothing; but a new creature;" all things becoming in such a transformation new; we ourselves turning from darkness to light, loving what we once hated, and hating what we once loved. This is the shortest definition of the change. Unless this deep inner change take place, we cannot walk with God; and if we do not walk with God we are not in the way to heaven, or destined either to be transferred or translated. On the contrary, we are in the way that leads from heaven, "dead in trespasses and sins," "walking after the course of this world," and approaching to the confines of that woe from which there can be no retreat or emancipation forever.

In order to walk with God, we must not only be reconciled and by faith united to him; but we must also have perfect, unwavering, or, if not perfect, growing confidence in God, as father and friend. I never could walk with a man with any measure of comfort of whom I had a silent suspicion that he would either kill me, or poison me, or lead me into a snare, if it should be in his power. I could not walk with one of whose designs I had constant suspicion. I would not consent to be the friend of a man who would betray me on the most convenient occasion, or cheat me on the first opportunity, or do me other mischief if he could only do so without the risk of exposure. With such a man I could not live, or walk, or have communion or converse of any sort. It is not otherwise in our relation to God. If I have suspicion of God, latent convictions that he is always waiting to catch me slipping, and then to destroy me; if I have a feeling that he really hates me, but is driven by a sort of constraining necessity to love me; if I have an idea that I must propitiate him by sufferings, and trials, and tears, and that by pleading what Christ has done I must make him thus love me, though he would otherwise hate me,—then I cannot walk with him.

Such ideas of God are so melancholy, and so unjust, and untrue, that I am not surprised that those who give them hospitality should say, Let there be no God. Such suspicions must be so dreadful, and so depressing, that the presence of Deity must be felt as an unspeakable calamity. Yet there is no sin of which real Christians are more commonly and more flagrantly guilty than that of having a constant suspicion of God, as if he were a hard-hearted taskmaster, ever waiting to destroy, and never waiting to make happy. It is all the reverse: God loved us, and Christ died as the consequence, not the cause, of that love. God asks that we would not walk with him as a maniac walks with his keeper, or as a slave walks with his master; but as a confiding child with a confiding and ever affectionate father, or approach as an unsuspecting babe nestles in the bosom of its dear and unsuspected mother. We are to walk with God, with perfect confidence in him, feeling that he sees us, that he knows us, and loves and studies our well-being, and is ever — ever — ever waiting and watching to make us happy; for if we are not happy, it is not because God is straitened, but because we are. But, you say, our sins — these are the causes of our suspicion of God. They ought not to be so: our sins are our shame, and are just grounds for our suspecting ourselves, but, in the light of Christianity, no grounds for our wanting confidence in God. We are to go to him, not because we are sinners, but in spite of our being so; believing that the heaviest sin that weighs on our conscience is nevertheless not beyond the efficacy of what is revealed in the Bible, "The blood of Jesus Christ his Son cleanseth us from all sin." And it is most remarkable that this very apostle, and in this very epistle, though in other words, tells us that we can never walk with God in perfect fellowship unless we have a perfect realization of this great truth, "The blood of Jesus Christ his Son cleanseth us from all sin." John states,

"These things write we unto you that your joy may be full. This, then, is the message which we have heard of him, and declare unto you, that God is light, and in him is no darkness at all. If we say that we have fellowship with him," that is, if we say that we walk with him, "and walk in darkness," "we lie, and do not the truth; but, if we walk in the light as he is in the light, we have fellowship one with another, and the blood of Jesus Christ his Son cleanseth us from all sin." A happy walk is realized in proportion as this text is felt to be actual, "the blood of Jesus Christ his Son cleanseth us from all sin." Let us, then, walk in perfect confidence with God. When the road seems dark, and the cloud hangs lowering, and thorns and thistles and sharp flints are in the way, with enemies before us, and traitors on every side, yet let us have perfect confidence in God, that he will lead us through all, and make us more than conquerors in the midst of all; that a mother may forget the infant that she bore, but "I will never leave thee, nor forsake thee." "Behold I have graven thee on the palms of my hands;" "nothing shall separate us from the love of God, that is in Christ Jesus our Lord." I cannot enunciate this too freely, that the great demand of the Gospel is confidence in God — that the great feature of a Christian is confidence in God. Let us lay aside that suspicion which shrinks from him as a foe, and manifest more and more the confidence, the unsuspecting and joyous confidence, that glories in his presence, and never doubts his love, as that of a friend. What is faith? Simply trust. And what is trust? Real confidence or *fides*, confidence in God; taking his word just as it is. Believe his word; cleave to that blessed word; rejoice in that word as a lamp to your feet, and a light to your path; have confidence in all that its Author speaks there of himself, and concerning us.

Having thus confidence in God, let us walk and live under a perpetual sense of his presence. Thus it will be delightful to us. "Thou, God, seest me," is a conviction that, if lodged in the heart of a man that hates God, must kindle an incipient hell within him; but "Thou, God, seest me," lodged in the heart of a believer, is the rich germ of heaven within: because the one's idea of God is that of a dread and terrible tyrant; and the other's idea of him is that of a loving, affectionate, promise-keeping father. The believer, therefore, walks under a constant sense of his presence, and enjoys it, not dreads it. He sees him in the counting-house as well as in the church, on the railway as well as on the hill of Zion. He sees and feels his presence in his going out and in his coming in. Every hill-top becomes to his purged eye a transfigured Tabor. Every day dawns on the Christian soft and solemn even as a Sabbath-day; every house looks sacred as a sanctuary; every thought becomes worship; and even his very business is part and parcel of his daily religion. When a Christian thus realizes God, and walks in confidence with him, he will taste the bitterest cup as preternaturally sweetened, and the roughest path will become smooth. He will eat the grapes of Canaan in the midst of his forty years' march through the desert, and he will see the sunlight of his Father's face, he once thought gone, now smiling through the darkest clouds. "Blessed are the people that know the joyful sound: they walk in the light of his countenance."

The believer walks like Enoch with God, not only in the exercise of confidence in him, but also in obedience to all that he says. When a Christian wishes to know whether a thing be right, he does not ask, Will it be profitable? as we are often apt to do; or, will it be very popular? or, will it be very unpopular? or, will it please that great man, or propitiate this influential man? We have nothing to do with such inquiries at all; we have simply to pursue the path of principle, and we shall see its end peace. In speculating in matters of business, we may say, I will do this, because it will lead to that result, provided the beginning and end be pure. But in every great act our great question must be, Does God sanction that? does God authorize it? is this according to his will? And, if it be so, then let us bravely do it. We have nothing to do with the profit, or the pleasure, or the pain, or the displeasure. We have to act from principle; and expediency, however it may be denied, always follows principle; principle does not always follow expediency. Do what is right, and expediency will follow it. Do what is expedient in the face of principle, and we shall see that it is neither expediency nor principle. God's great law is, "Seek ye first the kingdom of God and his righteousness; and all these things shall be added unto you." God says, "Not forsaking the assembling of ourselves together." "Thou shalt love the Lord thy God with all thine heart, and with all thy soul, and with all thy might." "Search the Scriptures; for they are they which testify of me." "Believe on the Lord Jesus Christ, and thou shalt be saved." "Thou shalt love thy neighbor as thyself." "Earnestly contend for the faith which was once delivered unto the saints." Some pious persons say, that we should not be so excited about the interests of pure religion, that we ought to be more moderate. Moderation is admirable when applied to things of this world. The apostle says moderation is good,—"Let your moderation be known unto all men." In your preference of form, in your love of the world, pray be moderate. But you cannot be moderate in Christianity. Did we ever hear of a man being moderate in honesty? Why, moderate honesty would be absolute theft. Did we ever hear of moderate truth? Moderate truth would be a lie. You cannot be moderate in being good. If a thing be right, you are to do it with all your heart; and if a thing be wrong, you are not to do it at all. It is the old story that one needs to be reminded of every day. Men will bear earnestness in commerce, in politics, in all that relates to this world; but the moment that a man is earnest in his attachment to the truth, that moment they think much religion has made him mad.

This walk is preëminently a safe walk. That we are sure of. "The Lord is thy keeper." "Behold, he that keepeth Israel shall neither slumber nor sleep."

It is a happy walk; for it will take from disease its disappointment, from sorrow its sting, from death its agony. It will lend the wings of an eagle to him that halts; and it will reveal, in all things, and in spite of all that is around us, God making all things work together for good to them that love him, and who are called according to his purpose. And when we come to die, as we must die, if we shall not be translated as Enoch was, or transfigured on the Mount of Tabor, as Jesus was, our death shall be so denuded of its bitterness, of its sting, and of all that makes it death, that when the Christian dies the great truth shall be fulfilled, it is not he, but death, that dies. If not translated living into heaven and happiness, as Enoch was, yet, when we come to lie down on the last sick bed, that will be our death-bed, we shall find that our death differs in name only from Enoch's, and that we too, like Enoch and Elijah, shall be translated. The present roughness of the road will make the end of the journey only more delightful. The stormy wind and the tempest will make the sweet calm of our Father's home only the more beautiful. "If ye be reproached for the name of Christ, happy are ye;" ye are in the path that your sainted predecessors walked, and they do not repent that they pursued it, for they are now in the presence of God and the Lamb for ever and ever. And we, having walked with Enoch, with Elijah, with Abraham, with Paul, with Peter, and with him the great author and the finisher of our faith, through all channels of this life, we shall find our closing sigh only the prelude of our great exultation, and the last groan transfigured into the first note of the everlasting jubilee, and wings imparted to the departing soul never seen by the soul in clay, on which it will be borne to the presence of him with whom it walked upon the earth, and in whose presence it will live and rejoice for ever and ever.

Are we walking with God? Are we believing the testimony that is given us? Have we confidence in him? These are voices from Enoch yet dead. The real question is not, are we Roman Catholics? or, are we Protestants? but, are we, what it is possible not to be, and yet to be either, are we Christians? Are we changed? are we walking in the light of God's countenance? If so, then we are walking with him from whom neither death nor life shall separate us; and when the enemy shall come in like a flood, we shall oppose him, and raise the standard of Enoch, and triumph. Such is an ancient and unspent voice, sounding from realms of glory; Enoch's voice, but laden and musical with God's truth.

CHAPTER IV.

THE ILLUSTRIOUS ELDERS.

But here a deeper and serener charm
To all is given ;
And blessed memories of the faithful dead
O'er wood and vale and meadow-stream have shed
The holy hues of heaven.

"For by it" (faith) "the elders obtained a good report." — HEBREWS 11 : 2.

THE first verse in Hebrews 11 is the answer to the question, what faith is, and the second verse tells us the fruit it bears: that "by it the elders" of ancient days, whose names are inscribed in this chapter on a monument far more enduring than brass, Abel, and Enoch, and Noah, and Abraham, and Moses, and Isaac, and Jacob, and Barak, and Samson, and Jephthah, and David, "obtained a good report."

Faith is perfect confidence in the truth of God, a perfect certainty that the least word that God has said is surer than the strongest foundation that man has ever laid; but it is a faith that never can be alone. It "worketh by love," it "purifieth the heart," says the apostle, "it overcometh the world." For a man to say, "You have faith, but no works," is absurd. If there be no works, there can be no faith. To speak of faith without good fruits, is just as absurd as to speak of the sun shining without light, or a fire blazing without heat. If there is no heat, there is no fire ; if there is no light, there is no sun above the horizon; if there are no good works, there is no faith, but very faithlessness, the absolute negation and want of it.

Now, these "elders," it is said, "by it obtained a good report." Not by deference to the fascinating sheen of splendid things that were before them, not by the power or the attraction of things visible at all, though such, doubtless, may have had their influence; but by confidence in what God had said, and the certain conviction that what he had promised he would abundantly fulfil, they "obtained a good report," which, like ointment poured forth, has not lost its fragrance, nor ever will.

This faith by which they overcame the world, which wrought by love, and by which they "obtained a good report," is not contrary to reason. Persons talk as if to disbelieve the Bible were the highest rationalism, and as if to accept the Bible were the highest fanaticism; as if it were impossible to be a rational man, and yet a believer. Where there is the strongest faith, there ever is the exercise of the purest and the noblest reason. Reason is not contrary to faith, but an ally to it; there is, however, this difference between them: reason leaves the conviction cold and outside, there to remain dead and barren; faith seizes the truth, appropriates it to itself, feeds on it, and unfolds its fruits in all the efforts of a beautiful, consistent character. Reason is valuable as a servant, and a subject to faith, but it is in no respect contrary to or inconsistent with faith.

It is remarkable, too, in looking throughout the Scriptures, how frequently faith is referred to. One does not wonder that some should have given faith so lofty a place in the creed; but one should wonder that any in the Christian church should have given such a low and subordinate place to it. If one should ask, "What shall I do to be saved?" the answer is, "Believe in the Lord Jesus Christ." When Jesus saw the centurion characterized by distinguished love, by beautiful humility, he did not say, "I have not seen so great love," or, "I have not seen so great humility in Israel;" but, "I have not seen so great faith, — no, not in Israel;" as if it were an indisputable fact, that where there is so much humility before man, there must be trust or confidence in God.

In another place, we are told, "Hath not God chosen the poor of this world, rich in faith?" And, again, when Jesus had met the poor blind man, who had fallen into danger in consequence of his recognition of Jesus, he asked him, "Dost thou believe?" And yet, this faith is not an indigenous plant; it does not grow in this cold, barren world of ours spontaneously. It is an exotic, planted by the hand of our Father, watered by ceaseless dews, fostered by an undiminished sunshine, so dependent upon him that if it were left to itself it would perish; but, guarded and protected by him, it receives fragrance to its fruit from his breath, beauty and tints to its blossom from his smile, and becomes alike comforting to man and glorious and honoring to God. By this faith, we are told, "the elders obtained a good report." In other words, "got a good name," or, to use a more modern phrase, "got great credit."

Now, this seems very remarkable: for, if there be one grace which strips man of every element of boasting, and gives to God all and exclusive glory, it is faith. If there be one grace that gives man no ground for boasting, and gives God all the glory, it is faith. Love brings a glowing heart to God. Courage brings an heroic heart to God. Obedience brings a quick foot and a working hand. Every one of these brings something to God. But faith brings nothing to God but an empty heart, an empty mind, empty hopes, and empty merits, and seeks to him for all, that it may have all the good, and he may have all the glory. And yet it is stated that by this faith, which gives man no glory, "the elders obtained a good report." How is this? It was just the fulfilment of that text, "Them that honor me, I will honor." The Christian shines in the reflected lustre of his Lord. He becomes glorious in proportion as he gives glory to the Lord. As Moses gazed upon the countenance of God, and carried off a portion of the lustre of that countenance, so the believer, by contact and communion with God, brings off a portion of the glory of God. All the world acknowledges that he has been with Jesus. It is the Father reflected in the countenance of his child. It is thus that God has arranged it, that he who seeks glory for himself shall never obtain his object, and he who subordinates himself, and seeks only the glory of his master, shall obtain a "good report." No individual ever yet set out by labors, by zeal, or by exertion of any sort, to elevate or dignify himself, who did not substantially fail; and no one ever set out to honor and glorify God, who did not succeed in giving glory to his Lord, and catching, as the glory passed by, some rays of that lustre which let the world know who he was, and to whom he belonged.

This "good report" may be partly in our own consciences. "He that believeth hath the witness," that is, "a good report," "in himself." And when one's conscience is pure, spotless, right in the sight of God, few have any idea what a load one can bear. A single ounce of obloquy will crush the man whose conscience falters in its principles; but a whole ocean-load of calumny cannot crush that man who has the testimony of a good conscience in the sight of God.

It may be true that this good "report" was mainly outward, and in the church. We mean, by having a good report in the church, being reputed upright, and fit as officers in it. Accordingly, when we are commanded to elect elders, it is said, we must select men of good report. And again, it is said that "Abel offered unto God a more excellent sacrifice than Cain, by which he obtained witness that he was righteous." And "Enoch had this testimony that he pleased God."

In the world, also, the Christian will have "a good report;" for there is no such thing as a world utterly denuded of every Christian influence. In its worst state, there are some of the restraints, checks, or motives of the Gospel left. There is the direct influence of the presence and the power of God; and there is the indirect or reflected influence of Christianity, by which all the world more or less is colored. The worst men have an irrepressible conviction that truth is beautiful, that piety is good, that justice is right, and religion holy. They know that such a conviction condemns themselves, because they do not exemplify it in their lives; but when they see one who sacrifices himself to the glory of his Lord, and, under the impulse of real and living religion, clothes the naked, feeds the poor, lifts up the down-trodden, and gives of his abundance to the oppressed, they may be the most wicked and the worst of the world, yet they cannot but admire, whilst in their wickedness they would rather be rid of the presence of one who, by the contrast, rebukes their selfishness, their inconsistency, and their crimes. It is thus that the holy obtain "a good report even in this world."

We read, in the account of the successive characters contained in Hebrews 11, that Samson was illustrious for his strength, Solomon for his wisdom, Abel for his religion, Abraham for his obedience, Moses for his learning, Joshua for his courage; yet all for faith. The distinguishing graces of these illustrious heroes are scarcely noticed; the victory they obtained, the satisfaction they gained, arose not from the obedience of the one, the strength of another, the learning of a third, the courage of a fourth; but all from one common grace, which they all possessed, each in his measure, even that faith which is "the substance of things hoped for, the evidence of things not seen." The reason is, that faith is the grace that feeds, sustains, gives tone, and imparts direction, to every other grace of the Christian character. It enables hope to pierce the skies, zeal to burn, obedience to persevere; and gives fragrance, ripeness and bloom, to all the fruits of the Christian character. It is the radical and vital grace in the Christian's heart, and therefore it is magnified by God, as "the victory that overcometh the world."

As we intend to speak of the elders under the Old Testament as their names are given in the eleventh of the Hebrews, let me try to fill up the catalogue, in some such way as we might suppose an apostle, if writing now, would have filled it up, by alluding to some of those elders, necessarily omitted by Paul, in whose bright catalogue the apostle himself was not the least conspicuous.

I may notice, first of all, the early Christian converts just after and about the day of Pentecost. Of these men it is said, they "sold their possessions," they took joyfully the spoiling of their goods, "rejoicing that they were counted worthy to suffer shame for his name." They felt, in all these things, that they had an enduring substance in the heavens no earthly aggression could touch. Faith told them it was so. They believed that men do not live by bread alone, and, therefore, there was no sacrifice they were not ready to make in their service and allegiance to the Lord, and loyalty to the King of kings. Hence, the names of these saints are venerated wherever the Bible is read, in palace or cottage, or battle-field, or on the deck: they constitute a glorious galaxy, and, as the centuries rush over it, they do not dim, but add to its splendor, presenting to every century, and every generation of the Christian church, glorious proofs of what the church was in its early purity; though even then an imperfect earnest of what the church shall be in its coming glory. The early church, by that faith, "obtained this good report."

We may fairly quote the very apostle who wrote the eleventh chapter of the Epistle to the Hebrews. What a noble illustration is his own biography of obtaining a good report by faith! He renounced the tempting prospects of ecclesiastical preferment. If he had remained a Pharisee, he might have obtained the chief priest's office; at any rate, he would have reached the rank and profits of a rabbi. But, in obedience to that sacred thing into which neither sacerdotal nor royal hand can penetrate, — the conscience, — and under the impulse of that divine principle by which "the elders obtained a good report," he braved perils by sea, perils by land, perils among false brethren, good report and bad report among the enemies of the Gospel, preached before Felix till he trembled, spoke before Agrippa till Agrippa was almost persuaded; and, in these and other cases, with such power and with such evidence that some believed and rejoiced in the truth, while others gnashed their teeth, and laid wait in order to destroy him. He also by faith preached in Athens, amidst a group of the most talented and accomplished philosophers that the sun ever dawned upon; and while these philosophers crouched behind the altar they had raised in their folly to the unknown God, he, the noblest character in the group, by faith proclaimed, in tones that the Gospel alone could originate, "The God whom ye ignorantly worship, him declare I unto you." In Rome, the capital of the world, in the midst of all its imperial splendor, in the presence of the Cæsars themselves, in the face of menace, proscription, imprisonment and death, Paul, by faith, said, "I am not ashamed of the Gospel of Christ." He gloried in infirmities, he counted not his life dear, that he might obtain the recompense of reward.

In prison he felt the chains of a prisoner for Christ's sake more honorable than crowns in his retrospect of the past, and in his prospect of the future. "I have fought a good fight, I have finished my course, I have kept the faith. Henceforth there is laid up for me a crown of righteousness, which the Lord, the righteous judge, shall give me at that day: and not to me only, but unto all them also that love his appearing." By faith, Paul has obtained that good report which suggests to us to follow him as far as he followed Christ. It may be and is perverted by some, who canonize him as a saint to be worshipped, instead of accepting him as a faithful Christian to be followed. Hence our apostle, lest the good report that he obtained should lead to the mischief that we have so faintly intimated, — after all these losses, sacrifice, perils, — after being in the third heavens, seeing sights that no man had seen, and hearing angel voices that no human tongue could ever echo, — after all this faithfulness in Athens, this heroism in Rome, this teaching proud philosophy what philosophy had never learned, — after victory over perils by land and perils by sea, and finishing his course, in order to guard the world against treating him as an angel, or canonizing him as a saint, he writes, "Though we, or an angel from heaven, preach any other gospel unto you than that which we have preached unto you, let him be anathema." And when he bids you follow him, he lays down the limit of it: "Follow me, as I follow Christ." And, lest it should be supposed, at any time, that what he was should be esteemed as the creation of his own excellence, he says, "The life that I live I live by the power of the Son of God." And again, "I live;" but, lest it should seem that he was striving to take one ray from God's glory, and thus take a curse into his own bosom, he says, "I live, yet not I, but Christ liveth in me." Thus, by faith, Paul obtained this "good report."

Another instance of the same is found in the apostle Peter; so frail and faltering in his confidence whilst his Master was on the earth, rashly trying to tread the waves, thinking that his feet were holy enough to awe them, and then sinking and crying out in despair, "Lord, help me, or I perish;" with so little faith that he unsheathed the sword to smite down the enemies of Christ, as if Christ had not come to be a victim; with so little Christian heroism, that a maid frightened him at the door of the judgment-hall, and made him deny, with an oath, that he knew his blessed Master; in whose breast faith and sense, belief and scepticism, seem to have struggled in mortal conflict for the mastery. Watch Peter, however, after the day of Pentecost. What heroism in telling those that had his life in their hands, "Ye have taken, and by wicked hands have crucified and slain him!" What faithfulness in preaching salvation for them all, whether Jews or Gentiles, announcing that "there is none other name under heaven given among men whereby we must be saved," than the name of Christ! His past failures seem to have never departed from his memory. One cannot read his epistles without seeing his sorrow for the past running through every sentence in an audible and continuous undertone, intimating, as it were, that the recollection of his great offence was never distant from his mind, nor sorrow for it quenched in his heart. And, when condemned to be crucified for his Master's name, he is said to have begged that he might be crucified with his head downwards, lest he should seem to take any glory from his blessed Master. In all this we see a trust that faltered not in the worst, and that wearied not in the best of circumstances; and so by faith Peter obtained what we cheerfully accord him, and accord him no more, "a good report."

By faith, the Waldenses, those noble witnesses for Christ, obtained a good report. When all Europe was involved in the darkest midnight, and they were persecuted by the inquisitors, and those who were under their directions, they fled to the valleys of Piedmont and to the rocks of the Cottian Alps, and there, amid hunger, and nakedness, and famine, and persecution, they preserved their faith — not their faith, but our faith — pure as the Alpine snows, amid which they lived, unstained during a thousand years, as at its first falling. And that faith they have handed down to us — that faith in which we rejoice, while they themselves were the true and resplendent links of that glorious succession — that true and only succession, which connects the Christians of the nineteenth century with the saints and martyrs of the first. These men had no trumpet to sound their names, no newspaper-column to proclaim their praises, no general council to back their sentiments, and no royal shield to protect them. They had only strong confidence in truth, enthusiastic love and affection for the Lord; and by faith they have obtained that "good report," which certain half-papists, and more consistent whole papists, are trying to cover with reproach; but good men and true men, like him of whom the great minstrel wrote, are attempting to scrape off the moss and the dust that have accumulated on their tombstones, that men may read the story of their noble deeds, and thank God while reading that, by faith, they obtained an imperishable report.

By faith, Wickliffe, not the least illustrious of all the ancient reformers, emerged from the obscurity of Europe, and shone alone but prominent in the sky, as he has been justly called, "the morning star of the reformation." Wickliffe exposed the tyranny of the Pope, despised the threatenings of his bishops, and, by faith, first translated the Scriptures into our mother tongue, exhuming God's truth from the grave in which the sextons of Rome had long and successfully entombed it; and, by faith, when he was cited to appear before the Pope, and answer for the awful crime of making God's word free, instead of keeping it chained and bound, he gave the noble answer, by which he "obtained a good report," — "Whether it be right to obey the Pope, or to obey God, judge ye." And long after he was gathered to his fathers, and buried in the church-yard at Lutterworth, which I never pass on the railway without earnestly recalling the event, his enemies dug up his bones, and cast them into the Avon, in order to express their detestation of the glorious Gospel. A poet has well said that, in so doing, they gave notice of their own downfall:

> "The Avon to the Severn runs,
> The Severn to the sea;
> And Wickliffe's dust shall spread abroad,
> Wide as the waters be."

He died after he had given his testimony; but the very efforts taken to extinguish that testimony were the grand means of spreading it abroad with greater speed from shore to shore. Wickliffe sought no honor from man, and got no favor from the Pope. He lived by faith, and died in faith, and so "obtained a good report." Let his enemies conspire to blacken his illustrious name; they only degrade their own, while his emerges brighter and more cherished than before.

By faith, another great elder of ancient days, the greatest of all since St. Paul, Martin Luther, "obtained a good report;" a report that grows in brightness, that shall never fade, whilst there is truth to be maintained and error to be put down, or gratitude to man or glory to God. By faith, he took his propositions, which condemned the dogmas of the Papacy, and pasted them on the doors of Wittenburg church. By faith, when he visited Rome, and saw what they said were the heads of Paul and of Peter there preserved just as they had been cut off, he pronounced in the midst of that city, and in the hearing of its assembled priests, that they were only wooden blocks made by a bungling and rude carpenter. By faith, he gazed on the catacombs in Rome, where the saints had sighed and prayed, "How long, O Lord most holy?" and recognized in those catacombs a glory and an architectural magnificence which St. Peter's in its richest array makes no approach to. By faith he took the papal bull which was fulminated at him, and did, what we should do with the last papal bull, burn it in the public street before them who feared it, revealing in its blaze the darkness from which it emanated, and the faithfulness of that servant whom God had raised up to oppose it. And by faith, too, when he was told that he must go to Worms, and appear there before the council, and have an opportunity to plead for himself and his cause, but was also told that Duke George and the priests would waylay and murder him, he answered, "If the skies should rain down Duke Georges for days together, I will go to Worms." He did the duty of his day, and by faith he "obtained a good report." By faith, that lonely monk stood in the presence of illustrious kings, in the midst of irritated and revengeful pontiffs, and enunciated, in all its native simplicity, with unrivalled sharpness and clearness of outline, and in words of thunder, the reverberations of which still agitate the air, the great doctrine of justification by faith; and that doctrine, thus let forth like lightning in the summer skies, shot from land to land, until great continents shone with its splendor, and men's hearts glowed with undying fervor, before which Rome shuddered and trembled till the nations heard her chains. The voice of that noble man still sounds in great congregations, and breaks in sweet music on cottage thresholds. By faith, Luther thus lived; by faith, Luther thus "obtained a good report."

By faith, an illustrious martyr of the land in which we live, Bishop Latimer, not the least illustrious or the least faithful of them all, "obtained a good report." When he was seized and made a prisoner for his faithfulness by those who hated the truths that he preached, and fastened to the stake, in company with Ridley, a co-presbyter or co-bishop, — which, it matters not, — because of his utterance of the same faithful testimony; and this is not a piece of romance, but what Rome did when she had the power, and what Rome has never repented of, and is now so far from being ashamed of that, in a little book called the History of England, drawn up specially for the use of children in the Roman Catholic Church, it is said that the burning of Latimer and Ridley was what they deserved, and that the church did well thus to put them to death; when Latimer was tied to the stake, and his brother Ridley to another stake beside him, as the flames rose up, he turned round to Ridley, and said (and said it by faith), "Be of good cheer, dear brother! This day we shall light such a flame as, by God's grace, shall never be quenched in England." These words were a prophecy. A short time ago, when what is called Puseyism was gaining ground every day, when one hundred Protestant ministers had gone over to the Church of Rome, when some bishops were fostering it instead of rebuking it, and others were making apologies for the men that professed it, instead of turning them out of the livings the responsibilities of which they had abused, — when the Pope of Rome by an allocution had declared that every man baptized is subject and responsible to him, and ought to be canonically punished if disobedient to him, and according to very clear appearances Latimer's prophecy was about to be reversed, it was really about to be fulfilled. Aggression quickened long dormant feelings: the heart of our fatherland was proved to be sound even to the very core. When some thought that the holy flame was utterly extinguished, they found it had been only smouldering, and feeding its strength in the sequestered places of the land, and in the secret recesses of the heart. It burst forth, at the approach of the papal power, from a thousand orifices; and prime ministers came down from their cabinets, and lord chancellors from their woolsacks, and fanned it. It now seems likely to blaze and spread with deepening and augmented speed, till all the chaff shall be utterly consumed, and the truth, dormant, not dead, shall mingle with the rays of that Sun soon to emerge, and create by his presence the splendor of the millennium. And thus by faith Latimer "obtained a good report."

I cannot omit to mention one as illustrious, as eminent, but grievously misjudged by many; I mean John Knox, a gentleman by birth, a thorough scholar by education, a true Christian by grace; and yet by some he is often denounced as if he had been either a great fanatic or a restless and a ferocious Goth. The truth is, he was constitutionally one of the most gentle of men, by grace one of the most heroic of martyrs, and when the crisis demanded it one of the most unflinching confessors. He was as gentle as a lamb in all the relations of private life; but when a great deed had to be done, he was courageous as a lion, and ever dared to do it. It has been remarked that men who have slow pulses are capable of the greatest things; for they are only, as it were, gathering their strength when other men's hearts are exhausted. It is such quiet and gentle men who, when inspired by the grace of God, and having a noble object before them, are capable of heroic deeds. By faith Knox "obtained a good report." And so faithfully did that man preach, and so powerfully did he speak, that Mary, then a Roman Catholic, said, "I fear more the words of Knox," because her conscience, in spite of her creed, told her they were true, "than all the long bows of England," the weapons that oft surpassed the claymore in effect, and were therefore at one time the terror of Scotland. He carefully preserved the cathedrals; it is a libel on his name to say that he pulled them down: the monasteries he did destroy, and, while men of antiquarian sympathies may deplore their ruins, by faith he did it, and Christians rejoice; and by faith he predicted that, when the rookeries were gone, the rooks would fly away; and what is the fact? That, in Scotland (at least in its national church), there is not such a thing as a Puseyite sermon preached, and the Pope as yet has not a hundred congregations of papists in the whole country. The Pope has admitted that Scotland is not yet ripe for his invasion; and he will find out that, if he attempt to invade it, he will have made a grosser blunder in the north than, as he has discovered by this time, he lately perpetrated in the south.

By faith, then, Knox "obtained a good report." It was inscribed on his tombstone, "Here lies the man who never feared the face of clay." Only, I may add, we must not suppose that the most conspicuous of the array were necessarily the most spiritual and devout. There were no less holy elders who are less renowned. Melancthon wrote in his study what Luther proclaimed on the platform. Calvin, whose Institutes are still referred to as the purest theology in Christendom, fed the flame that Luther kindled. Because a certain man does not preach so well as another, it is not just to say he is not doing God's work so well; he may be doing it much better. The words of Knox and of Luther have, except in their echoes, perished; but the writings of Melancthon and of Calvin still remain. I might refer to Pascal and Quesnel, and, in later days, to Whitefield, and lastly to Simeon, of Cambridge, who, after he had first begun to preach the Gospel in that university, regarded it as a token for good, and a reason for gratitude, that a servant-man lifted his hat to him, for he felt it as an acknowledgment of his labors. He lived to see dignitaries in the church and princes in the state acknowledge the service he had done; and he fell asleep, blessed by all the true Christian men, and obtained by faith "a good report." Need I mention Fox, and Oberlin, a recent missionary, and Brainerd, and Felix Neff, and Henry Martyn, and Wilberforce, who first originated that great movement of evangelical truth which one of his sons has just tried to extinguish by renouncing the principles of his father, and adopting the dogmas of Pope Pius IX.? These by faith inspired kingdoms, converted souls, and by faith "obtained a good report."

Men who have been misjudged by many, — the Covenanters in Scotland, — holding, I admit, great errors and exaggerated notions in many respects, whose indiscretions ought to be forgiven because of the testimony and the protest that they maintained, by faith have obtained, in the minds of all that can appreciate them, "a good report."

By faith, the Puritans in England protested against all the superstitions of a dominant party, and gave up their benefices, and their preferments, and chose rather to worship God in the humblest places, preferring by faith to obtain "a good report," than to sacrifice their consciences. By faith, a section of these Puritans went forth, and landed on the rocks that bound the iron coast of the western continent. By faith, they braved the storm, and kept their hearts firm, trusting in God, and their hopes undaunted; and by faith, they landed in the great western country, and, amid the blood of warm hearts and tears of weeping eyes, they planted that tree which has struck its roots deep in its now native soil, and has made America in her religion, and in her hopes and destinies, the sister of our own great England, rivals only in beneficence, fellow-workers in all besides.

By faith, too, in more recent days, men have labored, and we have entered into their labors; and by faith they have obtained, what they did not seek, "a good report."

Thus we find, by the records of modern times and from the catalogue of the past, that there never was but one true religion, and we may justly infer that there never will be but one true religion. The religion of Abraham the patriarch, and the religion of John Knox the reformer, were the same. The creeds of Simeon, and Wesley, and Whitefield, were substantially the same. Justification by faith was not a new star created at the Reformation. It has been standing over head for eighteen centuries, but was then clouded, and hid. All that Luther did was to dissipate the clouds, and let the star shine forth in its own pristine and native splendor. There has never been but one way to heaven; a way, I admit, very narrow, but a way, I must add, as clear, as plain, as if it were cloven through the everlasting hills, and the great mountains, and shining in the ever unclouded sunlight. No fog can permanently shade, no circumstances can really injure us. We walk in the way in which Abraham, and Isaac, and Jacob walked; in which Latimer, and Luther, and Knox, and Calvin walked; the way in which Simeon, and Oberlin, and Felix Neff walked, and entered into glory. Our lives may waste and wear like the dropping sand, and that sand may be swept away as the dust upon the floor, into the grave whose gates are ever opening and ever shutting, ever shutting and ever opening; but that inner life which Abraham had, which Knox lived, which Latimer enjoyed, which Simeon taught, never can waste or wear. Time writes no wrinkles upon its brow. It is no fleeting shadow, it is no vapor. It moves steadily along the way which God has opened up, and it will not cease to advance till it reach the lines of the cherubim and seraphim, and rejoice forever in the presence of God and the Lamb. All outward things die, all families change; but living Christianity lives forever. Of it, it is not written, "Thou shalt surely die."

This "good report," of which I have spoken, in many respects is most desirable for us. It is quite natural, wherever there is religious eminence, that there should be great contrast. It is a melancholy fact, in this evil world, that, the greater our light, the longer is the shadow we must project, and that the eminence on which we are placed is perilous in the ratio of its height.

The world knoweth us not, as "it knew him not." "We know that when he shall appear we shall be like him; for we shall see him as he is." But we know that a good name, even in the world, has the precious power of spreading the everlasting Gospel. There are Christian graces which the world can admire, though it cannot appreciate them. Justice, generosity, goodness, are admired by a world that has often crucified their advocates. Hence, the Christian should try to avoid what may be misconstrued, even the appearance of all evil, that the world may have nothing to say validly against him, and no reason to urge why it should reject, or despise, or undervalue the precious Gospel, which is its only salvation: "having a good conscience; that, whereas they speak evil of you as of evil-doers, they may be ashamed that falsely accuse your good conversation in Christ." Or, as he says again, "Having your conversation," that is, your life, "honest among the Gentiles; that, whereas they speak against you as evil-doers, they may, by your good works. which they shall behold, glorify God in the day of visitation." This we may be sure of, that, if the world will reject the Gospel preached by literally good men, it will much more readily reject the waters coming from a tainted fountain,—that is, the Gospel preached by a notoriously bad man. But our great concern must not be to please the world. These men that by faith "obtained a good report" did not seek its applause. We must let the "good report" come to us; we must not go after it. Our sole business is to have our eyes open to the duties, our ears open to the precepts, our heart accessible to the joys, of the Gospel. It is ours to sow the seed, and leave the fruits to follow. Duty first; praise next. "Seek ye first the kingdom of God, and his righteousness," and "a good report," and all these things "shall be added unto you." And let this "good report," above all, be from God himself. Let us seek to have our consciences right in his sight, to be Christians in deed; and "if God be for us," —our approver,—"who can be against us?" In every age there are special duties, and distinctive obligations, and we should try so to do them that we shall please God, and obtain "a good report." So the age in which we are now cast has, too, a great duty. A great duty of this age is contained in the words, "Earnestly contend for the faith which was once delivered unto the saints." But let not our hatred to our aggressing opponents dilute our love to precious souls. Let us be far more anxious to convert the victim of deadly error than to destroy that deadly error. Let us not be so excited against the cardinal's red hat as to forget that an immortal soul is beneath it. Let us not be more indignant as Britons than we are sorrowful as Christians. Let us be grieved for sin, rather than angry with sinners.

Nothing is more humbling than the mere "No Popery" shout, which leads to mischief; nothing is more precious than that hatred to error and protest against it which become a Christian. But deep compassion for poor perishing souls should blend grief with our anger, and should make us pray, when we contend for the faith, that thus we may win souls, and please God, and obtain by faith "a good report."

CHAPTER V.

BELIEVING PARENTS.

"Like warp and woof, all destinies
  Are woven fast;
Locked in sympathy like the keys
  Of an organ vast.

"Pluck one thread and the web ye mar;
  Break but one
Of a thousand keys, and the paining jar
  Through all will run.

"All which is real now remaineth,
  And fadeth never;
The hand which upholds now sustaineth
  The soul forever."

"By faith Moses, when he was born, was hid three months of his parents, because they saw he was a proper child; and they were not afraid of the king's commandment."—HEBREWS 11: 23.

THE instance of faith presented in the sacred passage prefixed to this chapter is an extremely interesting and beautiful one. We shall best discover its actual meaning by reference to a very few verses of the first two chapters of the book of Exodus. In the first chapter of Exodus, at the seventh verse, we find that, after Joseph died, "The children of Israel were fruitful, and increased abundantly, and multiplied, and waxed exceeding mighty; and the land was filled with them. Now, there arose up a new king over Egypt, which knew not," that is, did not approve of, the family of "Joseph. And he said unto his people, Behold the people of the children of Israel are more and mightier than we; come on, let us deal," as he called it, "wisely," that is, cunningly and wickedly, "with them; lest they multiply, and it come to pass that when there falleth out any war they join also unto our enemies, and fight against us, and so get them up out of the land." After he had pursued this course of infanticide in the case of thousands upon thousands, we read in the second chapter of the book of Exodus, "And there went a man of the house of Levi, and took to wife a daughter of Levi. And the woman conceived, and bare a son; and when she saw him that he was a goodly child," what is called a proper child in the text, "she hid him three months. And when she could not longer hide him, she took for him an ark of bulrushes, and daubed it with slime," or bitumen, "and with pitch, and put the child therein; and she laid it in the flags by the river's brink. And his sister," that is, Miriam, the sister of Moses, "stood afar off, to wit," that is, to know, "what would be done to him. And the daughter of Pharaoh came down to wash herself," or, rather, to perform sacred ablutions, "at the river, and her maidens walked along by the river's side; and when she saw the ark among the flags, she sent her maid to fetch it. And when she had opened it, she saw the child: and, behold, the babe wept. And she had compassion on him, and said, This is one of the Hebrews' children. Then said his sister," Miriam, the sister of Moses, "to Pharaoh's daughter, Shall I go and call to thee a nurse of the Hebrew women, that she may nurse the child for thee? And Pharaoh's daughter said to her, Go. And the maid went and called the child's mother. And Pharaoh's daughter said unto her, Take this child away, and nurse it for me, and I will give thee thy wages. And the woman took the child, and nursed it. And the child grew, and she brought him unto Pharaoh's daughter, and he became her son. And she called his name Moses; and she said, Because I drew him out of the water."

We have in these words the simple history of the incident we now proceed to investigate. The point that presses first for inquiry is, in what sense it could be said that Jochebed the mother, and Amram the father, of Moses, by faith took him and hid him three months in the river. It could not have been merely natural affection that prompted them to do so, because that natural affection was balanced between two possible contingent calamities. She risked, by one plan, the loss of Moses; or, as she had other children, if she had been detected hiding one, which was the grossest violation of the commandment of the king, she would have encountered the contingency of the destruction of herself and all her family together. If, then, it had been left to a mother to determine which she should do, — allow the child to be nursed by herself, and be exposed like the rest of the children of Israel, possibly to escape, possibly to come under the wrath of the king, while her other children remained untouched, — or to attempt the concealment of this child, and, in so doing, risk the destruction of the rest, — she would, no doubt, at the dictate of mere maternal instinct, have accepted the former alternative, however fearful, and lost the infant Moses to preserve his grown-up sister Miriam, and the rest of her family.

It was surely no ordinary persecution in the land of Egypt, when that became an element of terror which, to a Jewish mother's heart, was the signal for the intensest joy; that persecution must have been intense that made the Jewish mother in Egypt not to rejoice — to use the beautiful language of Scripture — that "a man-child was born in the world;" and to feel what was the joy of former times only a calamity, and not a blessing.

What was the special faith that prompted Jochebed, the

mother of Moses, to hide him three months, as she did? Paul says, both the parents did it; the actual history is, that one of them, the mother only, did it. The parents are said, by St. Paul, by faith to have done it. The history is, that the mother did all that is recorded of the parents of Moses. But this is a case parallel with that recorded in the Acts of the Apostles, where it is said Peter and John went together healing the sick and preaching the Gospel, and that the people took notice of them, that they had been with Jesus. They saw that Peter and John were "ignorant men," and they marvelled at them, and inferred that they had been with Jesus. Throughout the whole, Peter was the speaker, John was silent, and yet both are said to have contributed to the ultimate effect. So both parents may have coöperated here; faith may have been as active in the father's silence as it was in the mother's energy, in his advice and plans as in her execution of them. Faith may be in the silence that waits and hopes, as well as in the energy that acts, and is crowned with brilliant and visible success. By faith the father may have stood still; by faith the mother may have prepared the ark and hid her child.

But what was the ground of this faith, which is declared to be "the substance of things hoped for, the evidence of things not seen"? The mother of Moses simply had a promise for her faith to rest on; and this promise she heard sounding in her captivity in Egypt, — "I am God, the God of thy father; fear not to go down into Egypt, for I will there make of thee a great nation; I will go down with thee into Egypt, and I will also surely bring thee up again." The mother of Moses knew the promise, and that the destruction of her people in Egypt was an impossibility; and the ground of that impossibility was not political calculation, but the simple pledge and promise of that God that cannot lie. She saw that, if every Hebrew child were slain, the chosen nation must disappear as snow-flakes in the sea. She heard sounding as music in the depths of her heart a promise of perpetuity and safety. She saw upon the new-born babe's brow, by faith, some bright signature, from which she called him a proper, or a goodly, or beautiful child. From that bright signature upon the infant's brow, — the counterpart of the pledge and promise of God,— she believed that Moses was the destined liberator of her people, the child to be preserved in the purposes of God. She still cherished faith in God's promise, and she saw evidence on the child's brow that he was the individual by whom, and through whom, that promise was to be carried out; and she, therefore, in confidence in God, mingled with affection to her babe, hid him three months; and He, that cannot miscalculate or mistake, says, "By faith she did so."

We have in this a very different illustration of faith from what we have had in other recorded instances. By faith Abraham went to a strange land, fearing, trembling, yet confiding. By faith he offered up, or prepared himself, which was the same thing, to offer up Isaac, at the bidding of his God. But, in this passage, by faith the mother of Moses did what was not painful, but delightful to her heart, This is a new aspect of faith. Faith is obedience to God when that obedience crosses and cuts up our dearest and our most cherished preferences; and it is no less acceptable to him when it runs in the channels of our own deepest and dearest affections. A Christian enjoys what is pleasant by faith, not because he likes the pleasant, but because he obeys God; and a Christian endures what is painful, not because he does not shrink from the painful, but because he believes in and obeys his God.

It is God that thus sanctifies to a Christian the sweet, and sweetens to a Christian the bitter; enables him to be thankful for flowers when they bloom in his path, and to take with patience the thorns that are mingled with them. It is by faith a Christian marries in the Lord; it is by faith a Christian dies in the Lord; and in both cases he is acceptable to God, whose will, and word, and promise, his faith leans on and looks at. Thus, faith is developed in doing what is delightful to us, as well as in suffering what is painful to us. We are very apt to forget this. We often say, "I am in deep affliction; pray for me, that I may have faith." Yet it is no less appropriate, "I am in great prosperity; pray for me, that I may have faith." It needs just as much faith to enjoy the sweet as it does to bear the bitter. It was by faith that Abraham braved the painful, when he was ready to give up his child; it was by faith that Jochebed hid her babe, and gratified all the instincts, the deepest in our nature, of a mother's heart. It is by faith that kings rule, that subjects obey, that sick men suffer, that aged men die, that all men, if Christians, live. It is the bright silver thread that runs through the whole biography of the Christian man, giving continuity, consistency and glory, to all.

We see, in the next place, that God accepts this confidence in him, or obedience to him, simply because it is so. God did not command Abraham to offer up Isaac because he was delighted that his creature should suffer pain. He did not command Jochebed to hide her child three months because it was agreeable to the natural affection of a mother's heart to shelter her babe. But he commanded both to show their confidence in him by doing that which he pointed out as duty, simply because it was the prescription of duty, and nothing more. God regarded the faith that was prepared to give up an only son, not because of any felt pleasure in the pain that necessarily accompanied it; he regarded the obedience that goes forth to gratify the instincts of a mother's heart, not because it was delightful to her, but because it was the expression of allegiance to himself. God says, "Follow the pleasant in order to be happy, and you will fail; have confidence in me, and I will lead you to the pleasant, the beautiful, the good. Seek ye first the kingdom of God and his righteousness, and all these things shall be added unto you." Go where duty bids you, with a confiding heart, and an unfaltering footstep, and the desert itself shall become green, and all voices sound musical, and the wilderness before you shall brighten and blossom as the rose.

Another element of this overcoming faith is stated in another part of the verse, "They were not afraid of the king's commandment." Not that the royal commandment had no tyranny in it, or that there was no power in the royal arm to execute the devices of that tyranny; not that there was insensibility to pain or domestic affliction in the hearts of these parents; but they felt they had a clear commission from God, — their only duty was to do what was his bidding, knowing it was God's prerogative to take care of their ultimate and everlasting safety. And one can see that there must have been great faith when these parents thus dared that which was mightiest upon earth, and would not obey him who was the most exacting of Egyptian monarchs. One knows that words spoken by royal lips are arguments, and that power wielded from a throne is all but irresistible within its shadow. We have no experience of the conflict, too common in other times, when duty, as the apostle says, to God, necessitated disobedience to what seemed the equivocal command of the earthly magistrate. Men were then obliged to see "whether it be right" to "obey God rather than men." Times may come, and in other lands it may now be actually the case, that the command that issues from the high places of the earth shall run in direct antagonism to "Thus saith the Lord." Whenever such a collision comes, — and God grant it may never come to us, and there is no reason to believe it will come in this favored land, — we can have no hesitation in giving the reply, in the noble and impressive accents of Christianity,

"We ought to obey God rather than men." Yet this decisive step which the parents of Moses took is perfectly consistent with the loftiest loyalty. A Christian man is ever the most loyal subject; but even his loyalty has its limit; it ceases to be loyalty when he obeys what God forbids; it is in fact the noblest loyalty when it cleaves to every command that is not inconsistent with the allegiance that he owes to the King of kings, the Lord of lords. The noblest Christians have always been the most loyal subjects, — the most devoted in the camp, the most faithful in the field, the most loving to their home. But in so delicate a matter we must take care not to confound a crotchet in a scrupulous conscience with a solemn obligation to a Christian's God. We must not, in so weighty a matter, take any man's opinion as our ultimate guidance. Were all the counsels in Christendom that ever met, from Nice to Trent, to command me to violate the allegiance that I owe as a subject to my sovereign, I should disobey their rescript, and despise the anathemas that usually follow such disobedience. Were the Pope of Rome to command me to do what my Bible tells me is contrary to the allegiance that I owe to my sovereign, — obedience to magistrates being the express command of God, — I should retain undiminished my allegiance, notwithstanding. My duty must be drawn fresh from the fountain of duty, — God's word. The rescript that I shall obey must be drawn from the sacred Scriptures themselves; nothing patristic, conciliar, episcopal, presbyterial, has any force or conclusiveness, in the judgment of a Christian, on the conscience of a believer. These two parents did not fear the king's commandment, because they feared God, and obeyed God's will and word.

We learn another lesson from the subsequent incidents in the history of the parents of Moses, — that the most unbounded faith in the promises of God is ever accompanied by the most enduring energy in the path of duty. The mother of Moses might have said, "There is a promise that this child shall be preserved; God himself has promised it; I may sit still, have recourse to no expedient, employ no effort." But she did not do so; she proved that the faith which is evangelical, so far from being inoperative, "worketh by love, purifieth the heart, overcometh the world." It is the anomaly, the contradiction, if you like, which the world cannot explain, that the man who believes in an everlasting purpose is the most active and obedient to the precepts of Him who has made known that purpose. The world cannot understand how, if we are chosen to salvation, we nevertheless need to be saved through the sanctification of the Spirit, and belief of the truth; that, while we are not justified by any works of the law, we yet must live and do whatsoever things are just, and pure, and lovely, and beautiful, and of good report. Yet the very definition of faith given in the Bible implies that it is ever active. Did any ever hear of a sun without light, of a fire without heat, or of living faith without works as its holy and beautiful fruits? It is no faith at all if it be not followed by works,—it is very faithlessness and unbelief; for true faith is ever accompanied by things that are just, and lovely, and beautiful, and of good report.

We have a striking instance of the compatibility of an absolute promise with the use of means in the Acts of the Apostles, where we read of the perils of the ship in which the apostle Paul was carried to Rome. In this case there seemed the certainty of shipwreck and destruction inevitable to all. On that occasion Paul stated that an angel came from heaven and told him absolutely that not one in the ship, either of the crew or the passengers, should perish. He might have argued, "I have an absolute promise that we shall not perish; I will go down to my berth, and pay no attention to the crew or passengers, or use any means at all." But he did not do so; he stood upon the quarter-deck, and when the crew and passengers were rushing overboard to plunge into the sea, vainly hoping to escape, Paul said, "Except these persons abide in the ship, ye cannot be saved." Now, here is the seeming contradiction; he had an absolute promise that every one of them should be saved; and yet, so urgent, so essential, I may add, was the use of means, that he said, Except the means be used, and these men abide in the ship, ye cannot be saved. Here is the compatibility of an absolute promise of God with a dutiful attention to the means that are in our power.

In this spirit the mother of Moses acted. She arose with the promise still sounding in her heart, "This babe shall be saved, and be the deliverer of Israel;" but, in order to render possible that grand result, she constructed a boat of the frail papyrus, pitched it outside with bitumen to prevent the ingress of the water; a mother's fingers carefully, because inspired by deep affection, constructed it; a mother's keen eye, keen from the love that lightened it, watched every crevice, and laboriously filled it up; a mother's love — all affection to the babe, yet all confidence in the God that gave him — inspired her heart to feel and her lips to breathe the prayer, as never mother prayed before, that God would shut the mouths of the savage crocodiles, restrain the winds, allay and keep down the wild waves, and spare the precious treasure she was constrained, in obedience to a high command, and out of a sense of duty, to trust to the mercy of the waters, and the wild beasts, more tender than the Pharaoh that sat upon the throne. That mother, however, not satisfied with this elaborate provision against every possible contingency, or at all tempted to relax her exertions, set Miriam, the sister of the babe, to watch, as an unwearied sentinel, while she — the mother — went a little distance and watched the sentinel-sister, while the great God above stood the sentinel over all three; so that not a hair of the head of any one of them was injured, because they had faith and confidence in him. Soon after this, we read, in the passage we have quoted from Exodus, Pharaoh's daughter went to offer her accustomed sacrifices, or to perform the religious ablutions usual in that country, on the banks of the river. One can well conceive what was the trembling of the poor Hebrew mother's heart when she saw draw near to her most precious treasure the daughter of the very tyrant from whom she was hiding that babe. The wave — accidentally, the world would say — lifted the ark a little higher than the level of the Nile; the playful wind laid the rushes that grew up and hid it. The eye of the princess detected the unusual little boat rocking on the rippling waves, and, no doubt, made inquiry what it was. She sent her maid to examine it. She approached it, removed the lid that a mother's fingers had so well fastened, and there was disclosed what must have unsealed all the springs of tenderness and love in a woman's heart, — heathen as she was, — a babe in its lonely helplessness. Its bright face must have been thrilling eloquence; its very helplessness must have cried in piercing accents for protection; its big bright tears, as they coursed each other, must have been resistless appeals to pity. The heart of the daughter of Pharaoh was melted, and she resolved, under the inspiration of love and pity, to save the babe her father was ready and watching to destroy. Meanwhile, we may well ask, what must have been the mother's feelings when she saw the ark lifted from its place, and the daughter of Pharaoh inspecting its living contents? Surely her heart must have been ready to burst with agony, her faith in God's promise must have faltered, her expectation of Israel's exodus from Egypt must for a moment have been shaded and obscured; and in herself, and in her inmost soul, the poor mother surely said, "I thought God had given me a promise; I am mistaken. I thought Israel would be spared, and my child the great deliverer; I have misapprehended; God has forsaken me; my God has forgotten me."

But may I not ask, reader, of thee, Did you never doubt the safety of your soul? Did you never despair with a promise sounding in your ear? Have you had no suspicions of the faithlessness, no doubts about the truth, no fears of the love of God? Yet God's promise remains. Believer, that soul of yours, encompassed with frailty, doubting, trembling, often almost despairing, is just as secure, amid all its trials, its temptations, and its sorrows, as the babe of Jochebed in the little ark that was rocked by the waves. Heaven and earth may pass away, but that babe could not perish; your soul cannot be forsaken. A mother may forget the son of her womb, that she should not have compassion upon him, but "I will not forget thee; I will never leave thee, nor forsake thee."

But let us read the narrative. The mother's fears were excited; the loss of her babe was suggested to her mind. But man's extremity is always God's opportunity. Very remarkable it is, when the church of Christ has been at its very lowest degradation, or rather distress, God has been preparing her emancipation and her victory. At this extremity, as we read, the sister of Moses, under a divine impulse, ran to the princess, exhibiting a self-possession and quiet in which woman ever excels man, and skilfully suggested, "As your highness has found a Hebrew babe, what can be more proper than for your royal highness to select for that babe some Hebrew nurse?" Here was ingenuity, and yet there was no equivocation, no evasion, no deceit. Here is a specimen of exquisite policy, and pervaded and sustained nevertheless by inner and thorough principle. Miriam had been taught not to lie; but her affection prompted, and divine communication guided, her to suggest anything, except the sacrifice of truth, to save her infant brother. The moment that she made the suggestion, it came home to the heart of the royal princess, and she said, "Go and fetch a Hebrew nurse." With what a bounding footstep, with what a beating heart, must Miriam have reminded her mother alike of possible dangers that must have ruined all, of possible escape that might yet save all; and with what joy must the mother have seen the dawning vision of the safety of her beloved babe! Hope was rekindled from its smouldering ashes; the thought flashed across her mind, "Why should I have doubted the faithfulness of God?" and she learned that things may be brought to the very lowest ebb, as we know that the cause of truth may be at the very lowest pass, and yet God's promises shall not fail till they are lost in glorious performance; and that the least word that God speaks is stronger than the mightiest pillar that man can erect. The mother, we are told in the interesting history in the second chapter of Exodus, received the foundling back to her bosom. Ten minutes before, she would have given all the world to save her babe; now she is not only permitted to clasp him in her bosom, but, in addition, she is unexpectedly paid to be a nurse to him. Faith in God led her to leave the babe to the everlasting providence of God, and that faith is honored by him replacing that babe in the bosom of the mother, and making her the paid nurse to the child. "Them that honor me," is as true in England as it was in Egypt, "I will honor."

"Trust in the Lord, forever trust,
And banish all your fears;
Strength in the Lord Jehovah dwells,
Eternal as his years."

The wages of a nurse — and to a poor mother these were not unwelcome — were added to the joy of a mother. And now, lest a knock at the door might make her suspect the approach of the murderer, lest the shadow that swept over the casement of her home might lead her to fear that the emissaries of Pharaoh were approaching, the babe is not only saved from the waves, but it is protected by the very royal authority which was exercised against the rest; and she learned, what believers still learn, that, through faith in Jesus Christ, all elements that were against us are turned into our allies, and that all things work for good to them that love God, and are the called according to his purpose.

While noticing the feelings of the mother on her recovery of her babe, we cannot pass by the features displayed by a heathen princess on this interesting and touching occasion. It is doubtless true that man is fallen, perishing and corrupt; that he cannot think a thought that is perfectly pure, or conceive an act that is perfectly good, until the Spirit of God regenerate and inspire his heart; yet it is not true that even from the natural man every gleam of his pristine grandeur has passed away. Sometimes the worldly merchant on the exchange does things that put to shame the professing Christian at the communion-table. Many a time a lofty sense of honor has achieved what the grace of God in the heart has not yet enabled us to equal, still less to excel. There are traits in the natural man, many of them exquisitely beautiful; and all that we wish to teach is, not that these traits, which have so much of conscience in them, and are so beautiful in themselves, are bad, but that all, when woven and combined together, cannot either constitute a title to the regions of the blessed, or be a fitness in the heart for that rest which remaineth for the people of God. In the case of this heathen princess, we see tender natural affection, a susceptible heart, open to the impressions of the good and the beautiful as noonday itself; we witness in her conduct lofty courtesy, condescending kindness, as manifested in the reception she gave to the gratuitous, some would have called it the offensive, suggestion or remark of Miriam; we find, in addition to all this, a high sense of honesty in paying wages to the Hebrew mother for nursing the Hebrew child. She might have said, if she had been mean-spirited, "It is enough that the child is spared;"

but she added, "I will give thee thy wages." The grace of God teaches us to do justly. What a shame to us, if nature goes beyond us in this! That man who stints the laborer of his wages, who takes from his servant that which is his due, and, in order to enrich himself, will do bad things and dishonest things, may talk of his religion as he pleases, — the heathen princess of Egypt will rise up at that day and condemn him, since she did by nature what he does not, though professing to be actuated by grace. There was, in this heathen princess, munificent kindness, in thus taking a foundling, a foundling of the hated tribes of Jacob, receiving him under the roof of the palace of Egypt, and training him for high and lofty purposes; and it was great heroism, approaching to faith, that prompted her, in spite of her father's royal interdict, to watch over the child, nurse, and educate, and prepare him for a royal sphere. In all these respects, she manifested traits, surviving traits, of what man originally was. We may say, from these, that she was at least near to the kingdom of heaven. We may hope that she, who was instrumental in saving one who had so grand a work to do in the providence of God, saw a light struck out in the history of the babe whom she saved, that led her to believe in one like unto Moses, the great prophet and priest of the people, the Saviour of sinners, whose blood cleanseth from all sin.

Those words, uttered by the heathen princess, remind us, however, of another application. She said to the mother, "Take this child away, and nurse it for me." It is almost violence, but I hope it is pardonable violence, to imagine these words addressed by our Savior to every Christian mother. That babe that he has given you is to be nursed, not for the world, its pomps, its vanities, its ambition, its pride, its vainglory; or even for Cæsar, as its great and its ultimate end; but "Take and nurse it for me." Parents are, as they ever ought to be, the noblest sponsors for their babes. Having received their babes to be taken care of in virtue of the instincts that are deep and dear in a parent's heart, they receive superadded a new charge to take their children as Christians, and, as Christians, nurse them for the service, the glory and commands, of the Lord Jesus Christ. Do not despise a child; do not undervalue an infant; there is more in that babe than eternity itself will unfold. No parent knows sufficiently how responsible a charge is hers when an infant is given to her to nurse for Christ. It is not a castaway; it is not despised by Jesus; it is not a soiled, and a miserable, and an outcast thing; children are not vile weeds to be trodden under foot; they are beautiful but trampled spring flowers; they only need to have their heads lifted to the Sun of righteousness to be watered with the dews of heaven, to be embosomed in a mother's prayers, and their mothers may hope that they will yet be great and illustrious in Israel. Take this babe, and nurse it for me; for of such as these is the kingdom of heaven.

We hear many voices sounding from this interesting history. They are, shortly, these:

We hear, in every incident, the doctrine of a special, or, as it is frequently called, a particular providence. Take the chain that connects Moses' birth in the midst of Egypt with Moses' burial in the mount, no man knew where, and if one single link had dropped from that chain, the whole destiny of the world, so far as we can see, had been totally altered. And if we take a retrospect of the most prosaic, dull and bare biography, from the time we left our father's and our mother's roof-tree, till the moment that now sweeps past us, we shall find that if any one fact in our lives had been otherwise, it would have altered the whole tone and complexion and current of our present being. Was it not the turning of a corner that brought us where we met with prosperity? Was it not an accidental event that brought us within the walls where we heard the Gospel? Was it not an accidental meeting that made me a husband, a wife, a father, or a mother? Pins the most minute are the pivots upon which the wheels of the history of the world have revolved. Give me, as I have said before, the power to have put in a pin where I pleased, and I would have engaged to alter all the destinies of Europe. If God be not in minute and microscopic incidents, he is nowhere at all. If there be not a particular providence, there is no providence at all; for little things are the events and hinges on which great destinies constantly turn. And if this be so, it suggests an important advice: never despise a fact that occurs, an opportunity that opens, a suggestion that is made. The man shows little faith who says to us, "O, what is the use of my doing this? I have so little influence." Do not think highly of yourselves, but think most highly of God, and so seize every opportunity of good he presents. If you are in the senate of the land, amidst the senators of England, never say, "What is the use of saying anything? They will not listen to me." You may depend upon it that a word uttered there, containing a real truth, never returns to God void. It lives, and the movements of the next century may be the reverberations or the crashes of a sentiment spoken, amid the sneers of some, the coldness of others, the opposition of more, by some obscure man, of no party, in an obscure place of the great assembly of the land. Do not undervalue the least of things as openings or spheres of usefulness; for there is a God in minute things as in majestic. Just as the microscope reveals to us God as truly in the structure of a beetle's wing as in the creation of the elephant and the leviathan of the deep, so his providence is just as conspicuous in the tiniest and minutest movement as in the very greatest. The Highlander illustrated the usefulness of little things when he said to some one who thought that the little he could do was unavailing, "Do you see the dew-drops on the heather? Notice these dew-drops turn into little rivulets, these into larger ones, these into the mightier streams that roll to the great sea, bearing the navies of the earth upon their bosoms, and kings and princes at their helms; so the very least and minutest of things may embosom the very greatest results."

We hear another equally eloquent and impressive voice; our babes need no less the protecting providence of God than the child of Jochebed lying in the ark, upon the river Nile. The same helplessness is with ours as with hers, the same providence is pledged. If God be not around our babe's cradle, it is not safe. In this privileged land, it is true, there are no crocodiles ready to devour, nor rough waves threatening to overwhelm, nor wicked monarch on the throne determined to extirpate, — yet there are evils, invisible to us, but accumulating on every side; trials under the happiest roof; dangers lurking about the brightest fireside; our world is replete with temptations and difficulties; there is no safety for children or cherubim, except under the overshadowing wing of God; and there is no danger for the youngest babe embosomed in the fervor of maternal prayers, and directed by Christian tuition. The best protection is the providence of God. The best lesson a child can learn, or a mother teach, is "Thou, God, seest me."

The church of Christ has been before, and may be again, reduced into very little and very unimpressive space; the outward eye may see no prestige of material grandeur, and very faint prospect of ultimate victory. Yet what seems great to the eye is not always great in fact. The minutest acorn is great because it will quicken and develop itself into the gigantic oak; whereas, the greatest mountain is small, for it wastes down every day. Truth, even when minutest, is mighty; falsehood, even when it looks the greatest, has in it the elements of its own destruction. It seemed contingent on the casting of a die, to use a familiar expression, whether that ark should be the coffin or the cradle of Moses, whether the Nile should be the grave or the guardian of that babe; and there did appear but little hope for grand results arising from a case contingent upon so minute and microscopic an accident. Yet, it was predetermined, before the world began, that that babe should live and be the deliverer of his people, and the great and suggestive foreshadow of the Son of God. Over that tiny ark, rocked upon the wild waves, partially hidden by the bulrushes, there were marshalled all the cherubim of the sky; around that little babe were the everlasting arms that weary not, and will not give way; all things might perish, — it could not.

How great was the contrast between Pharaoh on his throne and Moses the infant in the ark! The natural man would say that on that throne and around it were all the elements, the certainty, the earnest of endurance, greatness, victory; and in that ark, and about that babe, all the symptoms of decay, of weakness, of death; but it really was not so: the one went down and perished with all his chivalry, like a ship, in the Red Sea; the other led forth the hosts of Israel to progress, to victory, to the promised land. In later days, we have seen Luther, a poor monk, speaking a great truth; Leo, the most powerful of the pontiffs that ever wore the tiara, treating him and all such with consummate contempt; and yet, the truth of God, whether in the babe rocked upon the waters of the Nile, or in the monk's bosom, half buried in a convent, is immortal and imperishable, and all besides is weakness. The arc that truth describes is not to be measured by a human foot-rule; it is to be measured, if measured at all, only by the inexhaustible promises and the eternal faithfulness of God. The Nile might sweep away Pharaoh's palace, it could not overwhelm that ark; the lightning may rend to atoms the gigantic oak, it does not touch the frail violet that blooms amid the rank grass at its roots; it is not the strength or bulk of the thing, but the presence of Deity, that makes it strong.

How wonderfully does God overrule the schemes, the passions, and the wickedness of man, to the furtherance of his own great ends! Pharaoh heard that a Hebrew child should dispossess him of his throne. Egyptian prophecies said so, — no doubt, the mere confused echoes of what was uttered in the oracles of God, — but, at all events, it was what Pharaoh believed. His fears aroused him to action. He determined, lest the feared Hebrew babe should grow up, to murder every infant that should be born. All he did, however, only expedited the great purpose of Heaven; for his own daughter became the guardian of the child that was to overturn his throne, his own palace became the nursery of the very babe that he dreaded. It was not the power of Moses, but the sin of Pharaoh, that broke his sceptre, and swept away his kingdom. Truly, God restrains the wrath of man, and overrules the remainder of it to praise him.

We have here an evidence of God's perpetual presence with his church. The church was represented in Moses, and its existence was contingent on a babe's life. Yet God was there, just as he was in heaven. Jesus is no more with the portion of the church that is in heaven, than he is with the portion of the church that is on earth. "Go and preach the Gospel; I am with you always, to the end of the world." "When thou passest through the rivers, they shall not overflow thee." Crowns may withhold their splendor, wealth its contributions, genius its eloquence, all things may conspire against Christ's church, but it is founded upon a rock, and the gates of hell shall not prevail against it.

Persecution always fails in promoting the ends it has in view. Pharaoh used its weapons, and they proved a miserable mistake. It has been tried by other men, and it has equally failed. We never can put down a lie by persecution, we never can sustain a truth by injustice. Truth repudiates every assisting weapon that is not drawn from the armory of heaven, and what is false shrinks from the aid of the pure and lofty in every age. Truth can only be supported by her own weapons; the weapons of her warfare are not carnal, and, because they are not carnal, they are necessarily and invariably mighty. Bless, and blessings will return upon you in a thousand forms. Curse, and the curse will return upon him that utters it. Wind a chain around the arm of a brother, and, by a great law, the other end of it will be wound about your own. He that unsheaths the sword in all probability will perish by the sword. We need to know this, and in the present day to act on it, more than ever. It may be that power will not be our protection, that high places will not be our shelter; but, blessed be God, if all power should cease to defend, and all law should be against us, the Bible remains, the God that wrote it remains; faith, hope, love, remain; and these are mighty, for to God they go, as from God they originally came.

CHAPTER VI.

THE CHOICE OF MOSES.

"Tears, what are tears? The babe weeps in its cot,
The mother singing; at her marriage bell
The bride weeps; and, before the oracle
Of high-famed hills, the poet hath forgot
That moisture on his cheeks.

"Albeit, as some have done,
Ye grope, tear-blinded, in a desert place,
And touch but tombs; look up, those tears will run
Soon in long rivers down the lifted face,
And leave the vision clear for stars and sun."

"Choosing rather to suffer affliction with the people of God, than to enjoy the pleasures of sin for a season." — HEBREWS 11 : 25.

MOSES chose, not only in heart, or in principle, as we may do, but in fact, when the alternative was before him, affliction with the people of God; and rejected, personally and practically, all the pleasures of a palace, because sin was there. We have recorded in this passage what was presented to the choice of Moses, one of two states. There was sin under the roof of Pharaoh, and amid the pomp and grandeur of a palace; there was affliction in the company of a poor, persecuted body of slaves, laboring at brick-making, and crushed by a terrible tyranny; — the one the prescription of his conscience, the other the enjoyment and delight of man's passions. On the one side Moses saw a path strewn with roses, fragrant with their perfume; but underneath the roses, serpents and poisonous reptiles, that would sting the foot that trod them, and the hand that gathered them. On the other side, he saw nothing but a black road, and a dark and a miry way, but over it the sunshine of the face of his God, and at the end of it joys at his right hand, and real pleasures, not the pleasures of sin, forever. His choice was between sin, whose pleasures were momentary and external, and holiness, with its afflictions, which also are momentary and external.

It does not imply that with a palace there are always sins and pleasures, nor does it mean that with the people of God there are always afflictions. Men have been, and may be, in a palace, holy, prosperous and happy, in the profession — the heartfelt profession — of the Gospel of Jesus. It is always, and everywhere, the heart that makes the atmosphere about us, and not the circumstances that make the heart. A holy man must be a happy man everywhere. A man whose conscience is racked with a sense of sin must be miserable, place him where we will.

We see still before us two great elements, between which Moses was placed, — the one, sin with its supposed, imaginary real, and, when real, momentary pleasures; and the other, God's people, God's cause, and God's walk and way, with its contingent accompaniments, in his case actual accompaniments, — afflictions.

What is sin? A word uttered in a moment, with a meaning inexhaustible forever. That monosyllable "sin" is the most awful, the most dreadful thing in the whole universe of God. It is essential evil. Disease is not evil, death is not evil, suffering is not evil; but sin is unmitigated, unrelieved, unmingled evil. It is what a discord is to the ear, what ugliness is to the eye, what disease is to the body, what death is to humanity; it is all these compressed into one. We cannot conceive fully what is in that monosyllable, sin. It rent a happy world from God, it still rends man from his fellow. In the strong language of the most gifted and noble spirit of his age, the late Mr. Howels, "Sin is a homicide, and would be a deicide."

Sin, rejected by Moses, in spite of its pleasures, is neither from God nor of God. God did not make sin. Wherever it came from, — and we shall find that the infidel who rejects Revelation will be far more puzzled to explain its origin than he that believes Revelation, — and for whatever reason it was allowed to interpolate its poison, God did not make it. God made the wild field-flower, and the overshadowing oak. He made the dew-drop that dances on the rose-leaf, and the great sea that girdles the earth with its bright zone. He made the youngest infant that prattles on its mother's knee, and the cherubim that stand before him, and cry "Holy, holy, holy, Lord God of hosts," continually. He made whatever in the depths the microscope detects, and he created whatever in the heights the telescope brings within the horizon of our view. But sin he did not create. It is neither of God, nor from God; nor on God rests the responsibility of sin, whose wages is death, whose issue is hell.

Sin, also, which God did not make, and for which God is not responsible, carries in its bosom always a curse. Man never can be happy in sin. He may have a pleasure which is external for a moment; but we know ourselves, when the sin that gave the momentary pleasure is gone, the long, lasting, gnawing pang known popularly by the name of remorse, — a pang as sure an accompaniment of sin as the shadow that accompanies our body in the sunshine remains behind. Sin's wages, we are told, is death. The spirit that welcomes it is ever a wounded spirit. The progeny of sin is violence, fraud, murder, battle, death; and its history is written in tears; and bleeding hearts, and crushed affections, and wounded spirits, are the wrecks it has strewn far and wide on many a strand.

Its history is written in tears. It laid a fair world waste. This world was once exquisitely beautiful, — so beautiful, that God, that made larger and grander worlds, pronounced it to be very good. What altered it? what broke it up? The answer is, Sin. There is not a cloud that darkens the brow of once conscious innocence, that is not the shadow of sin standing between that brow and the countenance of God. There is not a tear in the channel that furrows the cheek of child or aged man, that has not its spring in sin, and its bitterness, all its bitterness, there also. There is not a broken heart or a wounded conscience in the world, that has not something to do with sin. Graves are its foot-prints, battle-fields are its play-grounds, and the discordant trump, and the groans of the dying, and slaughtered dead, are its victims and its spoils. Sin's wages is death temporal, death spiritual, death eternal. Sin is hell, and hell is sin. According to my judgment, we need no material fire, no actual, literal worm in hell, to be its intensest agony. That language, "Their worm dieth not, and the fire is not quenched," is just the use of the strongest elements of bodily torture, to denote the terrible and the inexhaustible agony that flows from the absolute domination of sin. "The worm dieth not,"—its life is sin, — "the fire that is not quenched," — it was kindled by sin; — and that hell, in which sin is dominant, as I have often said, was never meant for man. "Come, ye blessed of my Father, inherit the kingdom prepared for you;" but "Depart, ye cursed, into everlasting fire, prepared," not for you, but "for the devil and his angels." And, therefore, he that perishes eternally in hell finds himself where God never meant him to go, where no decree drove him, where no coercive predestination sank him; he has landed there just as a stone dropped from a height falls upon the earth, or as a piece of lead thrown into the sea sinks to the bottom. The sinner finds himself in hell by the very gravitation of his character; and that character has carried him there, because he would not appeal to atoning blood for its pardon, and to a sanctifying Spirit for renovating influence. I have often said, and it is well over and over again to repeat it, there is not a lost spirit in hell that is not a suicide; there will not be one lost victim there whose recollection will not be, "I did it all myself;" and there will not be one saved and happy one in heaven whose constant song will not be, "I did none of this, I deserved none of this; Christ did it all. I was saved by grace, and grace alone."

But sin is shown not in its worst aspect in the facts that I have mentioned, but in this: It crucified the Lord of glory; this alone is evidence of its virus. It was not Pilate, nor Herod, nor the Jews, that crucified the Lord Jesus Christ; it was sin. To blame the poor Jew is unnecessary; let us blame ourselves. It was we that crucified him. He came to his own, and we said, "Away with him, away with him!" He came to redeem, and we said, "Crucify him, crucify him!" And it is remarkable that a section of the church, if church it can be called, whose supreme pontiff has driven back the Jew to the Ghetto, to which he is now restricted, and thus given an earnest of what liberty under such domination would be, alone as a church crucifies the Lord afresh, and puts him to an open shame. Yet, as if the Jew alone did so, she preëminently maltreats the Jews, and has stood an obstruction, for a thousand years, in the way of their conversion; so much so, that the poor Jew has often said, "I had better remain where I am than enter a communion where sculptures of wood and of gold are done homage to."

But sin not only crucified the Lord of glory, but it ruins the soul.

There may be momentary pleasure to the body in sin, —

and when I use the word sin, I mean the transgression in thought, in word, or in deed, of any one of the ten commandments, — that delights a nerve in the body; but it also strikes a sting that, if unsubdued by grace, will ruin forever the immortal and precious soul. I can conceive nothing more terrible than such a ruin — the ruin of my soul. We are so accustomed to see one drop out of our number here, or another disappear there, that we fancy there is an end of man when he is laid beneath the green sod; but it is not so. If it were the end of man, he would be the unhappiest creature in God's universe. I would rather be the meanest of the brutes that perish, than man, with those indomitable yearnings within him, and nothing to satisfy them, — with that strong, instinctive craving after immortality, and yet disappointment, certain disappointment. But it is not the fact. When the body is laid in the grave, the soul emerges as the sword leaps from its sheath, and appears naked, just as it is, just as it left the body, at the judgment-seat of Christ. And if sin is found to cleave to it an unforgiven thing, then — it is not my opinion, but it is God's word — that soul perishes forever. Nineveh may again be rebuilt, Jerusalem may be re-constituted in greater glory, Palmyra may be restored a nobler spectacle; but a soul once lost is hopelessly, eternally so. If you lose your health, you may recover; if you lose your fortune, you may regain it; if you lose the sense of hearing, God, by a beautiful law in his good providence, will make the sense of seeing more acute, and *vice versâ*: but, if you lose the soul, there is no possible reparation for it; the loss is fatal, final, irreversible. And, surely, that thing called sin, which can ruin my soul forever, must be a poison for which we can find no just and adequate expression. This is the sin that Moses fled from.

But what did he select in its stead? Affliction. Now, what is affliction? I said sin, which he shrank from, did not come from God. I now state that affliction, which he accepted, does come from God. Affliction springs not from the ground. The Lord gives, the Lord takes away. It is a stream from the fountain of life, it is a ray from the source of life. The most painful affliction that can overtake a Christian has not one atom of accident in it. It came from God, and it is meant and designed to do God's will; ay, and to do us good, the greatest good, eternal good. However painful affliction may be, if it comes from God, I will cheerfully accept it; however pleasant sin may be, it is not from God, — I will shrink from it by his grace, and crucify it. Affliction, moreover, is the very evidence of the love of God. This is not what nature says. We fancy that when we suffer God is angry. That is natural logic; but New Testament logic is, that God is well pleased. "He whom thou lovest is sick;" "Whom the Lord loveth he chasteneth." Afflictions are, in a Christian's family, angels unawares. Give them hospitality; receive them as come from God, and leading back to God again. In the pang that rends your heart, in the blow that falls with consuming weight in the loss of your property, in the death of your babes, in the departure of all that man loves, and in the happening of all that man dreads, if you be a Christian there is not one drop of wrath, not one; it is the exponent of love, it is the evidence that God loves you, for he chastens you.

We need not be afraid that God will ever add to one of his children — as Moses felt, as we too should feel — one atom of affliction more than we can bear; he will not send one drop more of sorrow than will do us good. He will not make our afflictions too few, or too short, as we would like them; but he will not make them too heavy, too long, as the devil would like; but he will just afflict us as may be best and most expedient for us. Sin, however pleasant, ruins; but affliction, wherever it is felt, however painful, always sanctifies.

God tells the Israelites that he led them, in his love, through the wilderness, that he might humble them. And who does not know that he never has so much of heaven in his heart as when he is in affliction? We do not like affliction, we do not like pain, — that is natural; but there is not a Christian that cannot testify that it was just when he lost some near and dear child that he saw the chasm left behind filled by him who cheered his sad heart with joy, with confidence, with peace. All experience shows it is in affliction that we learn and display most of God. The aromatic plant, when trodden upon, sends forth all its richest perfume. The brightest summer and the noblest autumn always follow the hardest winter. The highest Christianity is nursed and built up amid the severest and most painful afflictions. If we have no experience of afflictions, the presumption is that we are not God's people. If we have afflictions, let us, trusting in him, and leaning on him, regard them as expressions of his love.

Having looked, then, at these two, — sin, with its pleasures to be hated, whatever its pleasures may be; and grace, with its afflictions to be courted, however heavy or numerous they may be, — let us learn the very important lesson, that the church of Christ may be very often in a very poor and afflicted state. God's people in Egypt, we read, were in the depths of affliction and depression. In the Church of Rome the definition is given by Bellarmine, that outward prosperity is a "note" of the church of Christ. A strange definition! If it be so, then the church of Pharaoh was the true one, and the church that Moses allied himself to was the false one. But it was the reverse. A day comes when the sons of God shall be manifest, and when the church of Christ shall be all gathered into one, and made visible. Then, its prosperity will last like the sun; but, at present, the jewels are in the mire, and upon the street, amid storm and tempest; and

Christ is gathering them, and polishing them, and brightening them for his diadem, now hidden, but then to be revealed in everlasting glory and beauty.

The true church of Jesus may have no outward splendor whatever. Pharaoh and his people were adoring idols in those beautiful temples in Egypt, some fragments of which now remain to give us an idea of their stupendous grandeur; but the church of God was worshipping the Lord in dens, in caves, in sequestered and hidden places. And has not this been the almost continuous history of the church of Christ? When was the church the purest? Not when cathedrals were its coverings, and when prince-bishops were its ministers; but when the caves of the Alps were its lowly chapels, and when martyrdom was its chief confession of faith. Then the church of Christ was purest; for the mitre on its brow was the beauty of holiness, and the garment that adorned her, the raiment white and clean, the righteousness of saints.

The true church in Egypt, as we have already seen, was not the established church. One holds that the church established by the state is right, and another that it is wrong. Here, at all events, was a church established by the state, and yet it was wrong. And what does this teach us? That the establishment of a religion by the state does not make it true. If it were so, the communion established in Turkey would be true, and the Bible proscribed in Rome would not be sin. It is possible for a church not to be united to the state, and yet to be true; and it is possible for a church to be united to the state, and yet to be pure. The substance of a church is not the one or the other. In this case, the church of Pharaoh was the church of the state, and it was false. The church, on the other hand, that was cast out, persecuted, and trodden down, was the church rejected by the state; and it was true.

The Egyptian church of that day, the church of Pharaoh,

was by far the most fashionable. As far as pomp, splendor, circumstances, advancement, could be obtained, the right way was to belong to the church of Pharaoh; but, if persecution and contempt were not to be feared, it was duty to belong to the church of Moses. Yet Moses left the church in whose congregations were devotees, and crowns, and wealth, and splendor, — the embroidery of Egypt upon its altars, and the riches of the world upon its shrines. He left all, and allied himself to a handful of slaves, who had nothing to commend them before men, but hearts that beat true with allegiance and loyalty to God; and he chose affliction with them, rather than the pleasures of sin, royal as they were, which were but for a season.

No doubt, the church of Pharaoh was by far the most numerous. This teaches us that we are not to determine which is the true church and which is the false church, by anything extrinsic. The true church may be in a chapel; the false one may be in a cathedral. Christ's people may be a handful; those of Antichrist may be nations, and kindreds, and tongues. The Shechinah had a splendor just as real in the midst of the mean tabernacle, as it had when it blazed and shone in the temple of Solomon. It is not by its outer splendor, but by its inner glory, that we ascertain where is the true church of the Lord Jesus Christ. In order to join a congregation, we should not care how many attend it, or how rich they may be; we should go where the Gospel is most clearly and unequivocally announced, and where our souls needing bread can be best nourished, and most refreshed with hope, and peace, and joy.

Days are coming when sects shall be broken up, when connections and relationships, however dearly loved by some of us, shall be destroyed; and there shall be nothing left at last but that which was first, the little company met together in the name of Jesus, and himself in the midst of them; the church that man cannot build, the company that time can never waste.

Moses chose the people of God. This is the simple distinction. He renounced number, fashion, rank, wealth, the establishment of his country, all that could win the mere carnal man to any body, and he chose affliction with the people of God, a few despised, hated slaves, without anything to commend them to man, but with much to commend them to God. But who are the people of God now? Not all Episcopalians, not all Independents, not all Presbyterians, not all the Church of England, not all Dissenters. We are all very apt to try to maintain a monopoly of grace, and to think that our church is so much the best that there is no salvation without it. I believe that there is a people, however few, even in the Church of Rome, — I cannot state, nor am I called upon to state, their number, — where, through the murky cloud that envelops them, they can see the Sun of righteousness, and in their hearts feel the rebound of the touch of Jesus. They are there, not in consequence of their creed, but in spite of their creed; and they prove, not that the church that they are in is true, but that the grace of God is so mighty, so irresistible, that it can penetrate the greatest antichristian obstructions, and reach humble hearts, and transform them into its own celestial likeness.

The people of God are not they that pronounce a certain Shibboleth, or wear a peculiar garment, or display a certain badge, or hold a crucifix, or use a liturgy, or do not use a liturgy. None of these cover the distinction of the people of God. I do not say that we should not love the communion that we prefer; but, the instant that our love becomes equal to our love to Christianity, we are on Popish ground. The moment that our love to our party becomes stronger than our love to Christ and his, then it is a mere question of time when you will land in Popery. Popery is not a system that has the Pope at its head, but a creed that prefers the ecclesiastical element to a divine one, which makes more of a sect than of the people of God.

The people of God. What are they? Who are they? The people that live by faith, that are justified by a perfect righteousness without them, received by faith, and are sanctified by an almighty energy within them, the Holy Spirit of God; whose creed is not man's invention, but God's inspiration; whose law is the law of God, and it alone; who, resting upon Christ who died for us, and sanctified by the Spirit that now is, are looking in blessed hope for Christ, who will come again, and receive them to himself.

This leads us to conclude with three practical remarks, relating to the three great topics that we have been studying. First, there are those that remain where Moses left. There are, secondly, those that leave, as Moses did, and are the people of God. And there are, thirdly, those who cannot yet make up their minds whether they shall remain in Pharaoh's palace, amid the pleasures of sin, which are for a season, or turn to the people of God, and risk persecution with them.

First of all, there is a class that remain amid the pleasures of sin, where Moses left. We do not say that sin is inseparable from a palace. This is not our meaning. We only say, that, in the circumstances in which Moses was, sin was inseparable from his remaining. The matter was plain and clear, and he made his decision accordingly. But you, if I address such a class, are still determined to remain with the pleasures of sin. It need not be in the palace,—it may be in a hall, in a trade, in a business, in parliament, in medicine, in law. The place and the pleasures of sin keep you from God. Whatever it be, it is that which keeps you from God, and it is to you precisely what the splendor of a court, with its sinful pleasures, was to Moses in his day. And you have made up your minds, have you, to remain? Then the world is your all, you have taken its joys as your all; your creed then is, "Eat, drink, and be merry, for to-morrow we die." You ignore Christianity, you despise all idea of a future rest, you refuse to entertain — what a refusal! — this momentous problem, "What shall it profit a man, if he gain the whole world, and lose his own soul?" I ask, is it rational to refuse to entertain it? Does it indicate common sense to settle all or any questions that relate to our national, social, domestic, personal state, and leave this great one unsolved, unsettled? You say, It matters not, I have done so. Then, my dear reader, the angel within you is lost in the animal, the divine within you is buried in the human. All that should draw you, and lift you to God, is despised, repudiated, rejected. There is no dungeon so dark as that man's bosom in which there is no Christianity. Your house is, indeed, left to you desolate, and all the coruscations of the most splendid intellect can only reveal, what they do not remove, — a darkness denser than that which fell upon Egypt, and the precursor of a more terrible darkness yet to come. Either, speaking to such as are resolved to remain where they are, the Bible is a delusion, Christianity a dream, religion a lie, or your conduct is the most grievous guilt, and the most terrible inconsistency. There can be no medium. If this Bible be a lie, Christianity a delusion, then why do you go to church? Why do you keep a Bible? Why pay any homage to what you know to be a lie? Why accept in any shape what you believe to be a delusion? But, if it be not a lie, then the love of God is great, then the death of Jesus is wonderful. How will you answer at the judgment-seat of God for trampling under foot the blood of the everlasting covenant, and counting it an unholy thing? I ask, in the nineteenth century, what an apostle asked in the first, "If we neglect so great salvation, how shall we escape?" Surely, every reader of these pages, whatever be his present condition, has made up his mind that the grave is not the end of this life, that death is not the final scene. Has it never struck you to inquire how you must cross that deep chasm that lies between you and eternity, — how are you to escape that deep fathomless abyss? Surely, no man is so insensible to all that is terrible in prospective peril, that he will not entertain this question, When my soul leaves my body, how am I to get to heaven? Yet you do not, you repudiate it. Do you say, as I have heard some persons say, "O, it is very well for religious men"? Do you say, "One man is religious, another man is commercial, another man is medical, another is political, another is literary, another is scientific? If you like religion best, then be religious. If you like literature best, then be literary. If you like science best, then be scientific"? Alas! this is gross misrepresentation and delusion. It is right to be literary, scientific, political, it is perfectly right; but religion is not one of the professions, nor one of the pursuits, that one may despise, neglect, or prefer. A man may prefer scientific to political pursuits, but all are bound to be Christians. Religion is not a profession for a coterie: it is the cure of man's sin, the salvation of man's soul — that which every man is called upon instantly to study, and heartily to accept. Do not cease to be literary; but let your literature be sanctified by your religion. Do not refuse to be statesmen; but let your politics be read in the light of revelation. Be what your taste prefers in the sphere of human life; but, O, think again before you reject salvation, however despised, and remain with the pleasures of sin, which are but for a season!

But I trust there are, in every place, not a few, but very many, who have made up their minds, and have already left, with Moses, the pleasures of sin, and accepted the company of the people of God, with all their afflictions, which are but for a season. Do we address any who have made the sacrifice? Do we address any one who has given up a lucrative trade because he could not but sin in it? Are there any readers who have come down from a splendid position, in order that they might leave the pleasures of sin, and cleave to the people of God? Happy people! Beautiful poverty! Glorious descent! Magnificent decision! Blessed is the people that are in such a case. Rejoice and be exceeding glad! You have riches far more glorious than those you have left; You have an expectancy already revealed in this precursory act. The germ of everlasting joy is in your bosom. You are seeking the kingdom of heaven first, and its righteousness; and I am persuaded that neither life nor death shall be able to separate you from the love of God that is in Christ Jesus. "And no man has left houses," — mark these words, — "no man has left houses, lands, wife, children, family, for my sake, who shall not receive in this life an hundred-fold." We well know that to get rid of that corroding feeling of remorse, that disquiet, that dissatisfaction, that anxiety of mind, which all are conscious of who are living in a course which conscience will not applaud, is to get out of the region of death into the very region of joy and life. There is a natural blessed compensation within, and God will add without what is most expedient for you. Now that you have made the decision with Moses, you will be rich in the meanest hut, patient in the greatest tribulation, and tranquil amid the most excited crowd. You will now step into every relation of life with a new dignity, and you will enjoy whatever God gives you in his providence with a new and an unprecedented zest. Your heart has now regained its true polarity, your affections now do not oscillate; you are not drifting upon the currents of life, you are sailing across life's solemn main; and as you sail, you will touch at every place where a flower is to be gathered, a brother is to be cheered, a blessing is to be left; but you will only touch at it: you will again set sail and sweep onward toward that haven of happiness, that home and rest that remain for the people of God. You will not enjoy science less that you are a Christian, you will not be a worse statesman that you are a believer, you will not attend to your profession less because you love your Bible more.

Some reader says to himself, "Well, I am sure that the author is right." I know that some will say so, and more think so. I know that every conscience these words may reach will protest in favor of the claims of the Gospel. No reader dare contradict these truths that we here record. Each professor, whether he likes them or not, knows them to be God's truth.

But some under that conviction will say, "Well, I should like to leave Pharaoh's palace, with sin and its pleasures, and to join the people of God; but I cannot yet make up my mind." I believe this is a most numerous class; they are what may be called border Christians, — men who have sometimes a fit of religion, and at other times a fit of worldliness; who one day are all enthusiasm for the Gospel, and the next day all freezing indifference; who are rolling about unsettled, never becoming fixed friends of Christ and him crucified. You have too much light to reject Christianity, and you have too little to close with it. Your conscience will not let you despise the Gospel; your passions, calling for indulgence, will not let you accept it. You love the pleasures of sin so much, that you do not know what would become of you if you were to give them up; and yet, you dread meeting God at the judgment-seat so truly, that you do not know how you will meet him. Conscience has its paroxysms; then you must have a physician, and a priest is close by. Passions must be gratified; and for these you have indulgences. Between the pleasures of sin and the afflictions that accompany the acceptance of the Gospel, you are constantly oscillating. You fancy yourselves that you are perfectly safe, yet you feel you are in a sort of twilight, but you eventually hope that it is the twilight that will end in everlasting day. Christ has said, "He that is not with me is against me." Your twilight is just that which will infallibly end in everlasting night. Let me, then, beseech you not to remain loitering any longer. Your condition is the most miserable of all. I could not continue in such a condition: I must be one thing or another, out and out. You have all the misery of this condition, without its joy. You have not the world's peace, which is " Peace, peace;" nor have you Christ's peace, which passeth understanding. If Christ, then, be no Saviour, if the soul be not immortal, if death be an eternal sleep, then, my dear brother, why not say so, manfully say so? Burn the Bible, turn your back upon the sanctuary, do not enter it again. Why do you shrink? why do you hesitate? Just because you know that these things are truths, and in your solemn and sequestered moments you cannot get rid of the deep, inner conviction that the Bible is the truth of God. But, on the other hand, what does the Bible say? "He that believeth not shall be condemned." Then decide that, for you and yours, you will cleave to the truth as it is in Christ Jesus.

But perhaps you will say, "It is very easy for you to say, Decide." I know it is. It needs the grace of God to enable you to do so. But you must not make that an excuse for indecision. Is there anything upon earth that is worth having which we must not encounter great difficulties in obtaining? Did you ever get credit for knowing anything without labor in acquiring the knowledge? Do you think that those who make eloquent speeches among the members of Parliament do it by inspiration? Do you think ministers whom you consider eloquent have only to open their mouths and speak? All things excellent are the results of struggle, study, hard preparation by day, and deep thinking by night. If this be God's law, that nothing worth having is to be had without study, how should you think that it is possible to decide between God's truth and man's lie without thought, without study? You have learned to distinguish between a good sovereign and a bad one. Did it not cost you some experience? Can you distinguish between a good bank-note and a bad one? — have you not learned thus to distinguish by considerable practice? Have you made up your mind upon questions of finance, upon the papal aggression, and never made up your mind whether the Bible be God's truth or Satan's lie? Out of your own mouths I condemn you. Let it not be said that the children of this world are wiser in their generation than you.

But perhaps you say, you do mean to decide, but not now. "Wait till I get rid of this troublesome law-suit that I am involved in just now. Let me retire from business, and go to my country-house, and then I will talk upon religion in earnest." This seems very plausible; it is the most successful deception that the devil practises; let us see what is in it. You admit the duty of deciding, but, while you admit the duty, you violate it. God says, "Now;" you say, "No." God says, "To-day;" you say, "To-morrow." Felix tried this experiment; you have read of his success. He failed, he perished. When you retire to your country-house, when you have got over this law-suit, are you sure that God will wait all this time your convenience? are you perfectly satisfied that your heart will be so susceptible, and your mind so inclined to decide, next year, as it is at this very moment? It is needless to disguise it: it is only a more courteous way of rejecting Christ, and ignoring the Gospel.

But some one, perhaps, says, "We dislike extremes; we do not like to go to extremes in religion. We wish to maintain that smooth, quiet kind of Christianity which is characterized by moderation." Far be it from me to encourage anything like fanaticism; there is nothing more detrimental to real religion. But when you speak of moderation in religion, let me ask, Did you ever hear of a man moderately honest? Would you not think such a man was dishonest? Did you ever hear of a man moderately true in his statements? And is it possible to be moderate in the fervor of our love to God, in the intensity of our reliance on the cross of Christ? Such a plea needs only to be investigated to be seen to be utterly untenable; for, so far is moderation from being recommended in these high matters, that God says, "Thou shalt love the Lord thy God with all thy heart, and with all thy mind, and with all thy soul, and with all thy strength."

Then decide for Christ; count all but loss for the love of him; fling yourselves loose from all that fetters your feet in running the race that is set before you; lay aside every weight,—be Christian; and from that moment you will be far happier; you will tread the earth with an elastic step; you will look forward to a judgment-seat without a cloud upon your brow; every pulse in your heart will be a bounding one, because yours is a hope that maketh not ashamed. Do you think that Moses repents in glory the decision that he made on earth? And when you come to die, the only repentance you will have will be, that you did not sooner close with a faith that adds to the grandeur of the man all the glory of the saint, that makes earth's dark places bright, and smooths the wrinkles on the brow of age, and awakens in the fainting heart the voices of the skies, and has perpetuated its echoes in the biography of Moses, who "being dead yet speaketh."

CHAPTER VII.

REJECTED GREATNESS.

There is no wind but soweth seeds
  Of a more true and holy life,
Which burst, unlooked-for, into high-souled deeds,
  With way-side beauty rife.

"By faith Moses, when he was come to years, refused to be called the son of Pharaoh's daughter." — HEBREWS 11 : 24.

IN the preceding chapter, we showed what a beautiful and Christian faith, laden with many and precious truths, was lodged in the hearts and developed in the conduct of Jochebed the mother and Jethro the father of Moses. "By faith Moses when he was born was hid three months of his parents, because" — having a promise from God, and seeing on the brow of that babe the signature that indicated him the object of promise — "they saw he was a proper child; and they were not afraid of the king's commandment." We have now the same faith exemplified in the child of so faithful and excellent parents: first, by his refusing great honor in order to identify himself with the sufferings and vindicate the wrongs of the people of God; next, in "esteeming the reproach of Christ greater riches than the treasures in" even "Egypt;" and next, in forsaking "Egypt, not fearing the wrath of the king; for he endured" that wrath, and clave to this duty, because he saw "him who is" to human eye, to carnal eye, "invisible."

We have already seen that faith may sometimes be exhibited in doing what is pleasant, just as it may be developed in enduring what is painful. God prescribes the painful to faith, not because it is painful, but because he would nurse his child in loyalty and confidence in himself; and God prescribes what is pleasant, that he may show us that the Christian may live in sunshine as well as in clouds; and that, whether it be in the sunshine or in the cloud, in the heights of Pisgah or amid the tents of Mesech and the tabernacles of Kedar, a Christian's life is a life of faith. By faith the parents tried to save their child, — what the heart's affections chimed in with; and by faith Abraham left his country, — what the heart's feelings protested against; and in both they were accepted, not because the one endured what was painful, and the other did what was pleasant, but because both had confidence in God, and obeyed his will.

Here we have another contrasting evidence of what faith is. The same faith that compelled Joseph to remain in the court of Pharaoh, contradictory as it may look to the world, compelled Moses to quit the court of Pharaoh. This seems almost a contradiction; because, if faith prompted adhesion to place in one, how could it prompt the renunciation of place and power in another? Yet it did so. By faith Joseph held the place of dignity and power to which he was raised; by faith Moses quitted the place of dignity and power to which he had been raised; and both did that which was beautiful before God, and consistent with the Christian character by which they were distinguished.

In this we learn a very important lesson: that acts, which in themselves are not sinful, ought not to be judged by us till we see all the circumstances connected with them. To condemn Joseph for remaining amid the splendors of a court, on the plea that he loved pomp and dignity, would be just as rash as to condemn Moses because he left the splendors of a court, by attributing to him asceticism, or fanaticism, or folly.

The acts which are not obviously sinful are to be tested by their motives, their ends, their aim, their object; and when we see how many acts which appear to us sinful are just the reverse when analyzed, the longer we live the more we shall learn the lesson, to be slow to judge, and quick to pray for all men. Joseph remained in this court, and for the obvious reason that he could be a minister of good to the people of God. Israel had perished on the plains of Egypt if Joseph had not been at Pharaoh's right hand. And Moses, on the very same ground, namely, to be a minister of good to the people of God, left that court in which he could not have benefited them, and where he might have injured and weakened his own Christian character. The court that was friendly in Joseph's days had become hostile in the days of Moses. A Christian may remain in an idolatrous court, in whose idolatry he is not called to take a part; but a Christian cannot remain in a persecuting court, whose proscriptions he is compelled to carry out, and of whose fierce passions he must become necessarily the exponent. Thus Joseph remained in an idolatrous court, an evidence of true worship, and a minister of God to his people. Thus Moses left a persecuting court, because, as its chief member, he could not continue in it, and prove hostile to those who were dear to God, and therefore dear to him.

There is not necessarily sin in accepting the honors of a court, as Moses did when he was called the son of Pharaoh's daughter, or as Joseph did when he became the prime minister of Pharaoh. Obadiah lived in the court of Ahab; Daniel lived and did good in Nebuchadnezzar's; Mordecai had his mission in the court of Ahasuerus; there was a Christian prime minister in the Ethiopian Candace's court; there were saints in the house and amid the palaces of Nero. God sends men, in his providence, where there is something for them to do; and so long as they can do that which contributes to the glory of God and to the benefit of his church, without themselves catching the contagion of the court in which they are, so long they are called upon to remain. The truth is, sin is no more in royal purple than it is in beggars' rags. The sin is not a thing that cleaves to the circumstances: it belongs to the person. A true Christian can glorify God anywhere: a carnal heart must dishonor him everywhere. It is not the circumstances that make the man holy: it is the holy man that sheds a splendor on the meanest circumstances, and consecration on the least and humblest work. The true guide, therefore, in all these things, is that beautiful remark which has been made by our blessed Lord, "If the eye be single, the whole body is full of light." Steer by expediency, that is, apparent good, and you will leave your bark amid the reefs, the rocks, and the quicksands. Steer by truth, that is, everlasting and unchangeable good, and you will be guided to the haven of rest that remains for the people of God. Remember, that what seems expedient is not always really so, and if it be wrong it never can be so; but what is true, and good, and just, though it may seem to cross us, and to beat upon us with all the force of all the winds of heaven, its course is straight, its destiny is happiness, blessedness, and peace. Seek first in all things the kingdom of God and his righteousness, and all the rest will fall in as matters of course.

So it was with Moses and with Joseph. The one, having a single eye, took power; the other, having the same single eye, resigned power; and both did it, not because the one loved it, or because the other was weary of it, but because both by faith did that which they saw and felt was their allegiance to God.

But, it may be asked by some of those who are the advocates of that expediency to which I have referred merely by name, Would it not have been far better if Moses had tried to hold on by the circumstances of grandeur in the midst of which he was placed, and kept, what he afterwards abjured, an opportunity of doing so great good? When we hear of some person giving up a place of lofty influence, and subsiding into a meaner and humbler one, the first exclamation of many an excellent Christian is, "What a pity he resigned a place of so much influence, and selected one where his influence must be utterly lost!" That depends, first, upon the circumstances of the place, and next, upon the conscience of the individual. I do not say that conscience is always an infallible judge. There is sometimes a scrupulous conscience, sometimes a feverish conscience, and there is in some a conscience that never can be at rest; and, therefore, it needs to be illuminated by the light, and inspired by the Spirit of God, in order to be right. Your course must depend upon the circumstances of the place that is resigned. If you cannot keep that place, whether it be that of a servant in a private house, or of a servant in a great and public place, without doing that which is sinful, then it is not, and never can be, an opportunity of doing good to man, or giving glory to God: it must be an occasion of stumbling in itself. If a place be sinful, it ceases to be tenable to a Christian. It may be a place of the loftiest power, the most extensive influence, the largest prerogative; but, if you are compelled to do in it what your conscience, properly enlightened, protests as wrong and sinful before God, no possible expediency can tempt you, as a Christian person, to retain that place, because there you must violate the law and grieve the spirit of the Lord Jesus Christ.

Moses saw that, however lofty the place that he occupied, it must prove the occasion of his doing that which was sinful; and, therefore, he left it;—he saw that it must prevent him from allying himself with those that were suffering, whose wrongs were his, whose sorrows were his, whose God was his also.

It may be asked, in the next place, Did not Moses do what was an act of great ingratitude, when he refused to be called the son of Pharaoh's daughter, who had saved him from the Nile, preserved him from being destroyed by its ravenous creatures, nursed him with a mother's care, spread over him the wing of royal power, raised him to great dignity, taught him all that was worth knowing in Egyptian science, and in Egyptian literature? Was it not an act of base ingratitude to leave one whom he ought to have loved and continued with as if she were his own mother? Did he love her less because he loved God more? Affection to her was strong; but duty to his God was stronger still. He, too, heard what we have heard, and what so few have had magnanimity to exemplify: "If any man come to me, and hate not," that is, comparatively, "his father and mother, and wife and children, and brethren and sisters, yea, and his own life, also, he cannot be my disciple." Moses, therefore, however much he loved her who acted to him a mother's part, yet felt that there was an allegiance higher than that he owed to earthly relations — the allegiance he owed to his God; and, like him of whom he was the great type, he must have said to her, when she protested against his leaving, "Wist ye not that I must be about my Father's business?"

It is important to observe that Moses made the choice which is here recorded, not in the season of youth, when rashness might have prompted him to do so, but when he came to full years. "When he had come to years," that is, to full and ripe age; and in the Acts of the Apostles we are told he did so when he was full forty years old; for that it then came into his heart to visit his brethren, the children of Israel. If Moses had done what is here recorded when he was a young man, it might have been said that he had done a very rash and hasty act, and made a precipitate decision, which he might live to repent. Or, if he had acted thus in the wane of life, it might have been said that dotage and weakness of intellect had induced him to do so. But he decided, not hastily as a young man, nor foolishly as a very old man, but in the prime, in the strength and vigor of manhood. It seems as if God sanctioned the opinion, that the full strength of human life is at that period. Moses was for forty years regarded as comparatively young, he was forty years spending the middle age of human life, and then he lived forty years more, which constituted old age, having lived in all one hundred and twenty years. There has been no shortening of human life since that time; and, if we do not live to that age, I do not think that there is anything in the Bible that states that seventy years is the summit of human life. And, were the sanitary condition of our country what it ought to be,—and I look upon that sanitary condition as a fit subject for the pulpit of church, chapel or cathedral,—were our temperance much severer than it is, and had we fewer and less corroding cares, irritating feelings, ambition, disappointments, griefs, vexations, aches, —for these are the vipers that waste and suck out the very life of human nature,—were we, in short, humanly speaking, in better circumstances, moral and physical, I do not see why our life should not be still one hundred and twenty years. Some one will say, "Ah! you must forget the ninetieth Psalm: 'The days of our years are threescore years and ten; and if by reason of strength they be fourscore years, yet is their strength labor and sorrow, for it is soon cut off, and we fly away.'" It is not that I forget it, but that some misinterpret it. For where was that Psalm written? In the wilderness, when God's people were in a state of peculiar suffering, and Moses complained, and said, "The days of our years," that is, of Moses', forty as a young man, forty as a middle man, and forty as an old man—one hundred and twenty years in all, "are reduced to threescore years and ten. So great have been our sufferings in this wilderness, that our life has been reduced to threescore years and ten; and if we reach eighty, instead of just beginning to get old, we find that we are old already, and that our days are labor and sorrow." Let us learn this plain lesson, that when, where, and how we should die, must rest with God; but that, as far as sobriety, temperance, immunity from unnecessary care, anxieties, fears, perplexities, can go, we shall try to reach the limits of the years upon earth, influentially living to do good by walking with God, and dying to inherit good, and so be forever with Christ.

We come now to the peculiar exercise or expression of the faith of Moses as declared here. "He refused," it is said, "to be called the son of Pharaoh's daughter." What excellence was there in this? Very great; he was raised to the position of a prince. Josephus, the celebrated Jewish historian, states that Pharaoh had no son, heir, or successor to his throne, except the foundling Moses, the only adopted child of his royal daughter: and that, if Moses had remained in the palace, accepting the honors that were given freely and lawfully to his exalted position, he might have indulged the hope of reigning on the throne, and swaying the sceptre of mighty Egypt. Surely, when we see in this world ambition laboring so hard in order to attain honor, and those that have it struggling and striving so desperately to retain it, such as it is, we can discover in the conduct of Moses very great sacrifice, when he accepted the name of the hated Hebrew, and abjured the royal name of the son and heir of all the Pharaohs. We can see in this such denial of one of the strongest instincts of the human heart, such trampling under foot of the love of the world, the lust of the eye, and the pride of life, that we must admit that there was great faith in God, to enable him thus to lay aside all man loves, and to choose all man dreads upon earth, and to ally and identify himself with the persecuted and despised and contemned children of

Israel. The apostles once said, "We have left all and followed thee." There was much in this; but what did they leave? A few broken nets and leaky boats. But Moses left a lofty throne — a royal diadem. Yet, when we think justly, the sacrifice does not consist in the largeness of the thing that we leave. There may be as much sacrifice and faith in God in a poor man's leaving and sacrificing twenty shillings a week, as in the greatest noble's laying aside his coronet, and coming down from his hall to be an every-day laborer. It is not the amount that we leave, but it is the relation of that amount to us; and if there be faith which worketh by love, which purifieth the heart, whether it be ten thousand pounds or ten farthings, it is equally the victory that overcometh the world. The glories of a city that hath foundations shaded all the glories of Egypt in the eye of Moses. His eye rested on a crown of glory, his ear was filled with celestial harmonies; the rose lost its briers, and the desert lost its barrenness, because God was with him, and the blessing of the Lord was upon him, and the pillar of cloud and the pillar of fire guided him to the rest that remaineth for the people of God.

Nor was it, in the case of Moses, mere disappointment with his circumstances that induced him thus to give up this lofty place. Sometimes we hear of great persons resigning the dignities of a crown because they had felt disappointed ambition. Their subjects have risen in insubordination against them, or rival kings have excelled them in popularity or *éclat*. But in Moses there was no such feeling that could thus prompt him to give up Pharaoh's court.

Nor was there anything like fanaticism. He was the soberest of men.

Nor was there any of the ascetic element in the character of Moses.

We can explain his conduct in no other light than this, that it was Christian self-denial; that God's word, sounding in his heart, was to him dearer than all the pomp and splendor of Egypt; that he looked only to Him that was above him; and that he was ready to dare all, to do all, to sacrifice all, for the glory of his blessed Master, and for the good of his beloved people.

It is the motive, it is the inner feeling, that gives its tone and character to the outer act. It is not the outer splendor in which Joseph was that we are to look at, nor the abjuration of that splendor that Moses made, but that which was in the heart of each, — loyalty to conscience, allegiance to truth, confidence in God, which bade the one remain, and commanded the other to fly. It is not necessary to suppose that wherever there is a palace there only is pride, and that wherever there is a hut or hovel there must be humility; just as it is not necessary to suppose that wherever there is ten thousand a year there is avarice, and that where there are a few hundreds a year there must be liberality. It is the inner man that gives force, tone, character, to the outer circumstances. Prouder hearts have beaten under conventual robes than under royal purple. There has been often as much pride developed in descending from a palace as ever was developed in ascending or climbing to a palace. Cowls and hoods are not necessarily the exponents of humility. The crucifix has been held in a monk's hand with more superb hauteur, with more contemptuous pride, than ever a sceptre was grasped by a monarch, or a crown worn on an emperor's head. Abstinence has often nourished as much pride as indulgence, however sinful or wicked. Fasting in Lent has very often punished the outer man, whilst it has carried into the inner heart self-righteousness, pride, and "stand aside, I am holier than thou." Renunciation of self has often graced a throne; deep and unmortified pride has often been developed by a barefooted mendicant friar; and, of all pride, the most hateful before

God and the most horrible before man is the pride of religious distinction, privilege, superiority.

This act of Moses, in renouncing all the dignity of a throne, was not because he felt the circumstances themselves were necessarily unlawful; not because he believed that the circumstances of dignity in which he was placed were in themselves sinful. There is a class of Christians who have separated from various denominations, and who hold that, when a man becomes a true Christian, — that is, a true convert, — he ought instantly, if he has a seat in Parliament, to lay it aside; if he holds an office in the state, to renounce it. We believe that these men, with the best of motives, are dealing around them the greatest of mischiefs. God means society to be just what we find it, a gradation of wealth, gradation of rank, gradation of social, political and national circumstances. That seems to be the law of nature, and no less the recognition of the Gospel of Christ. Were all society macadamized into that dead-level road to which some would bring it, the very first to suffer would be those who had made the experiment. The valleys have flowers so sweet, and vegetation so green, because the black high hills above them contribute their showers and streamlets from their bosoms; and the humbler classes of society have, many of them, their chiefest blessing, the sweetest shadow from the other, because society is constituted as it is in our favored and privileged land, — the absence of tyranny in high places, the absence of insubordination in low places; and all because it is held together by the sweetener and the cement of life, the religion of the Gospel of Jesus. Moses did not renounce all this because he thought honor was unlawful or improper. We ought to take the place God assigns us in his providence, and to try to make it a place of practical usefulness, a fountain of munificence, by the grace that God gives us by his Spirit.

But we must not forget that, if a high place, such as a Moses occupied, has great honor, it has great responsibilities. Why was Solomon made wiser than his fellows? Not for himself. Why is another man richer than the rest of mankind? Not, surely, for himself. The order of God's providence, and certainly the law of Christ's Gospel, is, that wherever there is great power, lofty position, there is great responsibility, and a call to instant duty. If your house is very magnificent in its architectural splendors without, and in its furniture within, it is that you should look around you, and take care that the houses in the lanes behind shall not be so miserable and wretched as they are. London's grand palaces would not look less splendid if they did not cast their shadows over so many miserable dwelling-places, where there is neither air, nor water, nor the elements of healthy moral or physical existence. And let us never forget, whatever be our position, that the untitled name of the humblest peasant, who loves his God, and carries forth the mission of his Lord, sounds musical where the angels are; and that the loftiest title of the greatest noble, who is forgetful of his duties, disloyal to his God, selfish, narrow-minded, self-seeking, is not mentioned in heaven, or is mentioned only to be deplored as a curse, and not a blessing. When David was raised to a lofty place, his language showed that, in the Bible, which our sceptics say our age has grown out of, and in those Levitical laws which our modern philosophers allege were only fit for a barbarous people, there is a loftier humanity, a tenderer sympathy with suffering, and greater evidence of deeper and more earnest regard for man and beast, than in any other code of laws that the ingenuity of man, in ancient or modern days, has given birth to. David, when he came to a lofty position, said, "I dwell in a house of cedar," (that is, a house of great splendor), "whilst," he stated as an intolerable contrast, "the ark of the Lord is in curtains." And so every man, raised as Moses, Joseph or David was, should ask, "I have a large income; how much do I lay out on the claims of the poor? What do I to promote the cause and the kingdom of Christ? Have I ever denied myself a great luxury in order to do a great good?" Is it not true of us all, that we have rarely given beyond our superfluities; that we have rarely yet denied a right eye or a right ear its joy, or the human heart its appetency, in order to do moral, spiritual, physical, real good to the souls or bodies of mankind around us? Let us recollect David's expression, "I dwell in a house of cedar, when the house of the Lord is desolate." If I may now address some reader in high life, I would remind him that these places are always slippery places. There is no person so little to be envied as the very chiefest servant of our most gracious queen. The greater our office, the heavier are our responsibilities; and no man needs so much to be prayed for, or so deeply to be sympathized with, as he who treads the high and the splendid places of the world. I have often thought it a beautiful expression of Nehemiah, "O Lord, I beseech thee, let now thine ear be attentive to the prayer of thy servant, and to the prayer of thy servants, who desire to fear thy name; and prosper, I pray thee, thy servant this day, and grant him mercy in the sight of this man. For I was the king's cupbearer." He asks the greatest mercy because he held the highest office. Great rank, then, has great troubles, great responsibilities. Let us not forget this.

Moses, when he voluntarily left the dignity that he was raised to, although he did not judge it unlawful to hold it, yet, at the same time, estimated it at its due value. That expression employed by Luke in the Acts of the Apostles is a very suggestive one. He says, "When Agrippa was come and Bernice with great pomp." The Greek word means "with a great fantasy;" that is, with a royal magnificence, which was an empty splendor. Moses penetrated the outer show, and estimated it aright. All the glory of the world is as the grass; its greatest men only as the flower of the grass; and the flower falls first before the grass. All the splendor of lofty circumstance is little more, when we can look at it in the light of a judgment-seat, than the clouds of the west illuminated by the beams of the setting sun, or the poor man's casement lighted up with the glory of the rising sun, when the hearth may be cold within, and the heart may be pining in poverty and in want. The greatest sceptre, the most illustrious crown, is, after all, but a gilded toy, and the gilding soon wears off, and the owner soon feels and knows that it is so; and the procession of the noblest king and his meanest subject is alike a funereal procession to the grave. In the words of a poet I have often quoted,

> "Art is long and life is fleeting;
> And our hearts, though stout and brave,
> Still, like muffled drums, are beating
> Funeral marches to the grave."

Our last retrospect of life in the light of eternity rarely fails to place it in its due proportion, and show the emptiness of that grandeur which Moses resigned, without hesitation, for the sake of that glory which shone from afar.

Thus we learn the great lesson that spiritual and eternal things are alone great, precious, weighty and important. True and enduring greatness is moral, not circumstantial or physical. Neither the stars in the sky, nor the flowers on the earth, are so beautiful or abiding as the graces of a Christian character. We may very fairly estimate our sympathy with Christ, the amount of our sanctification and likeness to God, by this: Does a noble and a generous act, which we see done by another, thrill through our hearts like the noblest music? Does a great soul, elevated by the truths of the everlasting Gospel, appear to us arrayed with a grandeur far eclipsing the impression which the loftiest mountain scenery makes upon those that first behold it? Do we look upon the heights and depressions, the varied outlines and ways of human life, with an interest far greater than that with which we look upon panoramas and beautiful landscapes? Do we feel Moses renouncing the splendors of a palace, the dignity of a throne, to be a nobler scene, and covered with a richer glory, than Napoleon's victory at Austerlitz, or at the Pyramids, or Wellington's triumph at Waterloo? Is it true that moral things in our judgment are alone the majestic things? Can we hail the smile of God as dearer to us than the garlands of the most illustrious conqueror? Do we feel affections at peace with God through the blood of Jesus, and at peace with each other, as the sweetest harmony? Do whatsoever things are just, whatsoever things are pure, whatsoever things are lovely, honest, and of good report, constitute, in our estimation, the richest glory, the noblest possessions? Next to having strength to do as Moses did, is the grace of being able to admire and applaud it, and to pray that, when we are called, we may have grace also to follow his noble and holy example.

Perhaps there may be other reasons, one or two of which we may just notice.

Moses saw faithfulness in the favor of God, and precariousness in the favor of the court. The promises of a king are but threads of gossamer; the promises of God are sure and steadfast, entering within the vail. Moses learned what humanity unsanctified seems no better for learning. "Put not your trust in princes;" in one day their very thoughts perish.

Moses felt that sacrifice for Christ's sake was, after all, the greatest gain. If he had remained in the palace, his name would have been sounded for a season in its halls; it would have been written upon its pillars, perishable as the material on which it was graven; or it might have been carved upon its stone, or in the hieroglyphics of its pillars, or embosomed in its stony pyramids. Such would have been all his glory, if he had held fast to his place, and renounced his duty. But has he not a much greater glory? That name now lives in every tongue; it is mentioned still with admiration in every age; it is perused in the Bible as a word full of sweet music; and in heaven, it is said, they sing the song of Moses and of the Lamb.

We learn, from the whole of this, that faith resigns to God with as great cheerfulness what God demands, as it receives with gratitude that which he has given. When God takes away from us the property we have gathered, the possessions we have earned, the beloved, and the near, and the dear, he takes them, not as a spoiler, but as a proprietor. And, when called upon to surrender what we love, we ought to give it up, not as a reluctant exaction that we had rather keep, but as a free-will offering which we cast upon the altar of him whose are the riches of all the universe.

If Moses thus denied himself, let us recollect that he was excelled by One, a greater than Moses: "Ye know the grace of our Lord Jesus Christ, that, though he was rich, yet for our sakes he became poor, that we through his poverty might be rich;" and that "He took upon him the form of a servant, and humbled himself, and made himself of no reputation." If Christ has denied himself for us, do we ever deny ourselves for him? If he sacrificed so much for us, let us ask ourselves what have we ever sacrificed for him?

One more lesson let us learn in the case alike of Joseph and of Moses; they obtained dignities which they did not seek. Joseph was unexpectedly carried to Pharaoh's right hand. Moses was as unexpectedly educated by Pharaoh's daughter, and in the splendor of Pharaoh's palace. Let riches follow us; it is unworthy of us to follow them. Let honors seek us; but let us not seek them. Take the place that God may assign you, and in that place seek to glorify and honor him; but remember that there is as much faith in being satisfied with the position which God has given us as there is in renouncing at his bidding the glory and the honor that God has added. Jesus waited thirty years in obscurity before he went forth to preach, to suffer, and to die. Joseph, who had qualifications for a prime minister, was hid for a long time in a dungeon. David, who was able to sway a sceptre, learned first to feed the ewes and follow the sheep. And Moses refused the greatest honor when the time was come to renounce it. God will exalt us when it is good for us; and, if he has not yet exalted us, it is in love, and not in anger. A Christian can serve God best just where God's providence has placed him. Many persons say, "Ah! if I were raised to be a master, then how much better I should serve God!" But you will learn, my dear brother, that, if your wish were gratified, the old longing would revive, and you would wish again, "Ah! if I had a few hundreds a year!" and, having obtained these, you would next cry, "If any one would give me a lofty title, what influence I should have!" The man who cannot honor God in the humblest by-path of private life will not be able to do so in the high road of public existence; and the very way to lead God, in his favor, to elevate you to the highest place, is to discharge faithfully and tenderly all the duties of the low place. Do not think about a change of place; but be sure of a change of heart. This is the great thing. Wherever Christian character is, it shines beautiful as a star, whether it sweep a crossing, or sway a sceptre, or lead great armies to battle and to victory. Our present character alone is that which determines, and is the certain antecedent of, our everlasting state. We are now sowing what we must reap; we are now creating, in the providence of God, that character which will remain for ever and ever. If we prefer the splendor and the pomp of office in the palace of Pharaoh, and repudiate all allegiance to God, and scorn the people that belong to him, we laugh now, but we shall weep then; we have our good things now, but our evil things are yet to come; we barter an immortal crown for the wild field-flowers that lie in our path; we exchange, for an indulgence of the world's fleeting happiness, the joys which endure forever. Peals of bells may follow us on earth; the firing of cannon may announce our arrival; but, if we are not children of God, all the elevation of our present dignity will only make more terrible and disastrous our ultimate and everlasting ruin; and if we are passing to a judgment-seat with unregenerate hearts, with unbelieving minds, without an interest in the Saviour, without sympathy in his cause, whatever be the pomp, the place, and the splendor of our present position, yet dirges and funeral anthems are all that await us in the shape of weeping, and wailing, and gnashing of teeth.

But I trust I address many a reader who desires not to be in the place of Moses; and who, if there, would have no hesitation, at Christ's bidding, in instantly surrendering it. I trust that I write to some who, in poverty, can battle with it, who, in prosperity, can make a holy use of it, and who, whether rich or poor, offer up this daily prayer: that, in poverty, they may be patient; that, in their riches, they may be kept from temptation; and that, if they weep, they may pray to God; and that, if they rejoice, they may praise God; and that all that betides them may only bring them closer to him, with whom to walk on earth is to walk surely, with whom to be in heaven is to be in joy unspeakable and full of glory.

Such are some unspent echoes of the voice of one who "being dead yet speaketh." May they linger as sweet and sanctifying strains within us!

CHAPTER VIII.

THE REPROACH OF CHRIST.

"O thou who mournest on thy way,
With longings for the close of day!
He walks with thee, that Saviour kind,
And gently whispers, 'Be resigned:
Bear up, bear on; the end shall tell
The dear Lord ordereth all things well.'"

"Esteeming the reproach of Christ greater riches than the treasures in Egypt."—HEBREWS 11 : 26.

THERE shone before Moses in the future a recompense of reward that attracted him upward and onward continually. In reference to the past, he had a faith resting on the promises of God, which sustained and strengthened him, and became the victory that overcame the world.

We have, in this verse which I have selected as the subject of reflection, the true estimate of what the world dreads as its great calamity, "reproach;" and of what the world loves as its choicest treasure, "the riches of Egypt." We have here the instance of one who is not a solitary fact, but a precedent, a model for us; for nothing was done by the saints of God of old that may not in the same strength be done by us. God's arm is not shortened, God's ear is not heavy. It is still true, "My strength is made perfect in weakness." "My grace is sufficient for thee."

The two things that are brought before us in this passage correspond to the two we have considered, namely, "affliction with the people of God," and "the pleasures of sin for a season." Moses chose the first, and repudiated, in that choice, of necessity, the last. He esteemed the "reproach of Christ" — corresponding to the "affliction" of the former verse — as "greater riches;" or found in it a mine of richer gold than he discovered by his enlightened eye in all the treasures of the wealthiest land of ancient times, even "the treasures of Egypt."

Let us look at this reproach, here asserted as "the reproach of Christ," or the reproach that ever veils and clouds from the world the great beauty and glory of the people of Christ; and we shall find that in every age of the world, just in proportion as the lustre of Christian character has broken forth, clouds and reproach have been heaped upon the people of God. It is when the Christian character reaches its greatest brightness, that, provoked by it, the reproaches of the world are most multiplied and heaped upon it. It is well known that when the sun, by the very excess of his brilliancy and heat, draws forth from the earth the moisture that ascends into the sky, becomes consolidated into clouds, that ultimately seem for a season to darken his splendor, the very same beams that raised the clouds dissolve them into showers that fertilize the earth, and refresh the fainting violet and the parched grass, and give bulk and volume and speed to the rivers that water the earth.

And, looking at the history of the people of God, we shall find that reproach has ever been more or less their account. The persecution, so called, of Isaac, was reproach. Job, the patriarch, was reproached by his friends, and by Satan. The builders in the days of Nehemiah were treated as weak, ignorant and contemptible men. David says of himself, "I am a reproach to the people." The apostles also were reviled at the day of Pentecost as fanatics and drunkards, but they said, "Being defamed, we entreated." And, coming down to later times, what has been the predominant characteristic of the papal hierarchy ? — the habit of reproaching the people of God, and especially Luther, the Reformer. The fables they have invented, and the publications they have written, in order to blacken that bright character, are only evidences to those who know it, and know what he was, that reproach followed him because he was so much more truly in Christ than the multitude that were about him. Calvin's character has been also misrepresented as a fatalist. The descriptions given by Romish writers of his death are most horrible, but most untrue; for none so truly believed, none so purely lived, none so magnanimously and nobly died. But so it will be. The brightest light has always in this world the darkest shadow; the living epistles never will be without the comments, the blackening comments, of those that cannot endure their light. The reproach of Christ is the reproach of his people still.

But, whilst looking at it in this light, we must also recollect that every reproach we meet with as Christians may not be necessarily the reproach of Christ. Sometimes our own infirmities provoke the animadversion of the world. Sometimes the inconsistencies of Christians draw down reproach; and when our inconsistency, infirmity or sin, provokes the scorn of the world, it is not right to call such scorn the reproach of Christ, although it be perfectly true that the least falter in a Christian's footstep is by an Argus-eyed world denounced as a fatal fall, the least infirmity in a Christian man's character is magnified into a grievous crime, and an unguarded expression incidentally dropped is construed by the world that watches as a great calumny. The same world that most charitably construes its own sin denounces in a Christian the falter of a word. When the world looks at its own transgressions, it views them through a diminishing medium, by which they are diminished into infinitesimal molecules; but when the world views a Christian's failing, falter or infirmity, it looks through a magnifying medium, and sees it increased and exaggerated to the most gigantic size. We must, therefore, recollect that we live in a watchful world; that the more of a Christian one professes to be, the more need one has to walk watchfully, and circumspectly, if possible avoiding not only evil, but the very appearance of it; for they that know the world best will readily acknowledge its disposition to make a slight slip of the tongue, a short falter in the step, the least excess in the temper, a reason for rejecting the whole testimony of God, and blackening the claims of Christianity itself.

But, while we must guard against such reproach as this, yet there is a reproach incurred by the people of God which is here very appropriately called "the reproach of Christ." There is not a doctrine of the Gospel that is not perverted or misinterpreted by the world. The truths we hold, the graces we develop, are equally caricatured by the enemies that wait to do so. For instance, election is denounced by some as fatalism. Let a man only whisper that a Christian is saved by grace, and the least severe epithet for him will be Calvinist; and generally the world's estimate of a Calvinist is that he is a fatalist. Justification without works is denounced as a license for sin; the Atonement is thought an irrational provision, and the Trinity is pronounced simply a delusion, because an incomprehensibility. This is the language of men that do not know better; this is strictly so far "the reproach of Christ."

Again, let Christian graces be seen by the world, and they, too, are equally denounced. Zeal in the cause of truth is denounced as fanaticism. Excitement or enthusiasm for a client or a patient, or for or against the papal aggression, is all perfectly beautiful; but enthusiasm for Christ, for truth, for justification by faith, for missions, is denounced as downright fanaticism. Religion, in the estimate of the world, is hypocrisy, piety is mere pretence, and as for religious profession, it is well known, it will tell you, to be a mere passport got up for specific and ulterior purposes. You cannot please the world; there is no use attempting it. The right course is, to believe what God says, and do what God bids, and leave the world to reproach or praise, as it may be disposed. "He that judgeth us is God." Reproach, to be the reproach of Christ, must be incurred for holding Christ's truth, or exhibiting Christ's character; the world, in either case, turning what we believe, and what we do, into reproach. In fact, the world is much like the tarantula spider, of which we read that it draws the intensest poison from the fairest flowers and the richest blossoms, and turns what are elements of beauty into deadly bane, and the substance of good into evil.

But reproach, in order to be Christ's and for his sake, must not only be incurred because of what we believe, and what we do, but it must be borne also in a Christian spirit. It is Christ's reproach when incurred for holding Christ's truth, and doing Christ's work, and especially when it is borne in a Christian spirit. How beautiful is that expression, "If any man suffer as a Christian"! And again, says Paul, "Let us go forth out of the camp, bearing his reproach." And again, "If ye be reproached for the name of Christ, happy are ye." And yet, how often is our language, "If I had been reproached for what is true, I could have borne it; but, not being true, I cannot bear it"! Now, it ought to be the reverse; because it is not true, how composed and satisfied ought we to be! And, at all events, if it be true, yet, if it be borne in a Christian spirit, it is so far Christ's reproach. An ancient heathen, and a distinguished philosopher, Xenophon, on being reproached, made a remark which might have been a reflected ray from Christian truth, — "You, my friends, have learned to reproach, and I have learned long ago patiently to bear it." There may be as much grace and Christianity in patient endurance of reproach, as in courageous aggression on error. "He reviled," it is said of our blessed Lord, "not again."

If we are reproached for Christ's sake, and bear it in a Christian spirit, how satisfied should we be with the thought we wear the livery our blessed Master wore before us, we tread the same path that he so beautifully and meekly trod; we are in this matter followers of Christ, and are in the world as he was in it! If we be God's people, God writes on our heart the benediction of his own lips, "Blessed are the pure, and blessed are the meek, and blessed are the humble;" and all the clouds and reproaches of the world cannot dim one feature of a Christian character, or destroy one element of faith, and hope, and joy, which God has fixed there. Reproach, then, thus borne, is in more respects than one "the reproach of Christ."

In what sense may such be called his reproach? The answer is, "In all their afflictions he was afflicted." Let us recollect what he said to Saul, "Saul, Saul, why persecutest thou me?" Saul was persecuting his people; but Christ was so identified with them, that the blow struck at them had its rebound beside the throne, and a reproach on them flung its shadow across the throne where Christ is. The vine feels when its branches are torn, or tossed violently by the wind. The head sympathizes when the members of the body are wounded or persecuted. The reproach, however, cast upon a Christian because of that Christian's adhesion to Christ, is really not cast upon him, — at least, it does not rest there; it rebounds, and lights ere it stops upon Christ. "Inasmuch as ye have done it unto one of the least of these my brethren, ye have done it unto me." "In all their afflictions he was afflicted."

Again, we learn from this statement that "the reproach of

Christ" was borne by the children of Israel, — that Christ existed in the days of Moses. How often do we hear the popular remark, that Christ came into the world eighteen hundred and fifty-one years ago! Christ was in the world when the world was made, and "without him was not anything made that was made;" and by calling here the reproach incurred by the children of Israel "the reproach of Christ," it only confirms what previous passages had vindicated, that the rock in the wilderness was Christ. "Neither," says the apostle, "let us tempt Christ, as some of them tempted him in the wilderness." There was not a great fact in the life, the character, or the death, of Jesus, that Moses did not see, more dimly, but no less truly, than we. His glory blazed in the bush, his guidance was seen in the pillar of cloud by day and the pillar of fire by night, his sufferings and his humiliation in the passover lamb; and Moses himself was the type of a great prophet like unto him that God should bring into the world.

If Christ was thus in the days of Moses, Christianity is not a modern invention; it is the ancient faith. Adam was a Christian; Noah was a Christian; Abraham was a Christian; all the prophets were Christians; — only they saw the truth by moonlight, we see the same truth in sunlight; they saw it dimly, but truly, — we see it clearly and distinctly. Christianity, therefore, is not the invention of yesterday; it is not a blaze that has flashed upon the world soon to disappear. It dawned amid the ruins of Paradise; the light grew brighter as it shone upon the ark resting on Ararat; it brightened still more when it illuminated the prophetic mind; and it is now moving like the shining light, that shineth more and more unto the perfect day, to its meridian throne, its everlasting and never to be clouded splendor.

It is thus we learn what is meant by reproach incurred for Christ's sake, borne in a Christian spirit, because of holding Christ's truth, or exhibiting Christ's character. But how, we ask, was this reproach, as we are told in the case of Moses, "greater riches than the treasures in Egypt"? How can reproach be riches? or, to vary the expression, how could Moses find profit and advantage in bearing reproach? Reproach has great advantages, and teaches grand lessons, when it is Christ's reproach. Where the richest gold mines are below, there the soil is most barren above. So reproach is a barren soil, but in its bosom there is greater riches than all the treasures in Egypt. In what respect is it so? When you bear Christ's reproach, you have the evidence that Christ is with you. The pillar of cloud by day and the pillar of fire by night was the token to the children of Israel that Christ was with them. So, if I am told that reproach is one of those things I must meet with in my journey heavenward and homeward, then my meeting with it would be to me most convincing evidence that I am in the right way. If I had lost my way, and were told by a friend that I must pursue such a route, and were also informed by him, "You will meet with a very miry road at that part, you will meet with a very narrow lane at a second part, a very rugged path at a third, and plunderers and robbers at a fourth;" when I came to any or all of these, it would be very unpleasant in one sense, — "no tribulation is joyous," — but in another it would be most delightful to be assured that I am in the road that leads to my everlasting and happy home. It is so with reproach borne for Christ. In itself it is most offensive and bitter to flesh and blood, but that very bitter grows sweet by the prospect of its issue, and there follows or precedes it the pillar of fire that proves that I am on the right march to immortality; and so the brass becomes to me fine gold, and is indeed more precious than that. The crown of thorns is a stronger evidence of grace than a diadem set with gems. The chaplet of thorns is a more sure token of victory than the garland of the Olympian wrestler. To be like Christ, and to meet with his reproach, is evidence to us, and so far it is great riches, that we are in the way that leads to heaven.

In the next place, such reproach is rich to us in consolation, because it is evidence that the quiet of Satan's kingdom is disturbed, and that we are doing some good in the world. A man that passes through the world without praise and without censure has made very little impression on the world. If a person does very great good, or very great mischief, he is sure to meet with remarks laudatory or condemnatory, at least with notoriety. If a person, in going through the world, feels darken over him the reproach of Christ, he recollects from whom that reproach comes, and so enjoys this evidence that he is doing some good in his day. Satan is still as long as he is untouched or unexposed. Stagnation is his delight, stillness is his joy, darkness is his element. Luther made the remark most just and most true, "It is to me unspeakable joy that Satan rages and blasphemes; for it proves that he is hurt." So it should be to a Christian; it is itself painful that any man should reproach Christ, but delightful to him that his consistent adhesion to Christ has provoked that reproach. It is evidence that he is making an impression in the world. The strong man will not stand the intrusion of the stronger man quietly; he will resist with all his might; and reproach is one of Satan's as well as the world's weapons with which they assail the character of the people of God. The evil spirit did not leave the demoniac without tearing him; and Satan will not leave the world, in which he is a usurper, without rending it almost to pieces. Sentimental quiet may be the love of mere man, but a sublime struggle is the path and duty of a true Christian.

Reproach for Christ's sake is very great honor, and therefore a Christian counts it greater riches than all the treasures of Egypt. I know I speak what will be parables to some, and what it is difficult for even Christian men to realize. It is very easy to speak of it abstractedly, — we all know this, — but when we come to be reproached for Christ's sake, flesh and blood does not like it; and yet it is by knowing it, and comprehending it, that we shall be able, by God's grace, suitably to bear it. "If ye be reproached for the name of Christ," says the apostle, "happy are ye," and why? "for the Spirit of glory and of God resteth upon you;" as if the Spirit of God selected the bosom of the calumniated Christian as the special place of his residence and presence. "Happy are ye, for the Spirit of God resteth upon you." If you be more reproached with Christ's reproach than the rest of those who are about you, what is that the evidence of? It proves that Christ has put special honor upon you. An accomplished general would not place the weakest men in the front of the battle. It is the brave, the tried, who in time of battle are placed in the posts of difficulty and danger. And if you are called upon, not only to suffer, but to suffer reproach for Christ's sake, it is proof to you, and therefore richer consolation than the treasures of Egypt, that the great Captain of the faith has selected you for greater enterprise, for illustrious duty, and for richer and ultimate regard. Wherever we see a great sufferer, if a Christian, there we see a special favorite of Christ; wherever we see one reproached very much for Christ's sake, there we find one honored by him. It is given to angels to serve Christ simply; it is given to Christians to suffer as well as serve for his name's sake.

In the next place, such reproach, wherever it is borne for Christ's sake, is always rich in personal and heartfelt improvement of the whole character of man. It is when the outward world is dark that the inward light in the Christian's heart burns more brightly. Luther, whom I have already quoted, made the remark again, "They most profit me who speak the worst of me, and call me by the worst names." Christians are thus driven from looking to the world, to find something within that will stand them instead, and give them a joy which the world cannot darken, or take away. Grace, better than the fabled touch of Midas of old, not only turns stones into gold, but reproach into honor, suffering into joy, and the circlet of the world's scorn into a garland of beauty, a crown of joy. The darkest reproach, endured for Christ's sake, is to a Christian the means of personal and practical improvement. Thus the voice of dead Moses cheers the believer in his journey, sounding at one time a warning, at another an encouragement, and evermore certifying to the sons of God that they bear upon them the signs of the heirs of God — the followers of the Lamb.

CHAPTER IX.

THE RECOMPENSE OF REWARD.

"The light of smiles shall fill again
The lids that overflow with tears,
And weary hours of woe and pain
Are promises of happier years.

"There is a day of sunny rest
For every dark and troubled night;
And grief may bide an evening guest,
But joy shall come with early light."

"He had respect to the recompense of the reward." — HEB. 11 : 26.

SUCH reproach as that which Moses endured for Christ's sake must issue, for God himself has promised it, in a recompense of reward. Paul says, "If we suffer with him, we shall also reign with him;" and in the twentieth chapter of Revelation it is said of those who died for Christ, "I saw thrones, and they sat upon them, and judgment was given unto them; and I saw the souls of them that were beheaded for the witness of Jesus, and for the word of God, and which had not worshipped the beast, neither his image, neither had received his mark upon their foreheads, or in their hands; and they lived and reigned with Christ a thousand years." Their special reproach borne for Christ's sake was visited with special honor for a thousand years. And so it ever will be.

The Israelite of old brought his lamb, it might be his pet-lamb to the altar to be slain; it was returned to him with unexpected and incalculable blessings. Even so, all the shame with which the world surrounds the believer becomes the back-ground of a splendor on which the sun never sets. The curtain of reproach falls upon a Christian as the curtain of night falls on the earth, revealing above far greater glory than it conceals below; and he feels in all its sweetness the force of this benediction, "If ye be reproached for Christ's sake, happy are ye."

In these respects, and in others that could be mentioned, the Christian finds wealth in reproach far greater than the riches of Egypt. Those riches of Egypt have all passed away. Pharaoh's chariots and cavalry are buried in the depths of the Red Sea. The stores of the Ishmaelite merchants, once so large, have disappeared. The pyramids of Egypt alone remain, as if to mark the height to which the tide of its magnificence rose, and to be instructive proofs to future generations how thoroughly it has ebbed away. Where the glories of Egypt once were, are now, few and far between, caravans passing through the desert, or pilgrims of Mecca going to the tomb of the false prophet. The riches of Egypt have fled away; but the wealth of Moses endures, for unsearchable riches never fade. Moses does not repent beside the throne, nor regret for one moment that he preferred the reproach of Christ to all the treasures of Egypt; "for," it is added, in the next place, "he had respect unto the recompense of the reward."

Some eminent divines have tried to prove that the Israelites lived exclusively under a temporary economy; that no prospect of immortal joy beyond the dissolution of the body and the grave dawned upon the heart of the ancient Jew. It has been attempted to be shown that earthly rewards were all they were taught to anticipate, and that a rest of beauty, and of glory, and of joy, far beyond the land of Canaan, never entered into the heart or mind of a Jew. If this be so, Moses was bitterly disappointed, and God proved himself untrue. Moses, it is said, " had respect unto the recompense of the reward." If that reward be not the glory in which he now basks, where could it be? Was Pisgah, from which he saw the land he was not allowed to enter, the fulfilment of his hope of a recompense of reward? Were the forty years' sorrow, trials, vexations, sufferings, in the desert, the only bright recompense that cheered and illuminated the vision of Moses? Can we ascertain any one thing that happened to Moses upon earth that can be called "the recompense of the reward"? No; Moses believed in the immortality of the soul, just as we do. He saw on his spirit a signature that was the token and the earnest of its glory, and the pledge of its immortality. Abraham's great heart had a hope that the land of Canaan could not fulfil. Moses' "respect unto the recompense of the reward" was a far nobler and bigger expectancy than Pisgah could ever satisfy. He felt, it is true, the reproach of Christ, but he saw also from afar the glorious church of Christ. His ear heard borne from the heaven the same sustaining encouragement that the seer of Patmos heard in exile, "Be thou faithful unto death, and I will give thee a crown of life." Our home is not here, it is beyond the stars; our hope is not an earthly flower that fades, it bears its richest blossoms in eternity; the hopes of the Christian sparkle with the rays of immortality, and prove to him that he is but a pilgrim upon earth, to be crowned a prince and a priest in glory hereafter. Standing on Calvary, one can see a panorama in the future far brighter than poets can sketch, or prophets even reveal.

This soul of Moses, this soul of mine, has nothing in it that the grave can claim, it has nothing in it that death can hold fast. My body, in which that soul lives, is but the outer garment; and the soul's swelling and majestic hopes and lofty communings with God, — its yearnings after a glory that is never to be realized on earth, its deep anticipations of heaven, and of happiness to come, — all this is not woven so deep into its texture in order to perish with it. The soul is as distinct from the body as is the light of noonday from the clod of earth that it temporarily illuminates. The body is but the temporary tent; its inhabitant, the soul, lasts forever. It is to me one of the most beautiful thoughts in a Christian's death, that he does not die. We all shrink from dying; but I believe it is just on the same ground that we are unwilling to leave an old house. We have been so accustomed to the old tenement that we do not like to leave it. But death is not one moment's suspension of conscious life; it is not the interruption for an instant of the continuity of man's conscious existence. He lays down the body that he may live; it is not that he then ceases to live. That expressive eye of the departing babe, that speaks, as it appears to me, so eloquently, has in it the sheen of the glory that is to be revealed; and that last cry of the dying infant is not from agony that it dies, but in anticipatory joy that it is about to live; and the old man's gray hair seems to me so white because the near rays of the future glory already illuminate them; and the heart of the dying Christian is so happy because it dilates with a foretaste of the joy that is to be revealed. When a Christian dies, it is not he, but death, that dies. So Christians die in order to live, anticipating in earth's darkest shadow, as Moses did, "the recompense of the reward."

Whilst this hope of Moses thus reveals the soul's immortality, it shows, at the same time, that the true process by which we are to dislodge the love of that which is sinful is to bring to bear upon it the higher and the richer glories of something bright, beautiful and hóly. We here learn that the reason why Moses preferred the riches of heaven to the riches of earth, — the riches of heaven, set in reproach, to the riches of earth, surrounded with the pomp of royalty, — was because he saw shining in the future something brighter and more glorious. As the lesser light is always put out by the greater, as the wild field-flower appears pale and sickly in the presence of a more beautiful one, so Egypt's wealth seemed worthless beside the riches of Christ, and its palaces but as clay huts, when Moses brought into comparison with them the grand sketch portrayed to his eye, of "a house not made with hands, eternal in the heavens." So the true way to deal with a worldly man is, to bring to bear upon the earthly things he loves supremely a brighter thing and a nobler thing, that he will learn to love vastly more. Man's heart will never submit to be laid desolate. It is positively cruel to take from a man the little joy that he has, however frail that joy be, unless one can supersede it, and substitute for it a brighter and more enduring one. What comfort would it give to a poor man, were I to tell him of the bad effects of hunger? What comfort should I impart to a ragged boy shivering in the snow, were I to tell him of the wretchedness of his ragged covering? What would be the use of my going to a laborer working for a shilling a day, and reading him a long lesson upon the inadequacy of his remuneration? Such lecturing would do mischief, not good. What, then, shall I do? I will bring to bear upon the first the living bread that cometh down from heaven; I will tell the second of the raiment white and clean; and speak to the third of the unsearchable riches of Christ, while I try to relieve all three. You may speak to the miser for years upon the vanity of his avarice, on the perishable nature of his wealth; but the more you denounce it, the more closely he will grasp it, just because you are denouncing it; for we always love an object more when it is the subject of assault. But, if you show that miser that there is a wealth far richer and better, that communicates intenser happiness, which will dilate the soul with more enduring joy, he will let go gradually the wealth that perishes in his admiration of that which endures; and his avarice for earthly gold will depart before a new thirst for the unsearchable riches of Christ. Do not put out the poor man's tiny light, unless you can bring near the big, bright sun. Do not take away from him his cup of water, unless you can bring him to the grand fountain. If we drive out of the soul of man the love of literature, of horse-racing, or of card-playing, we merely sweep and empty the house, and seven spirits ten times worse will instantly rush in; but, if we can drive out the evil passions by bringing in the sublime preference, if we can only make pale the earthly joy by the splendor of the heavenly one, we not only expel the evil, but we bring in its place a good worthy of supremacy. Take not his Koran from the Moslem, his Shaster from the Hindoo, his breviary from the priest, unless you can substitute for them that more precious than them all, the word of the living God.

It is of no use to preach against Hindooism in India, unless we are prepared to supply the people with Christianity. It is vain to preach against the errors and the superstitions of Rome, unless when we do so we bring into contrast with them, as candidates for hospitality, the richer glories of Christ Jesus. Not extinction of what man has, but exchange for what man loves, is the mission of a Christian minister. It is most important that we should always keep this in view in dealing with the men of this world: they will not cast away what they love, except in exchange for something better; and I justify them so far; I will keep what I have, unless you can convince me that there is something better ready to take its place. Therefore, when asking the young man to give up indulgence, and the old man to resign his avaricious hoardings, knowing that I ask them to do what is painful, I will not be satisfied merely by telling the one to crucify the flesh, and the other to give away his wealth, but I will bring before them "the recompense of the reward," and thus they will give up the taper of a day for the Sun of righteousness, in whose wing is healing. It is thus that Moses felt dislodged the love of the earthly by seeing and feeling approaching the hope and joy of "the recompense of the reward."

We learn, in the next place, another important lesson, that the future recompense of reward is very much in the line and direction of present character. In other words, when we shall land in heaven, we shall find it is not introduction into a new course, but the continuation of the course we commenced on earth. Have you, for instance, sent your riches abroad in acts of charity, in deeds of magnanimous beneficence? You will receive in heaven by grace a richer reward, riches that thieves do not break through and steal, and that do not take wings and flee away. Have you resigned honor upon earth for Christ's sake? have you given up the pursuits of literature, in which you might have attained eminence, for the apparently humbler and lowlier services of Christian duty, in which you will meet with reproach? Your name shall be pronounced in heaven; it shall be inscribed upon a pillar from which it shall not be erased. Have you borne patiently, and without murmuring, the afflictions of the world? the cup that your Father has given you to drink, have you patiently drank it? Yours shall be the radiance of immortal youth, joys that are at God's right hand, and pleasures that are for ever and ever. Whilst the mere money-makers, the mere pleasure-hunters, are borne down by a gulf-stream that drives them into an ocean of misery fed from their own souls, and inexhaustible also, you shall move with a Pilot at the helm, and under the impulses of a breath that wafts you onward, till you end your voyage in the haven of everlasting rest. For whatever we have sacrificed upon earth we shall be rewarded in the future in some way proportionate to it, and yet not by merit in any shape, but by grace. In other words, one man shall be fitted for one sphere in heaven, and another for another sphere: our capacities shall vary. The characters and the tastes of men will differ, whilst all may be truly and indeed Christian. In that grand cathedral in which we shall worship there are many chambers, in which different Levites shall serve. One man is fitted for one chamber, another for another, and yet the way into the cathedral itself is Christ himself, "the way, the truth, and the life." There are many parts in the music of that choir in which we shall each take his part, and yet all the parts have one grand keynote, Christ Jesus. There shall be a vast multitude, we are told, there in "the recompense of the reward." There shall be one catholic tongue, and yet there will be many dialects of that tongue, for there are many kindreds, and nations, and tongues. There will be a majestic recompense of reward, the title to which is Christ alone; and yet there will be various pursuits, the vehicles of varying pleasures for the varied tastes of the saved. There shall be many stars, and yet one star shall differ from another star, and one flower from another flower. And thus "the recompense of the reward" may be suited to each taste, and rise to each capacity, whilst the right to enjoy it is by Christ, and by Christ alone.

Lastly, we here see, from this statement, that hope as well as faith is part of the great animating motives of Christian progress. Hope is spoken of as "the anchor within the vail," at which we may ride securely. A Christian keeps his eye always on the future, his faith and trust always in the past. He looks to the past for strength and for acceptance; he looks to the future for a joyful and a glorious reward. And so long as a Christian keeps his destiny in his eye as the alone bright and magnificent attraction, so long the inferior things that he meets by the way will appear to him comparatively of little value. A man who has been long in a distant land, and who is hastening as fast as he can to his home, may look upon the spring-flower by the wayside, but he will not sit down beside it to rest. We are going to a bright and everlasting home, and we are so smitten with its magnificence and glory that all present things we feel unworthy to be compared with it. We see, indeed, on all sides around us many a sparkling stream, rolling, it may be, upon golden sands; but every chime of its waves tells us, "Whosoever drinketh of this water shall thirst again;" but we can hear sounding from the olive-shades of Gethsemane, from Bethlehem, from awful Calvary, from the heavenly Jerusalem, from "Jesus the mediator of the new covenant," "But whosoever drinketh of the water that I shall give him shall never thirst, but the water that I shall give him shall be in him a well of water springing up into everlasting life."

Seeing, then, we look for such things, "be ye steadfast, immovable, always abounding in the work of the Lord; forasmuch as ye know that your labor is not in vain in the Lord;" and, resting upon the Rock of Ages as our only foundation, let us look for the crown of glory as "the recompense of the reward" earned by Christ, bestowed by his hand, and received by grace, — the blessing ours, the glory his. The voice of Moses, from the reward in glory he anticipated on earth, comes down in bright waves upon the shores of time. It bids us doubt not, — it eloquently urges us to follow. May its echoes deepen within us, and every memory be a whispering-gallery, in which his accents shall not die, and his teachings not cease, till we sing the "song of Moses and the Lamb!"

CHAPTER X.

THE HEROIC CHRISTIAN.

"Thoughts of my soul, how swift ye go!
Swift as the eagle's glance of fire,
Or arrows from the archer's bow,
To the far aim of your desire!
Thought after thought ye thronging rise,
Like spring-doves from the startled wood;
Bearing like them your sacrifice
Of music unto God.

"And shall these thoughts of joy and love
Come back again no more to me?
Returning, like the patriarch's dove,
Wing-weary from the eternal sea;
To bear within my longing arms
The promised bough of kindlier skies,
Plucked from the green immortal palms
Which shadow Paradise.

"O, would I were as free to rise
As leaves on Autumn's whirlwind borne,
The arrowy light of sunset skies,
Or sound, or ray, or star of morn,
Which melts in heaven at twilight close,
Or aught which soars unchecked and free,
Through earth and heaven that I might lose
Myself in finding thee!"

"By faith he forsook Egypt, not fearing the wrath of the king; for he endured, as seeing him who is invisible." — HEB. 11 : 27.

THE first instance of the triumphant faith of this ancient servant of God is, that when he was come to years of discretion, that is, to proper age, he refused to receive the honors that belonged to him as the presumptive heir of the crown, and refused them under a divine impulse; and accepted an humble and a lowly place in preference to being called the son of Pharaoh's daughter. He chose affliction because it was set in piety, rather than prosperity and honor which necessitated sin.

We are told, in the next place, that he esteemed the very reproach of Christ,—the reproach incurred by the maintenance of Christian principle, and adhesion to Christ's people, though darkening the path of duty,—in preference to the pleasures of sin that sparkled like gems in the path of worldly prosperity.

And lastly, we are told, "By faith he forsook Egypt, not fearing the wrath of the king." Moses thus held fast a sustaining principle throughout—a principle which we need not merely to be convinced of; for convictions in the intellect are often like icicles, only doing mischief where they do no good; what we need is the conviction, fixed by the Spirit of God in the heart, and then it will prove an element of indomitable power, a spring of inexhaustible virtue in the life, prompting not only to do, but to think what natural men have never dreamed of, and to do what natural men have only thought of, and to triumph where natural men have attempted, and have failed.

Moses being dead, yet speaketh. By faith he left Egypt. True faith cannot live where it has a divine notice to depart. A Christian will struggle with difficulties in the position in which God has placed him, and if it be possible he will triumph over them; but, if the necessity of sinning is inseparable from the place he holds, then, like Moses, by faith he quits Egypt, and endures, as seeing Him who is invisible. At the same time, we must not gratify indolence under the pretence of obeying Christian prescription. Some men leave a place, whether it be power, or rank, or office, or dignity, or influence, or trade, because they say they cannot honor God in it. But it has often turned out that they were too indolent to make the experiment. We must not leave the place which God in his providence has assigned us, if it be possible. As I understand it, the Great Captain of the faith has placed us as sentinels here, and here it is our duty to watch and wait. But, if it be impossible to keep our post without doing and sanctioning what is evil, then by faith we must forsake Egypt. But let each of us make the experiment first, and then, if we fail, we have the satisfaction of knowing that we have tried by God's grace to do our duty.

We read that the parents of Moses feared not the king's commandment, — and in that they showed true Christian faith; but Moses showed himself to be possessed of a yet stronger faith, for he, it is said, feared not the king's wrath. He feared not man, he feared not a king — the greatest of men; he feared not a king's wrath, that is the most powerful and formidable wrath of all. And this not fearing the wrath of the king was not the result of insensibility. Some men are calm in danger because they are stupid, other men appear to be heroes when really their heroism is iron nerve and insensibility; but it was not so with Moses. He had a heart open as day to all that was fair, and tender as woman's in time of sorrow. It was not insensibility, but Christian faith, that enabled him not to fear the king's wrath, because "he endured," we are told, — and here is the secret of his fearlessness, — not that he did not feel, "as seeing him who is invisible." There are men on the field of battle who do not fear, just because they do not think; there are men who do not fear, simply because they are strong and invincible in their physical constitution; but there are other men who can see with an eagle eye all the perils of their position, but who, in the exercise of that which in human nature is nearest to Christian faith, can remain unmoved, and occupy a commanding place, and put forth a controlling power, because they have faith in something higher than man, and in the possibility, if not in the certainty, of victory and of success.

When Moses fled from Egypt, not fearing the king's wrath, he did not depart because he was a criminal. He had quarrelled, it is true, with the Egyptians, but he did not flee because he had violated their laws; for the verse tells us that the spirit of his fearlessness was his appreciation of a present God. If Moses had fled as a criminal, the natural history would have been that he had fled in terror. A criminal is always in a state of terror. His own shadow frightens him; the rustling of a leaf alarms him. But when one flees from a country, composed, and calm, and self-possessed, and in nature not insensible, but the very reverse, he must have a Christian principle within him, a consciousness of a Christian duty in which he is engaged; a grand hope before him, and a good cause behind him. Without this, Moses would not have left Egypt, not fearing the king's wrath, but seeing him who is invisible.

When Moses left Egypt, he did not leave it as a rebel. At the first blush, when reading such a history, one might say, "What right had such a man, in the midst of such a country as Egypt, with its proper laws, to raise up a mighty multitude, somewhere about five hundred thousand men, who were originally the king's subjects, and without asking the king's leave?" Certainly, if any man were to do so here, he would be guilty of rebellion. But Moses showed credentials from the King of kings, which settled his right, and irretrievably proved that his was not a rebellion, but a lofty Christian enterprise. It is asked, What credentials? He authenticated his divine mission by the divine works, or supernatural miracles, which he wrought in the presence of the king and his people. Now, those men who want to imitate Moses must take care that they have Moses' credentials. You must not act upon this precedent unless you can show that you have the very same position, and the same credentials, and can do the very same works, that Moses did. Until you can show the same supernatural or celestial commission, we shall denounce you as a rebel in trying to originate a movement for which you were not sent, and which was not obviously designed for you.

When God has anything great to be done, he is sure to raise up a suitable agent to do it. There is something very beautiful in this, that, whenever God has a work to be done in the world, he invariably finds men to do it, and often men who appear to us very unlikely to succeed. Moses, forty years before this, wanted the Israelites to march out from Egypt, but they did not; and it was well; for he was not then trained and disciplined as he needed to be for so great, so trying, and so vast an undertaking. The crisis was not ready for the man; or, rather, the man was not ready for the crisis. But, as soon as God's predictions were finished, and the era of Israel's deliverance was come, and all things were ready, then Moses presented himself, and he was found the man made for the crisis. God did not interpose too soon; he would not delay too late; but, the hour having struck for their exodus from Egypt, the chief who was to lead them forth came also. And so it has been in all the past history of God's dealings with mankind. Paul, the apostle, was just the man fitted to reason with the subtle and accomplished Athenians, schooled as he was in all the syllogisms of a masterly and cunning philosophy, and with the warlike and educated Romans, open as they were to the influence of demonstrative and indisputable facts. Peter was adapted to the Jews; Martin Luther was fit for the Reformation in Germany; Knox, for the same in Scotland; and Ridley, Latimer, and Cranmer, for their great mission in England. And, at a subsequent period, Whitefield and Wesley did their work;

and, at a still later period, Wilberforce among the higher ranks, and Simeon among the undergraduates of Cambridge, fulfilled their respective and precious missions. And these men were prepared and fitted by the great Head of all to carry out the peculiar functions which they had to discharge.

Having thus noticed the facts connected with the exodus of Moses from Egypt, let me turn your attention to the basis of all, his enduring because he saw, or, as the right translation is, because he continued constantly to see, Him who is invisible. It was not a light that flashed upon his vision with the splendor and with the evanescence of an aurora borealis, but it was permanent, noonday light in his heart within; one which he saw, and in which he realized the presence of the invisible God. In other words, Moses acted constantly as seeing God. Yet some men will tell you that the secret of all heroism, and fortitude, and peace, and all comfort, is to get rid of God; and that they have peace and happiness,—and I can understand it,—just in proportion as they keep out of their minds the sight of an imminent, ever-present, ever-controlling God. They belong to that class of whom the psalmist speaks, "The fool hath said in his heart, There is no God." It is worthy of notice, too, that, wherever there is an atheist denying the existence of a God, there is an intense proselytizer; but it is not from a conviction that his creed is true, but that, by the reflex influence of his zeal, he may convince himself of its truth. Some men are so convinced of a great truth that they are all anxiety to teach it; other men are so insecure about the truth of what they believe that they teach it the more earnestly, in order to try to persuade themselves, what they are not yet persuaded of, that what they believe, or, rather, wish to believe, is true.

In discussing the subject of the invisible God, let me show (not supposing that I am addressing a pagan reader, unconvinced of God, but a Christian man or woman, who likes not only to have convictions, but to give good reasons for such convictions) some of the difficulties felt in accepting an atheist's creed, and a few of the arguments in favor of accepting the God and Father of our Lord Jesus Christ.

It has always appeared to me that the conviction that there is a God, and that God my maker, and my preserver, and my guide, is so precious in itself, that the man who goes about to destroy it ought to have very good grounds for his conclusions in the opposite direction; because this impression of this great fact, true or untrue, is, to a Christian in the rugged and dusty road of daily life, as a pillar of fire by night and a pillar of cloud by day. This majestic thought, that there is a God, and that God my God, opens to me so many sweet springs in the desert, sheds down upon my footsteps so much bright sunshine, occasions to me so many happy, so many delightful convictions, that no man is warranted in spoiling me of that precious thought, unless he has such powerful and overwhelming proofs that they satisfy him, and may fairly satisfy me, that what is happiness to me is but a delusion and a dream. It would therefore seem to require all but irresistible proof that there is no God, in order to warrant any one doing what ought to be, to a feeling person, a most painful thing, dispossessing a happy man of what is the spring and fountain of his happiness. Of course, if it be a stern duty, one can tread down every other feeling, and take in hand that duty; but it will require very strong and overwhelming proof to warrant any one going forth on the mission of atheism, and trying to persuade men that there is no God.

Now, what is the amount of proof that an atheist produces for no God? Let us see. All that he can say is, "I have not seen God; I have not heard God; in the course of my experience and researches, I have not found out God." This is all he can say. But is this basis sufficient for such a withering superstructure as no God? Are there not many things in the world that I and you have not seen? Are there not thousands of things in the heights and in the depths that we have not noticed, or even heard of? It appears to me, therefore, that to base the conclusion that there is no God upon the fact that I have not seen him, is to build a very lofty and a very awful superstructure upon a very slippery and insufficient foundation indeed.

But, if such a one still says, "There is no God," let us notice, to use a well-understood phrase, the *reductio ad absurdum* to which this leads. He says, There is no God. Well, the man who says there is no God must have a transcendently powerful intellect; for Socrates, and Plato, and Xenophon, the greatest of ancient times, were able to catch some gleams of his glory as he passed by. Yet this man, who finds that their arguments were not only insufficient, but pure sophistry, must assume to himself a wonderfully powerful intellect to come to such a conclusion. Moreover, such a reasoner must have ages for his life, and omniscience itself for his knowledge; and, in short, he who says there is no God must be at least omnipresent, or how can he be sure that, in the very place that he has not visited, there may not be the very Being whose existence he denies, that is, God? Such a man, too, must certainly be omniscient; for, unless he knows all in the height, all in the depth, all secret and all open things, he never can be sure that the very agent that he does not know may not be the Being he denies, that is, God; or that the very place which he has not penetrated with his intellect may not be the very shrine of an existent and all-glorious God. And such a man must have a memory all-capacious; for that memory must be able to contain all the propositions of universal truth, or how does he know that the proposition which he does not recollect, or which has not been lodged there, may not be this sublime one, There is a God? Such a man must know all that is in the height, and depth, and must himself be a God, in order justly to conclude that there is no God, which is absurd; and therefore it is impossible for any one to prove that there is no God without assuming to be what he disproves. Hence, the man who would lift humanity from its sheet-anchor, who would take from the widow the certainty of a husband in heaven, and from the orphan, weeping, pining, desolate, the bright and blessed hope and conviction of a Father beyond the stars, on so flimsy, miserable, untenable a pretext, must have something else as the basis of his efforts than love, and some other reason for his proceeding than the ground or conviction of soberness and truth. Hence, I have always doubted, either the sanity of his intellect, or the state of his heart, who goes about to make people believe that there is no God, and no truth in the Bible, and that Christianity is mere superstition.

But let us now look at the positive side of this question, the creed that there is a God. I notice one or two points merely, well aware that Christian men feel its truth for deeper reasons than syllogisms can supply. Yet there are some thoughts that may be satisfactory, or are at least expository of the text. Dr. Beattie, a distinguished professor of metaphysics or moral philosophy in the Marischal College, Aberdeen, and who wrote some noble defences of Christianity against Hume and others, one day went out into his garden, and traced the name of his eldest child upon the fresh mould, and sowed in the channels of each letter some common mustard-seed. In the course of a very short time, the seeds germinated, and the name was legible in the garden. The boy one day walked out, and saw with amazement and surprise his own name in the plants growing in the soil; and naturally asked his father for an explanation of this. He said we must suppose that the winds and the rains had sowed it, — "It is, no doubt, an accidental thing, mere chance; the winds and rains have done it." But the boy would not be satisfied with this.

He said he could not find that the winds and rains had done any such thing before; and why should the winds and rains select his name? and why should the winds and rains do it so well? The boy first of all insisted that there must be a cause for it, and, secondly, that there must be an adequate and an intelligent cause for it; and that adequate and intelligent cause, as that young child reasoned, must be a designing, intelligent being, whoever that intelligent being was. It is no less so with us. God writes his own name with the bright stars above, and with the fragrant flowers below; and as sure as that child's name, written with green things, pointed to the parent or an intelligent being who did it, so surely that name of our Father, legible in the splendor in which it was written, demonstrates the tracing of his finger, and imprints and impresses upon the youngest child, and upon the oldest cherubim, There is a God, and that these, and such as these, are the traces and the evidences of his action, and of his power. It is thus we come to the joyous conclusion that there is a God by the numerous things that indicate design, and so lead the mind to contemplate and believe in a designer. Of course, this is a very limited and superficial view of the question. We cannot ourselves look abroad on the world in spring-time, or go into the country when the trees are bursting into leaf, and the flowers into blossom, and conceive that all this is chance. Some one will say that a certain mixture of earth, and of carbon, and of siliceous matter, and of rain, and of oxygen, and of sunbeams, and other component parts, constitute all our summer glories. Collect a few sunbeams, a little oxygen, and a little carbon, and a little rain, and try the experiment of making summers. You will fail in constituting the humblest of these appearances of nature. Though chemistry may put us one step on, yet it does not satisfy us. There is such beautiful consistency in nature, — one grand law keeping the ephemeral insect fluttering in the sunbeam, and holding the monarch on the throne, one grand pervading vitality running through all, and developing itself in such beautiful variety, — that conviction is forced upon us, that chemical laws will no more explain the world without a Creator, than they will explain intelligence in man without an intellect. It used to be the explanation of man's mind, — in fact, I believe it is still held by some materialists, — that the pineal gland is the soul. This gland has been analyzed, and found to be phosphate of lime. Can I conceive phosphate of lime originating Milton's Paradise Lost, or Shakspeare's dramas? It is just as absurd to explain Milton's Paradise Lost by phosphate of lime as to explain the universe by chemistry. Wonderful it is what difficulties a man gets into when he dares to refuse the truth that there is a God reigning over all, and governing and controlling all. We are sure that there is a God; and, like Moses, we too see him who is invisible.

It is one thing to be satisfied with such arguments as these, which might be multiplied; it is another thing to do as Moses did, — see him who is invisible, and act under the presence of him who is all-present. Moses saw him everywhere. In all the variegated paths of hill, and dale, and valley, in all flowers, and fruits, and blossoms, Moses saw him. In all sounds he heard his voice. Even upon the blackest spots of the desert he saw God's grand footprints. He lived in an atmosphere lighted up with Deity. He walked constantly as in the presence of God, but not as a slave walks with his master, nor as a madman or a lunatic walks with his keeper, but as a child, a loving child, walks with an affectionate and a loving father. He saw everywhere him who is invisible. He saw his hand balancing the orbs in the sky, and giving their polarity to the minutest atoms of dust. He saw God polishing the planets in the firmament not more elaborately than he polishes the beetle's wing, or the sting of a bee; the microscopic insect seemingly so worthless has as much labor, if I may use the expression, expended upon it, as the greatest and most magnificent thing in the world; perhaps more. The microscope reveals in the depths more of the wisdom and the greatness of God, than the telescope, as it sweeps the horizon and scans the sky, reveals in its most majestic expanse. Moses saw God directing lightnings, sustaining planets in their orbits, feeding the ravens, clothing the lilies, superintending the sparrow's fall, not letting a single hair fall to the ground without his cognizance and control. It is a sad blunder to say that God is in great things, and not in little things. We, it is true, can only hear God's voice in tremendous crashes; but the circumcised ear can hear God in the murmur of the smallest brook, and the eye of faith can see him in the tiniest flowers, as well as in the greatest and noblest productions. A Christian like Moses can see him who is invisible, and hear him who is inaudible.

A Christian, however, does all this not so much as the result of a conviction forced upon his judgment, as of faith. "By faith he saw him who is invisible." I am quite satisfied that a Christian receives an inner moral organization, perfectly distinct from what a natural man has. If a natural man were to take an angel's pinion, and to rise higher than an angel's wing can soar, and faster than an angel's wing can clip, he would not see God. If, like the Apocalyptic angel, he were to stand upon the sun, and gaze upon all space, and take in all time, he would not see God: God must be within, before God can be seen without. There must be the light of Deity within, before, even in the light of Deity, you can see him without. Hence, a Christian by faith, which is this inner light, this new appreciating power, can see God everywhere; and accordingly, like Jacob, he builds and consecrates an altar in the desert, the green sod becomes its faldstool, and he sees the shadow of Divinity sweep past him in all movements, and hears his Father speak in all voices; and because he has, if I might use the expression, a world of God within him, he sees God, God, God, still in the world without him. "By faith he saw him who is invisible."

But, if God in creation be so transparent, by faith, that is, to the Christian eye, he is not less so in the course of his administrative providence. Fallen as man is, he is not destitute, utterly destitute, of all perception of piety and impiety, truth and error, virtue and vice. We must take care, in describing the results of man's fall, not to exaggerate; it is quite true that we ought not to diminish, but it is equally true that we ought not to exaggerate. If man's heart in its worst state be not a Paradise, there is no use in describing it as a Pandemonium; for, laid sadly desolate as it is, there is no soul in which the image of God is so expunged that it carries not even yet some inmost traces of the departed glory; there is no heart so utterly degraded and debased that even in its listening moments it hears not within, amid the silence of its own sanctuary, voices of Deity. Lost as he is, the reprobate that we abhor for his crimes has moments when better thoughts flash across his mind, and at least tell him what he has left and lost, if they are unable to make him what grace alone can accomplish. In the heart of the worst of mankind there are still uneffaced traces more or less vivid of the distinctions of virtue and vice. We find natural men sometimes showing a greater regard to honor and truth than even the professing Christian. Merchants are in this land of ours whose word will be received in every part of Europe, Asia, Africa, and America; whose promise will be regarded by all as a solemn oath, who would scorn to do a mean thing, and who would not stoop to do a wicked and an evil thing. One must hail all this; yet we must add more than this may be, and yet there may not be that heart which is fit for the kingdon of heaven: all this may be, and we may admire it much, but yet must proclaim, not on these must you rely for acceptance by a holy and sin-punishing God. Man so far sees in his ruins distinctions between virtue and vice; that when he does what is sinful there is a feeling called remorse, and when he does what is right there is some measure of complacency and satisfaction. Remorse is felt even by the vilest; at least, enough is felt to show the shadow that always follows sin: and, in the bosom of every one that does a good act, — and there may be nothing like self-righteousness in it, —there is a feeling of satisfaction whilst doing it. Beneficence is the purest joy upon earth; it is ecstasy to do good to all as we may be able. If there be a joy that angels may envy, it is the joy of benefiting those around us; and if there be anything that makes us Godlike, it is doing good to men who despise us, and speak despitefully of us. This sense of remorse for sin, this satisfaction at virtue, indicate a law, and consequently rewards and penalties; and, wherever there is a law, there must be a lawgiver, — God. Thus man's conscience tells us from its solemn oracle that there is a God.

And, if we extend our view to nations, we shall find that nations, ambitious, grasping, trying to extend their dominion over weaker states, careless of their feelings, their sufferings, or their pangs, — nations personated in an Alexander, or a Napoleon, and other men of that stamp,—have sooner or later fallen completely; because they violated the great law that devolves on nations as well as on individuals, that of doing to others as we would like others to do to ourselves. Whereas, nations that are pervaded by real religion, that do justly, and love mercy, and seek peace, and pursue it, prosper. Such nations have the germ of immortality within them. With all our faults as a nation, which we lament, there are in the midst of us so many redeeming, pleasing and beautiful traits, that, when the crash of the next earthquake comes, and shakes all Europe to its foundations, we may hope this great land of ours will yet be that in which freedom shall find its footing, in which humanity shall never be without a champion, and pure religion shall have its holiest and its noblest altar. And it is to my mind the most pleasing thought, that the two greatest nations that are swaying the destinies of the world — England and America — are the two races that have the purest religion, and the largest amount of abounding, living Christianity in the midst of them. It is God's purpose, I trust, to make these two great nations instruments in his hand for working out vast and glorious results. But this fact, that nations live as they are virtuous, and perish as they are naturally sinful, leads us to the conclusion that there is a law; and if a law, a lawgiver, and that lawgiver God.

And if this law is seen in great things, and in national experience, I need not add that it is seen in individual things, and in personal history also. Take away the conviction from me and my heart that there is a God, either in nations or in families, and what a dismantlement it is! I have no Father in heaven; I have no home when this weary, agitated, melancholy world is broken up; I must court annihilation as my only comforter, — surely more miserable than Job's; — when I get grand blessings, if there be no God, I have no one to unload my heart in praise to; and if I suffer and am bowed down under oppression, I have no ear to pour into the cry of the broken heart, and no hand put forth to bind its bleeding wounds. If there be no God, insensibility, annihilation, are all that I have to look to. If there be no God, then I do say that graves, and sick beds, and suffering, and poverty, do indicate that the world has lost its proper order, and that there is no hope of restoration; and man is the unhappiest wretch in the universe, for he has intellect to see that everything is wrong, and yet he cannot put it right, and a wish to live, and he cannot. O, take away from me, not the cold conviction, but the living inspiration in my heart, that there is a God, and that God my father, and my friend, my home, and my fortress, and my high tower, and my deliverer, and you take from me the only thing that makes life happy and death welcome, and the hope that alone is worthy of being cherished on earth.

But we see a God not only in creation, and in providence, but in revelation also: all our doubts are dissipated when we open that book, brighter than creation, more instructive than providence, — God's holy word. It is a very important thought, and one that we can easily appreciate, that a religion which is inferential is never so satisfactory as a religion that is simple testimony. The Scottish mind, it has been remarked, is often more satisfied with a process of reasoning, but the English mind prefers one fact to the most ingenious syllogisms that can be strung together. Hence one text in God's word, that declares that God is, is more satisfactory to me than all the inferences in providence and creation. The Bible as the book of God confirms creation as the work of God; and creation as the work of God points out the Bible as the revelation of God; and both, like the twin lips of an oracle, say, "God is."

Some have objected, that they cannot conceive that God should have condescended, or descended, to give such a revelation of himself. Now, it has always appeared to me that the most natural thing in the world to expect from God, if there be a God, is a revelation of himself. Surely it is the most natural feeling to expect a revelation from God, if indeed there be a God. What says analogy in this world? That the father teaches the son, that the elder teaches the younger, and, if we still extend it, that previous generations, by their discoveries, teach the next generation. Well, if we find that each link teaches or influences the next, why should we not conclude that He who sits upon that throne to which the whole chain is attached should teach and instruct his successive generations? But we know, on other grounds which it is not necessary to enter upon, that God has given a revelation of his favor to us, in which he has lighted up the otherwise undefined shadow which falls so darkly upon the revelations of creation and providence, — namely, what God is to us. "God so loved the world that he gave his only-begotten Son." "God was in Christ reconciling the world unto himself." "Not that we loved God, but that he loved us, and sent his Son to be the propitiation for our sins." One of these texts is more satisfactory to my mind than all the flowers in the fields, and all the syllogisms of philosophy. One single text from this blessed book, clear, distinct, emphatic, I can lay all my prospects on, and feel that it is worthy of him whose word is truth.

But this blessed book not only discloses a God giving Christ to die for us, but also God a Father. It reveals to us God our Father. That religion which can teach me to say to the great and the holy God "Our Father," carries on its very face its own credentials. All natural religion makes me shrink from him, but this religion bids me welcome to him. If there was a spectacle in Jerusalem that exceeded in beauty all history, or creation, it was when Jesus knelt upon the street, and the group of apostles knelt around him, and he, as their mouthpiece and spokesman, said, "Our Father, which art in heaven." It was the evidence that the link which was lost in Paradise was reünited and replaced in Christ; and that we, who were outcasts, prodigals, rebels and sinners, are by grace brought back again through Christ Jesus. Then the voice I hear in nature is my Father's voice; then the hand guiding me is my Father's hand; I have a personal heart in heaven that sympathizes with me. The Fatherhood of God, and the brotherhood of man, are two of the noblest truths in the pages of Christianity.

But God is revealed in this blessed book, as well as in providence and in creation, as taking care of the greatest and of the least, — probably, we may add, as much of the least as of the greatest. I can fear no accident if I am persuaded God in his providence takes care of me. Every Christian may feel, what I think is a most true persuasion, — I am immortal till I have finished the work that God has appointed me to do. God has given each man his mission, each his place, and each the limits of his life. It is perfectly compatible with our free will and responsibility to believe most heartily that we shall not fall till we have finished the work that God has assigned us to do. The tides of life ebb and flow through channels extremely delicate, yet not one can fail till God gives permission. The road of life is full of pitfalls and snares, but God still keeps my eyes from tears, my feet from falling, and my soul from death. Little and lowly as we may be, the overshadowing wings are over us. We may be tossed upon the billows, but God is greater and mightier than the great sea billows. In the height or in the depth I am safe, because I am in him who is my Father, and he takes care of me. What comfort is in this conviction of the individual providence of this God, while we thus "see him who is invisible"! What comfort is it to the sufferer, when called upon to suffer, to know that no cup is presented to his lips, however bitter, which is not placed there by a Father's hand! I know the difficulty of feeling this, and I know the facility of telling this; but, whether it be difficult or not, it is strictly true, that there is not a suffering that betides us, if we be Christians, that is not from God our Father: that cup he has tempered, before he gives it; and that affliction shall not be too heavy, too long or too severe, as the devil would like, nor will it be too light, too short or too lenient, as we ourselves would like, but it will just be what God's love sees to be best for us, — it is meted out by a wisdom that can never err. The most solitary sufferer in the most sequestered spot may be assured of this, that God as much superintends and watches his case as if God and he were the only twain in the universe. Can we conceive this? and yet it is true. Such is the character of God that the most solitary sufferer may feel that God waits upon him, and ministers to him, as closely as if there were no other sufferer in the whole universe. We have seen, from the analogies we have pointed out, that the frailest flower has its tints pencilled out as beautifully as if the only thing that God had to do in creation was the coloring of that flower. The tiniest insect that flutters in the sunbeam has as exquisite an organization as if God had had nothing in the universe to do but to frame it. It is a most precious thought, that the most minute things are not beneath the inspection of God, and that the greatest things are not beyond it; and that the superintendence of great things does not in the least respect modify the manifestation of his care displayed towards the very least sufferer in the whole household of the faithful.

Moses thus saw God, and endured because he saw him, though invisible. It is thus that faith sees God, and makes the invisible visible. "Faith is the substance of things hoped for, the evidence of things not seen." And wherever there is this faith in the invisible, there shall be perseverance. "He endured." "He that endureth to the end shall be saved." "I am persuaded that neither death nor life shall separate us."

And wherever there is this true faith in the invisible there will be love. "Whom having not seen, ye love; in whom, though now ye see him not, yet believing, ye rejoice with joy unspeakable and full of glory."

And wherever we see God we shall have perfect courage. We shall hear the footfall of our sleepless Sentinel around us everywhere. We shall fold ourselves everywhere in the omnipresent love of the Watchman of Israel that sleepeth not, nor slumbereth; and be at peace with him, and so at peace with all.

This will keep us from sin. "Seeing him who is invisible." "Thou, God, seest me." "How shall I do this wickedness, and sin against God?"

Wherever there is this faith, it accepts the conclusions of reason, it accepts the inferences of natural theology; but it also opens a door in heaven that is bolted to sense, and sees the presence of One that to sense is invisible, and enjoys the controlling influence of One who slumbereth not, nor sleepeth.

This faith is the gift of God, and yet it is no less our duty. You say, "How can we believe? I can believe the Bank of England, I can believe a merchant, I can believe a statesman, I can believe a tradesman, but I cannot believe God!"

Is this possible? Faith is simply confidence in God's word; and then in the strength of that word it goes forth and does whatever God bids us; man's smile not drawing us into a sin, man's frown not driving us into error, and God's faith teaching us to live soberly, and righteously, and godly, in this present world, looking for that blessed hope, the glorious appearing of Jesus Christ our great God and Saviour.

As Moses left Egypt because he could not remain without partaking of its sins, we are to leave this present evil world so far as its sins are inseparable from it. We are to come out of the world as Moses came out of Egypt,—not to go into a convent, which is a mere mechanical and pretended separation, for the nun and the monk carry the world within them, and recent revelations show that very little of the world has been left behind them; but to come out in principle, in sympathy, in solemn duty to God, in hatred of its sins. Separation from the world does not mean separation from it mechanically It is not drawing a line, and saying, "On this side of the line is the world, and on that side is the church," but it is coming out in heart, coming out in life, and rising above it, and growing into sympathy with a purer and a nobler one.

Thus, the world will be under our feet, while God is over us, and heaven before us.

God calls us to leave this world, as far as it is sinful, just as he called upon Moses to leave Egypt. We are summoned to decide, and not halt between two opinions. If the world be your all, take it; but, if you are satisfied that there is a better and a brighter one, where Christ is, aspire to it. The only beings that can afford to be spectators are God and angels. We are not and cannot be spectators; we are on, not beside, that stream which rushes with ever-accumulating speed to the great ocean of eternity. Despise the riches of Egypt. Count all but loss for the excellency of him who has a throne that endureth forever, "seeing him who is invisible." Then will the voice of Moses prove to us a voice of power; and his dead speaking stir us as his living presence stirred the Israelites of old. Egypt will be surrendered for a better hope, and the things of sense will yield before the attractions of everlasting prospects.

CHAPTER XI.

THE GREAT DELIVERANCE.

When to the cross I turn mine eyes,
  And rest on Calvary,
O Lamb of God, my sacrifice,
  I must remember thee !

"Through faith he" (Moses) "kept the passover, and the sprinkling of blood, lest he that destroyed the first-born should touch them." — HEBREWS 11 : 28

NOTHING magnanimous or noble is done on the earth that is not done through something out of self. There is nothing that gives glory to God, or lasting benefit to mankind, that is not, in some way, the child and the creation of faith.

By faith, the least things recorded by St. Paul, in Heb. 11, were done. By faith, the greatest things were not left undone. "Through faith, Moses kept the passover:" the word translated "kept" is rendered differently in other passages of Scripture. It is, literally, Moses "made the passover." It is translated, in another place, "ordained the passover." It is the same word that is employed by the evangelist, when he declares that "the Lord ordained twelve," or, literally translated, "made twelve." In Matthew 26: 18, the same word is rendered, "I will keep the passover;" it does not mean, therefore, that Moses invented the passover, but that by faith he kept what God had previously prescribed as an ordinance of his own.

Faith ascends to the highest, and descends to regulate and control the very lowliest things. It is a great mistake that only the grand things of Christian life are done by faith, and that the little things, so called, of Christian life, may be left to themselves. True religion, and the faith which is the exponent of that true religion, goes with the whole force and splendor of a celestial power into the commonest walks, and to adjust the most ordinary duties, of every-day Christian life. It is by faith a tradesman keeps his shop. It is by faith a Christian minister preaches his sermon. It has to go into the one, and make business religion. It has to go to the other, and make religion business. The business of this world, divorced from religion, becomes a selfish, ungodly, unsatisfactory scramble; and the religion of this world, divorced from business and every-day duty, becomes a revery, or quietism, or fanaticism. In the absence of religion, the Royal Exchange would become but a gambling-house, the House of Commons a place of personal rivalry and acrimonious dispute, and all our institutions mean, senseless, low; but, when entered by faith, and their duties done in faith,—that is, under the inspiration of the sense of a present God, and of responsibility to him,—the lowest duty of Christian life becomes lofty; for it shines in the lustre of him whose care extends to the minutest, and beyond whose control the greatest things are not. Real religion surely is not a thing for the Sunday, to be left behind us when we enter on the week. We come to the house of God on the Sunday to learn what religion is, and we go out from the house of God on the Monday to show in practice what religion does. The business is only begun when a sermon is preached: the practical part of it remains. The doctrinal part we hear from the pulpit: the practical part we are to carry into our every-day duties. True religion is not a Sunday dress, which we are so careful of that we will not bring it into the dust of the world, lest it should be defiled, or into the excitement and vortex of its trial, lest it should be rumpled. Our religion is not something upon us, but something in us; a principle, a power, a life, meant to go into the world, and to master the world, and in the world to enable us to glorify our Father who is in heaven. What does the apostle say? "Whether therefore ye eat, or drink, or whatsoever ye do, do all to the glory of God." How completely does this disturb the creed of those who say it is very well to think of God's glory on the Sunday, and very proper to do things to the glory of God when we propose to send out a missionary to the ends of the earth! This passage teaches us that the very minutest and most ordinary employment of human life is to be inspired, elevated, ennobled, consecrated, by the power of real religion. By faith, then, we learn life's great things were done, and life's little things were not left undone. In short, true Christianity is not a pompous display to be made upon the first day of the week, while the remaining six days are left empty of it, just as the pews we occupy are for six days left empty too. We are to begin the week by learning grand truths; by receiving them into our heart and our conscience; and then to go forth clinging to those things, inseparable from them in heart, as our responsibility and our immortality, going down into life's lowly places, ascending into life's high places, and, in all and always, according to the measure of our strength, making the world to reflect the splendor of the skies, and the image of God to shine upon the brow of the very meanest of his creatures. The honor and reverence that Christ demands is not a splendid procession along the aisles of a beautiful cathedral; nor glorious banners and impressive rituals does Jesus ask as the greatest honor we can pay him. Poor man is so foolish that he thinks he is most honoring his Lord when he is accumulating splendor, and form, and pomp, and ceremony; but that is not the honor that Jesus requires of his true and his faithful worshippers. He asks us to leave the consecrated pavement and the cathedral aisle, and to come out into the dusty road of ordinary life with him, and to the common floor of every-day duty, and to show that the religion which we gather, like the manna, on the first day of the week, has virtue to feed our souls, and to sweeten life's bitter things, and sanctify life's sweet things; so that, in the by-nooks of every-day life, as well as in the broad walks of public life, the world may take notice of us, that we have been with Jesus, by his spirit, his temper, and his life, being reflected and shadowed forth from our own. Our religion, in one word, is not a thing confined to a place, or to a day, or to a form, or to a ceremony. No one can read the eleventh chapter of Hebrews without seeing that, if by faith Moses kept the passover, it was by faith also that Abraham left his country; it was by faith that Rahab received the spies with peace; it was by faith that Samson exerted his energies; it was by faith that Samuel lived, and that the walls of Jericho fell, and that they passed through the Red Sea, and many other acts related of it in the same chapter. It is, in short, by faith, "the substance of things hoped for, the evidence of things not seen,"—that is, the bringing of a divine power into human life, and of a higher life into the humblest sphere and province of human life,—that we make heroic sacrifices and bear domestic trials equally, and at the same time. Our religion is not, like the electric element, gathered into the church as that is gathered into a jar, there to sparkle and make a little noise as it leaps from point to point; but, like that great element out of which the jar is filled, which runs through all the universe, gives fertility to the soil, balance to the orbs in the sky, order and equilibrium to the earth on which we tread, felt by its constraining, gentle, but persistent power, not heard by noisy crackling, or loud profession, on one day of the week. In short, real religion consists, not merely in saying prayers, but in being righteous;

not in speaking precious truths, but in living beautiful lives. Religion is not Christianity secularized, but it is secular business Christianized. What the age in which we live wants is not theological magazines, theological newspapers, but secular newspapers conducted on religious principles, and sustained by a religious element. What we want is not discussions in the columns of the papers of religious dogmas, but that the paper, the magazine, the book, whatever it is, should show, by its heavenly aim, by its holy advocacy, by its unswerving principle, that real religion is behind the scene, its life, and light, and truth, and that its influences are thrown out upon the world, felt rather than preached, in whatsoever things are just, and beautiful, and lovely, and of good report. Such is faith, or the apprehension of living truth, as it flows through and pervades the whole of the checkered circle of the Christian life, beginning in infancy and ending in old age.

Now, by this faith, by which he did things merely secular in their character, Moses celebrated one of the divinest and most solemn sacraments of the ancient Christian church. If, as it is said, by faith he esteemed the reproach of Christ greater riches than the treasures of Egypt,— if by faith he forsook Egypt, not fearing the wrath of the king,— if by faith he refused to be called the son of Pharaoh's daughter, —by faith also, in the sanctuary as well as out of it, "he kept the passover, and the sprinkling of blood, lest he that destroyed the first-born should touch them."

The origin of the rite here referred to is given in the twelfth chapter of the book of Exodus in these few words: "And the Lord spake unto Moses and Aaron in the land of Egypt, saying, This month shall be unto you the beginning of months: it shall be the first month of the year to you. Speak ye unto all the congregation of Israel, saying, In the tenth day of this month they shall take to them every man a lamb, according to the house of their fathers, a lamb for an house: and if the household be too little for the lamb, let him and his neighbor next unto his house take it according to the number of the souls; every man according to his eating shall make your count for the lamb. Your lamb shall be without blemish, a male of the first year; ye shall take it out from the sheep, or from the goats; and ye shall keep it up until the fourteenth day of the same month: and the whole assembly of the congregation of Israel shall kill it in the evening," literally "between the evenings;" "and the priest shall take of the blood, and strike it on the two side-posts and on the upper door-posts of the houses, wherein they shall eat it. And they shall eat the flesh in that night, roast with fire, and unleavened bread; and with bitter herbs they shall eat it. Eat not of it raw, nor sodden at all with water, but roast with fire; his head with his legs, and with the purtenance thereof. And ye shall let nothing of it remain until the morning; and that which remaineth of it until the morning ye shall burn with fire. And thus shall ye eat it; with your loins girded, your shoes on your feet, and your staff in your hand; and ye shall eat it in haste: it is the Lord's passover. For I will pass through the land of Egypt this night, and will smite all the first-born of the land of Egypt, both man and beast; and against all the gods of Egypt I will execute judgment: I am the Lord. And the blood shall be to you for a token upon the houses where ye are; and when I see the blood, I will pass over you, and the plague shall not be upon you to destroy you, when I smite the land of Egypt. And this day shall be unto you for a memorial; and ye shall keep it a feast to the Lord throughout your generations."

The historical origin of the facts is simply this,— Pharaoh and his people were resolved not to let the children of Israel go. He felt, or believed, that his power was able to wrestle, and to wrestle triumphantly, with Omnipotence itself. God tried, if I may use the expression, many fearful and terrible experiments, in order to subdue his heart, and constrain him to do what he was determined not to do. He smote the whole land of Egypt with plague and pestilence, with fire and with tempest; the water of the river, which the Egyptian held as his god, was turned into blood before his eyes; the cattle were destroyed upon a thousand fields; the very dust beneath the Egyptians' feet was kindled into animated hostility to every Egyptian that trod upon it. All this, however, signally failed to melt the obdurate heart of Pharaoh, King of Egypt. God, therefore, to show that he had not yet reached the limits of his resources, resolved to strike a blow that would be felt in every home, and that would penetrate the heart of Pharaoh on his throne, and the humblest heart in his dominions, with the most poignant sorrow that flesh and blood is heir to. He commanded an angel to spread his wing, and to sweep, on strong and untiring pinion, through every lane, and alley, and thoroughfare, and square, and enclosure, in the whole land of Egypt; and to go into every house, except certain specified ones which we shall describe by and by, and there to strike the first-born; and the heart of the first-born, whether twenty years, or twenty months, or twenty days old, should instantly be still.

One can well conceive, when the angel swept through the whole length and breadth of that land, in some still, dark and silent night, and when nothing was heard without but the rush of his pinion, and nothing was heard within but the wail of neighbors that lamented the dead that should live no more, how the parents rushed forth from one home to seek the sympathy of the next, only to meet the next neighbor coming to seek sympathy from them; — the very silence, and the very secrecy, and the universality of the stroke, increasing the awful national confusion that fell as a thunderbolt on every household; till at last one wild and piercing wail rose from every family of every Egyptian throughout the whole land. And the sun of the next day rose upon a city wrapt in sackcloth, and upon homes that echoed lamentations and crying; and all Egypt felt that a blow was struck in comparison with which all their previous judgments were but as playthings. One can well remember, when the terror by night and the pestilence by day was amongst us, what an anxious feeling pervaded the whole population; but that was nothing to be compared to the wide-spread feeling of Egypt, when every family's first-born was, by a mysterious touch, numbered with the dead.

But there was an excepted class. We read, that the Israelites, a certain class, took the blood of a lamb which they slew,—a painful thing,—and sprinkled that blood upon the lintel and the door-post of the house; and wherever that was, there the angel did not dare to enter.

There was no virtue in a lamb's blood any more than in the blood of another victim; it was because it was the ordinance of God, and because it was the foreshadow of another Lamb, and because it was teaching what all God's dispensations did teach, that without shedding of blood there could be no remission of sins.

Let us, in order clearly to apprehend the great deliverance of the Gospel, which is good news to all, mark well the only reason of the Israelite's safety and exemption.

He was circumcised, but that was not the ground—just as we are baptized, but this is not the ground of our exemption from judgment. The Israelite belonged to the people of God; but that was not the ground of his exemption. If a single Israelite, of the purest character, the most spotless repuation, omitted to slay the lamb, and sprinkle his threshold and his lintel with its blood, the angel entered that Israelite's home, and smote the first-born. It was not the Israelite's moral character, nor was it the Israelite's ecclesiastical character, that exempted him and his, however real, from the stroke of the angel. It was not his virtues in his past career, however manifold or beautiful. The only exemption was nothing in the Israelite, but wholly and solely in the blood sprinkled on the threshold, and the lintels, and the door-posts, of his house.

The whole of this passover is a lesson most instructive to us. We read in another passage of Scripture that Christ is our passover. We are told that Christ is "the Lamb slain from the foundation of the world." The Baptist cries, he is "the Lamb of God, which taketh away the sin of the world." We are told that, by his blood alone, there is life and defence. But, are we exposed to the same peril to which the Israelites' and the Egyptians' first-born were exposed on that night? We are exposed to a worse. Every swing of the pendulum carries a soul to the judgment-seat of Christ. What a solemn fact is this, that we meet in our churches at eleven, and depart at one; and during that interval, in the metropolis alone, some half-dozen will have passed into eternity, — either sprinkled with that blood and saved, or strangers to it and lost! Death walks amid our homes — the great messenger of God enters every household. There is not a home of any reader of these lines that has not some chair empty that used to be filled. There is not a threshold that has not ceased to be darkened by a welcome shadow that once lightened, or rather beautified it. There is not a heart that has not in it memorial tablets, on which dear and bright names are written, legible in the love in which they were originally inscribed. We walk amid the dying, — the angel of death is ever busy. In many a family he has smitten the first-born, and made the home for a season dark and drear. We, too, writer and reader, are subject to removal without notice; we, too, must be swept away from the place we now call our own. Not a face looks upon this page that in a very few years will not be beneath the green sod. There are more of the population of London beneath the soil than there are above it. Every day we are dying. Every pulse of the heart, especially in the case of the aged, and the very sickly, and the very delicate, is the curfew-bell that tells them that the day is fast closing, and the night is just about to begin, in which all earth's passions should be quenched, and they should prepare to put off "this mortal."

In the prospect of that great change which surely awaits us all, let us ask ourselves, each one solemnly for himself, Have I sprinkled on the lintel and the threshold of my heart the all-preserving and protecting blood which cleanseth from all sin?

Faith in Christ is our true deliverance. It is not enough to have been baptized. The Israelite had what is an equivalent to baptism, but that was not his safety. It is not enough that we have paid every man his due, and have been charitable and liberal. All these things are beautiful, but they are not the elements of our safety. It is not enough that, as far as we can see, we are the most spotless characters in Christendom. It is right, it is very beautiful, but this is not our safety; the only safety for the soul is the blood of the Lamb. The Israelite was saved, not by what he was, but because that blood was on his threshold. The believer is justified, forgiven and saved, not from what he is, but from that blood which cleanseth from all sin. Our fears, our doubts, our misgivings, do not destroy the efficacy of that blood. This is a very precious truth, which we are very apt to forget. Many a Christian have I met, many a dying one have I visited, who had fears, and doubts, and misgivings, just upon the very brink of the grave. But it was to such great consolation when I told them of that night when the angel swept through Egypt. I can conceive an

Israelite family waiting the result that long night. They had sprinkled the lintel and the door-post with the blood; and when the sound of the angel's pinion, passing along the street where that house was, echoed in their ears, and deeper still echoed in their hearts, I can conceive that every child crept to its mother's knee, and the family group gathered closer to the fireside; and that every joint trembled and shook like aspen-leaves smitten by the wind, whilst the angel swept by. But, because they doubted, the angel did not therefore enter. In spite of their misgivings, they were perfectly safe. It is not our doubts, nor our fears, nor our misgivings, that will dilute the protective efficacy of the blood of Jesus, or that will provoke the judgment of God to enter in. Our safety is in this, not that we have no fears, but that the blood of Christ cleanseth from all sin. In spite of our misgivings, doubts and fears, we are safe, because we have washed our rcbes and made them white in the blood of the Lamb. Thus the blood of Christ, and that alone, is our only protection.

Of course, when I speak of the blood of Christ, I do not suppose that any reader can be possessed of the Romish idea, that turns every spiritual truth into a material and carnal thing. The poor Romanist cannot think of the cross of Christ without thinking of pieces of wood; or of Christ's blood without thinking of material blood. It is by faith in our case,— not feeling,— it is by an unseen grasp of an unseen and real Saviour, that we live. In the Romanists' case not one individual feels that he is safe until he can touch the hem of the Saviour's garment. With him it is not expedient that Christ should go away. When I speak of the blood of Christ, I mean the sufferings of Christ in our stead. It is not unlikely that the blood of those wounded hands and of that bleeding side trickled down and fell upon the soldiers, and upon the Pharisees that shouted and hooted below; but it did them no good; whereas, the poor criminals on the day of Pentecost, who never saw the Saviour, nor heard his voice, yet believing, were safe, forgiven and happy. "Whom having not seen, we love; and whom, though now we see him not, yet believing, we rejoice with joy unspeakable and full of glory." I mean, therefore, by the blood of Christ, his death and sacrificial sufferings in our stead and in our room

Christ is the antitype of the paschal lamb; and the Lord's supper is still the festival that was celebrated after the sacrifice of the passover lamb.

Christ, I say, is the antitype of this passover lamb, and I might trace out, as I have done before, minutely, the resemblance, but I do not think it necessary to do so.

The lamb was set apart, and slain between the evenings; he was a lamb without blemish, in full strength and vigor; and in all these respects the lamb was the type of the Lord Jesus Christ.

The lamb was slain as a sacrifice. This is important; because, in the sense in which the passover lamb was slain, Christ was offered. Now, can it be said that the passover lamb was slain as an example? Can it be said that he was slain as a symbol of patience and gentleness? No. Then Christ was not slain in order to show that he was a martyr, and had a martyr's constancy. He was slain as a sacrifice, in order to show that except through his blood there could be no forgiveness of sins for guilty mankind. No one can deny for a moment that the passover lamb was slain as an expiatory offering. Its blood sprinkled on the lintels protected against the deserved and threatened peril. So Christ, our passover, was sacrificed and slain for us; not as a martyr, sealing the sincerity of his convictions, but as an atonement, making an expiation for the sins of all that believe. If the apostles and evangelists understood their own language, it is impossible to conclude that they did not mean to teach that

Christ died as a sacrifice. They used the language of sacrifice, they used the very figures of sacrifice, and they attribute to Christ's blood such efficacy and virtue that it is impossible to attribute the same efficacy and virtue to any other blood whatever. For instance, we are told that we have access through his blood, that we are purchased by his blood, that we are redeemed by his blood, and that the way to the holiest of all is opened through his blood. Can we say so of the blood of any martyr? Peter died a martyr, Matthew and Luke also so died; but could we say that we are redeemed by the blood of Matthew, that we have access to God through the blood of Peter, that we are purchased by the blood of Luke? The very statement shocks our truest and holiest impressions. It is impossible, from the virtue ascribed to that blood, to doubt that it was of an expiatory and atoning victim, by whom alone we are redeemed and restored, and in whom we have redemption, even the forgiveness of sins. I cannot see a single crevice in the New Testament for the creed of Socinianism. I cannot see in that cold, hyperborean religion any relationship to that warm sunshine that tints every page of the Gospel, that gives me life when it gives me light. If Christ be not my atonement, what is my state? Worse than that of the Jew. The Jew had the old law, which he could not obey; but we have the new law in addition; and if we cannot obey the one, how shall we obey the other, or the old and the new together? If the Gospel be not a remedy, but simply a direction, then everything is altered. The church is but a school, the New Testament is simply a transcript from Sinai; I am not sick and needing to be divinely cured, I am not condemned and needing to be divinely pardoned; I am only a little out of my course, and only require a little conciliatory direction to get into it, and work my way to heaven with vigor, energy and success. If this religion be true, when I stand in heaven, I shall say unto myself, who gained the day, and secured the victory, and made good my passage — "unto myself be glory, and honor, and thanksgiving, and praise." But it is all the reverse. I am lost; Christ is my only Saviour. I am condemned; that blood is my only ransom. I am guilty; that sacrifice is my only acquittal. I have lost all right to heaven; that righteousness is my only title. And when I shall mingle with the choirs of the blessed, I shall there feel it to be the deepest and the holiest instinct of my nature to say, Not unto me, not unto me, but unto him that loved me, and washed me from my sins in his own blood, be glory, and honor, and thanksgiving, and praise, for ever and ever.

And now, if we are not pardoned and saved by that blood, the whole reason is in ourselves, not in the blood. If the Israelite's first-born did not escape the destruction of the destroying angel, where was the fault? That he did not take the lamb's shed blood, and sprinkle it on his lintel. And if we are not saved, if we do not escape the destroying angel of the second death, it is not because there is no efficacy in Christ's blood, but because we will not take it and sprinkle it upon the lintel and the door-posts of our hearts. The reason of the whole failure is, not that the blood has not adequate efficacy, but that we really do not deliberately and truly apply it. And if any find themselves on the left, and in the number of the lost, upon that day, they will see then that it was no predestinating decree of God that stood between them and the blood of the Lamb; that it was not mere want of power, but want of will; never, never, I believe, has one been lost that would be saved, and never has a soul been saved except through Jesus Christ.

Can we this day say, I have forfeited heaven, I have forfeited all right, title, fitness, qualification for it; but Christ is my passover, that precious blood was shed for me? But one may say, Ah! is it for me? I just reverse the question, —Why not for thee? Is there anything upon thy brow that excludes thee from it? Is there any depth and dye in thy transgressions that this blood cannot expiate? Not if you can from the heart say, I take that blood as my only atonement; I look to that death as my only sacrifice, my only trust, the only ground in the whole universe of God why the earth should not be expunged, and all its people swept into hell; and I go to the judgment-seat persuaded, because I am sprinkled with it, that neither life nor death shall be able to separate me from the love of God which is in Christ Jesus my Lord.

Some one may ask, especially of those who do not regard Christ's death as a sacrificial offering, What was the necessity of this sacrifice? Why was a sacrifice required at all? God so loved us that he gave his only-begotten Son, that whosoever believes in him shall not perish, but have everlasting life. And here I correct, as I have often done, the erroneous idea sometimes indicated in preaching Christ's sacrifice as our only ground of salvation, namely, that God loves us because Christ died for us. I just reverse the maxim, — God loved us; therefore, Christ died for us. Christ's sacrifice is not the cause of God's love to me: it is simply the medium of God's love coming to me.

But, if God loved me, could he not provide a channel for that love, so that that love might reach my heart? So he has; and that channel is "the Lamb slain from the foundation of the world."

But you say, Why was such a channel required? The answer is simply this, that God's love could only reach me in a way that should show him to be holy, just and true, whilst he loved me. Humanly speaking, God's omnipotence cannot save a sinner without the atonement of Jesus; because by no other process that we know can he be seen to be consistent with himself, whilst he sheds down the expressions of his pardoning mercy upon the chiefest and the guiltiest of sinners. Christ's death makes it clear to the universe that God is just while he justifies, that he does not cease to be holy when he receives the sinner to his bosom.

You say, How does it make that clear? Christ stood in my place, he suffered in my stead. That holy, innocent, spotless Lamb wrapped himself in the unholy, tainted fleece of the lost sheep of mankind; and God saw the tainted fleece, and would not see the spotless One that was within it; and he let forth his judgments on the substitute who exhausted them. And just in the same manner now; because of what Christ has done, I, the guilty, the stray and unholy sheep, shall be clothed in Christ's innocent, and spotless, and perfect fleece; and when God looks at me in the judgment-day, he will not see the fallen one that is within, but he will see only the spotless fleece that is without; and I shall be accepted and acquitted as righteous through the righteousness of him which is laid upon me. When Jesus died upon the cross, there was nothing in him that deserved death; when I shall be admitted into glory, there will be found nothing in me that will deserve heaven. As it was just in God to let forth the expressions of his wrath upon Christ bearing my sins, it will be just in God to let forth the expressions of his glory upon me bearing Christ's righteousness. He was made sin for me; I am made righteousness by him. And when God, therefore, forgives the guilty sinner, he shows himself just, holy, faithful, true; his law kept, and yet the violator of it safe; his word maintained, and yet the sinner saved; in one word, "Glory to God in the highest; on earth peace, and good-will toward men."

We have thus considered this sacrifice, the passover sacrifice, Christ Jesus, by whose blood alone we are ransomed. Now, when the Jew had slain the passover sacrifice, we read that he kept what was called a passover feast. We must distinguish between these two. The secret, I believe, of what is called the Tractarian superstition, that has overflowed the country during the last ten years, and the secession of so many gifted minds to the Romish apostasy, lies in a very great degree in the fact that they confound the passover lamb or sacrifice with the passover feast or festival. The two things are perfectly distinct. The passover sacrifice was the slaughter of the lamb; the passover feast was taking the flesh of the lamb that had been previously slain, and roasting it, while the whole family gathered round the table, and fed upon it. Now, Christ is our passover sacrifice; the Lord's Supper is the passover feast after the sacrifice has been completed. There were two parts in the sacrifice. There was the painful part, which the Jew went through when he slaughtered an inoffensive lamb, and shed its blood: there was after that the pleasant and the delightful part, when the family gathered round the table, and ate its flesh, and drank of the paschal cup. Now, the Jew had first to do the painful thing, which was to kill an innocent lamb; he had then to enjoy the pleasant thing, which was to eat and drink of the festival after it. In our case our Lord took all the painful part, and finished it when he said, upon the cross, "It is finished;" and he has bequeathed to us the passover feast, not to add to the passover sacrifice, but that we should eat it with the bread of sincerity and truth, commemorative of the completed sacrifice. The very fact that there is a Lord's supper amongst us is an evidence that the expiatory sacrifice has been made. The Jew did not at the passover feast make the passover sacrifice. Therefore, for a priest to say that a sacrifice needs to be offered, and that the communion-table is the altar on which it should be offered, is to give the grossest caricature of the glorious Gospel of the Son of God. When Jesus said "It is finished," that moment all Romish, Tractarian or expiatory atoning offering, as needful to us, was swept away forever. Jesus said, "It is finished;" the blood is shed, the sacrifice is complete, the atonement is made; we have not now to make an atonement, but to trust in one; we have not now to celebrate a sacrifice, but to accept one; we have not now to plunge the knife into the throat of the lamb, but to trust in a Lamb already slain; we enjoy the feast after it, and we take this bread, and drink this cup, in remembrance that the sacrifice is complete, and that his blood cleanseth from all sin.

How were they to do this? They were to do this, says an apostle, in this manner, "With the unleavened bread of sincerity and truth." "For," he says, "even Christ our passover is sacrificed for us: therefore let us keep the feast, not with old leaven, neither with the leaven of malice and wickedness; but with the unleavened bread of sincerity and truth." I have heard persons say, We are going to the great passover sacrifice, and our title to it is "the unleavened bread of sincerity and truth." Such is a complete misapprehension. The sacrifice made and finished is our only title to the feast that is prepared; but, whilst that sacrifice is made and finished, and is our only title, the accompaniment of the celebration is to be "the unleavened bread of sincerity and truth." Our only title to the Lord's supper is just our title to heaven,—that the Lamb is slain; but the feeling with which we should celebrate the Lord's supper is that which we are to have in heaven,—"the unleavened bread of sincerity and truth."

I stated, at the commencement of my remarks, that the punishment of the death of the first-born was partly a retributive judgment upon Pharaoh for his refusal to let the children of Israel go. But what, in the midst of this refusal, was the special sin of Pharaoh? He ordered that all the first-born of Israel should be slain, lest the Israelites should grow and multiply, and become a nation that should be a match for himself. In this we see the illustration of a great fact that we all need to learn,—that the sins of a nation are always visited with punishment in some way connected with them. There is no more intimate connection between a tree and its seed, between an effect and its cause, than there is between sin and the judgment or punishment that follows it. A nation's judgment is generally the rebound of a nation's sin; so much so that we can read in the light of that nation's punishment the specific sin of which it has been guilty. A Romish hierarchy, thrust upon our country in spite of our queen, our constitution and our people, seems to me a judgment from on high for Tractarianism, long tolerated and indulged in England.

And we should do well if in this matter we learn another lesson from Pharaoh. When Pharaoh wanted to get rid of his punishment, he prayed. Take away the punishment; but he would not put away his sins. Now, if we want to get rid of our punishment, let us put away the provocative; and instead of praying to God to take away the cardinal, the right way is to set about ourselves to get rid of the Puseyism; and when the seed is destroyed, the upas-tree will soon fall. We read in this the true nature of our nation's sin.

The punishment of children, as here seen, is a very painful thing. Was it just in God to punish the poor babes, the first-born, because their fathers or their forefathers had sinned? It may seem unrighteous to us, but the unrighteousness is not in God, but in the obliquity of our vision. When the Bible says that God visits the iniquities of the fathers upon the children unto the third and fourth generations, it does not mean that God punishes with eternal punishment the child for the sin of his parents; but it does say that God chastens the children to the first, second and third generation, for the sins of their forefathers. You say, Is it just? I answer, Is it true? Do we not find it so in providence? Let a father indulge in drunkenness, and in habits of intoxication. It may seem a cruel thing that his child should suffer for his intemperance, and yet his child does suffer. If a nobleman should commit high treason, what a cruel thing that his child should not wear his coronet! and yet he does not wear it. If a parent commit a crime, does not the punishment fall upon his children? When we read of some parent in the dock begging that the sentence might be more lenient on account of his family, the answer has been an expression of surprise, that, with so large a family, he should dare to rush into so heinous an offence. We thus see, throughout the whole length and breadth of society, that the children do suffer for the sins of their parents. If it be said that the language of Scripture, as to visiting the sins of the fathers upon their children, is an argument against the God of Scripture, I answer that the facts I have mentioned go to show that, if there be no God of Scripture, there is no God at all; which more and more confirms what I have found, that no man can banish the conviction that the Bible is true, except by rejecting the conclusion that there is a God at all. You cannot escape what you think one absurdity without plunging into a worse. I believe that there is no solid ground on which I can stand save this, "All Scripture is given by inspiration of God, and is profitable for doctrine, for reproof, for correction, for instruction in righteousness."

It being fact that children are punished for their parents' sins, it teaches parents to be more careful, more prayerful, to set a nobler example, and to feel the lofty impression, that they have a trust of life not for themselves only, but for others that are to come after them. And thus the lesson that seems at first an unjust one will elevate parental relationship into a magnanimous and noble tie, and enable them to feel that they live not for themselves, but for others; that they have a sort of vicarious mission, that what they are, and what they do, will tell upon generations that follow, when their bodies are beneath the green sod, and their souls at the judgment-seat of Christ.

We learn, from the connection between the passover lamb with its passover feast and the Lamb of God with the Lord's supper, that the religion of the ancient Hebrew and that of the modern Christian are the same. There is difference of development, but identity of principle. Error is an innovation. Truth has been, from the beginning, gradually maturing itself. Romanism is but the rank grass that grows up in the summer sun; but true, evangelical, Protestant Christianity is as old as Paradise itself. Like the precious diamond, it has been maturing in the secret caverns of the earth whilst whole generations have passed away above it; and now it is coming forth to shine and sparkle in the risen sun; and soon it will emerge, yet more beautiful and brilliant, when Christ collects his jewels, and sets them in his own diadem, the glory of heaven, the beauty and the riches of the earth. Abraham was a Christian, just as I am. Patriarchism was Christianity; Judaism was Christianity. Moses and Matthew preached the same Gospel. Levi and John, like the overshadowing cherubim in the holy place, looked upon the same sacrifice; — they, in type; we, clearly and distinctly as he is.

I might show, from the study of the passover, how absurd is the dogma called transubstantiation. "It is the Lord's passover." These are the words of the sacred penman. Was the lamb slain, and placed upon the table when thus slain, for the purpose of the feast, concerning which it is said, "It is the Lord's passover," transubstantiated at such festival into an angel passing through Egypt, and destroying the first-born in some homes, but passing over and not entering into others? No. Then the almost identical words, "This is my body," are not to be construed that this bread and wine upon this table are transubstantiated into the body, and blood, and soul, and divinity, of the Son of God.

When Jesus said, "This is my body," his words were significant, not miraculous. They were declarative, not in any sense creative. And, if it should be said that Christ did change the elements into his body and blood, it does not follow that a priest can do so. Just as, although Christ said, "Let there be light, and there was light," yet a priest cannot make the darkness flee away. Were I to grant that Christ made such a mighty change, it would not follow that a priest is able to do the very same thing. Christ could say, "Walk," and "See," and it was so; he could raise the dead; but it does not follow that we can. And, therefore, were we to grant the first demand of the Romanist, the next would not follow.

And further, when Christ did miracles, he used a particular form of language. For instance, he said to the waves, "Be still;" to the dead, "Come forth." And, had he intended to change the elements of bread and wine, he would have said, "Be thou turned into my body;" "Be thou turned into my blood." He spoke thus in all his other miracles; and, therefore, his sacramental words were simply declarative.

And it is most interesting to select, from the most ancient of the Christian fathers, instances at least parallel to this. I have at least a dozen. One father says that, when you look at the head of Homer, you say, That is Homer; yet you mean It is his statue. When you see a map of Rome, you say, That is Rome; by which you mean to say, The map of Rome. And so, when he said, "This is my body," he did not mean, This is my true and real body; but, This is the sign of my body; for, says Augustine, "Christ called the sign by the name of the thing signified." One can only wonder that such a master mind as that of Archdeacon Manning, of all others, ever could be persuaded to accept such gross and revolting delusions; and one can only feel that it is explained by a very awful sentiment, perhaps too severe for frail man to utter, but yet the very same sentiment that occurs in relation to that great mystery of iniquity into which, we believe, he has unhappily plunged, that "for this cause God shall send them strong delusion, that they should believe a lie." Whenever man tampers with truth, he does not know the obliquity of the career upon which he enters; and still less does he know the awful issues into which that course may precipitate him. Dear reader, act up to the light that you have, and God will give you more; but tread out or misuse the little light that you have, and God will take away that little light from you. I believe that a sincere mind, even sceptically disposed, if he pray and search for what is truth, will not be left by God to ultimate darkness and error. But, if the most enlightened mind be living in opposition to what he knows is truth, let him take care lest he be given up to strong delusion, that he should believe a lie. In these days of sophistry, let us not, to gratify a miserable curiosity, go into Romish chapels in order to hear Cardinal W. or Bishop D. You have no business on Satan's ground, seeking God's protection. God will protect you everywhere in the path of duty. You have no right to expect protection when you leave that path. On God's own ground, we are conquerors over every opponent. Off that ground, we are needlessly perilling our own souls.

And one word more, and I have done. Hold fast great, precious truths, and you will escape deadly errors. Live in the sunshine of light, and the little Italian tapers will have no charm for you. Live on the bread of heaven, and the husks of Babylon will have no sweetness to your taste. If the old creed of Luther, and of Calvin, and of Ridley, and of Latimer, and of others in that noble school, could only be more clearly and vigorously preached and studied, you would have the heart so crowded with all that is true, and solid, and precious, and good, that you could afford to look down contemptuously upon the efforts of the advocates of error to ensnare, entrap and deceive you.

CHAPTER XII.

A TRAMPLED FLOWER.

God scatters truths on every side,
Freely among his children all ;
And always hearts are lying open wide,
Wherein some grains may fall.

There is no wind but soweth seed
Of a more true and open life,
Which burst, unlooked-for, into high-souled deed,
With way-side beauty rife.

" By faith the harlot Rahab perished not with them that believed not, when she had received the spies with peace." —HEBREWS 11 : 31.

IN this lecture, we have a new character introduced to our notice, who, being dead, yet speaks; Rahab, who " perished not with them that believed not," or were disobedient to the warnings they received; and whose faith was seen in the circumstances connected with her reception of the spies with peace.

What strange variety of character is brought within the horizon of the Gospel! Men of every nation, and tribe, and country, are its subjects. The great vineyard has every variety of tree, and fruit, and flower. There is not a land on which the sun sends his beams that waves not with the fruits of the Gospel, nor any specimen of the human race that may not be found in the happy and holy fold of the great and the good Shepherd. Illustrious patriarchs, like Abel, Enoch and

Abraham, are in its glorious muster-roll. Devoted women, as Sarah, the mother of Moses, Rahab, once the harlot, the woman of Samaria, and she that washed his feet with her tears, reclaimed by love, and transformed into monuments of grace, are found in that catalogue. Vast multitudes that crossed the sea, men, and women, and children, of different degrees of faith, of hope, of sorrow and of joy, were all numbered in the shining list of those whose faith became the victory that overcame the world, working by love and purifying the heart.

The history of Rahab is interesting; I need not say it is difficult and delicate; but it is a subject beautiful, instructive, and strikingly exhibitive of the power of the Gospel of Christ Jesus. Two confidential persons, we read in the book of Joshua, were selected by Joshua to visit Jericho, and from thence to bring back a report to the commander of its strength, its resources, and its population. It was the frontier, or capital city of Canaan. It was inhabited by the Canaanites, a depraved and abandoned race. These spies entered the city, into which they found easy and unexpected access. They sought for a place of refuge or shelter from the inspection of the police, and a covert from the suspicions that the entrance of Jews, who were known enemies of the capital, would naturally create. They found the house of a person despised for what she had been; for she had ceased to be what she once was; and, in this sequestered house, the spies, secluded from the rest of the social circle, found a shelter and a home. A report spreads (for it was difficult to elude the watch of a police such as they had in ancient times; or, rather, a rumor reaches the city authorities), that Jewish spies had been seen surveying the capital, taking its dimensions, measuring, probably, the depth of its trenches, and the strength of its walls, with a view to its destruction, if such an attempt should seem feasible. Still worse, the rumor spread that these spies had entered the house of Rahab. Instantly the gates are closed; the detective police are sent after them; the possibility of their retreat is cut off; their capture and destruction seem imminent. These officers, on visiting the house of Rahab, of course inquired first, as the narrative suggests, whether such persons as spies from the camp of Joshua had been seen within the walls of Jericho, and if they had visited or were in her house; and, of course, they required, at the risk of her life, that she should instantly deliver them up. If she had been, at this moment, an unprincipled person, her first dictate would have been to betray those who had cast themselves on her compassion, and under the shelter of her roof, and, for a consideration which would have been ample, to give up the spies to the vengeance of their foes. She did not do so. She gave a plausible, but untruthful excuse; not simply an equivocation, but a statement positively untrue. We must not disguise or seek to palliate what is strictly sinful, or to vindicate a character otherwise bright from an obvious stain. We must hail the good, and accept it, and acknowledge the evil, and reject it. By a false and untrue statement she covered them, and declared that they were not there; that they had gone another way; and, what shows that she could not have been a notoriously bad character, the detective police, not very easily cheated, as we know, accepted her statement as true, and believed every syllable she uttered, with apparently implicit confidence. These two traits should show that, if she had great faults, she may not have been without great excellences; and that the faults were forgiven by the blood of Jesus, and the excellences that merged them shone forth with richer lustre because of the humbling recollections in which they were embosomed. To give a very short summary of all that occurred, she hid the spies under the flax-stalks that were drying on the flat roof of her house, situated on the walls, and outside; and, on the departure of the police, she opened the gate, and let her guests go free; only she exacted a promise, first, for her own life, very naturally; but, what was still more beautiful, and indicated the Christian frame of mind of this woman, she exacted a pledge that they would be kind to her parents (she was at this time about seventeen years of age), and to the friends that were connected with them; all which they pledged. And, in due course, we read, that whilst the walls fell beneath the earthquake that upheaved them below, and the houses of Jericho crushed the inhabitants in their ruins, that frail house, under which grew in silence the transplanted flower, stood firm as if it had been based upon the everlasting rocks; all the attributes of Deity, like the mountains around Jerusalem, shielded and protected it.

Some have tried to show that the proper translation of the word which is here rendered "harlot" is "hostess." Now, those who have done so, as Moses Stuart, an accomplished Hebrew scholar, have drawn the Hebrew word from a wrong source, or, rather, have overlooked the proper derivation of it; it does not and cannot mean hostess; we must conclude, from the whole history, that "hostess" or "innkeeper" is not the proper translation, and that the translation, as given by the apostle James, when he alludes to her, is the right and true one: only, recollect, such she had been, but such she had ceased to be; and "such were some of you, but ye are sanctified, but ye are justified in the name of the Lord Jesus, and by the Spirit of our God." In other words, the epithet attached to her name originally would cleave to it after the character that deserved it was gone; the reproach clung to her character, after the evil it represented had been put away; her name could not be mentioned without the early discord being heard—"Rahab, the Christian, but once the harlot."

I have not demonstrative evidence of this, and therefore all may not accept this solution; but it seems at least a very natural and a very plausible one. One can only regret in this, as in other cases, what is so true, and what the great poet and reader of human nature has so well said:

> "The evil that men do lives after them;
> The good is oft interred with their bones."

It is very strange that our consciousness of sin in ourselves should make us the less sympathize with others, and more prone to condemn our neighbors. It looks as if we felt that, under the shelter of a brother's condemnation, our own iniquities should be more rapidly merged. The solution of her past history seems to be this: The customs of India are not modern or recent; and certainly, if antiquity can prove a thing to be true, India's religion must be the true one. In India, the native parents devote their daughters, in their earliest infancy, to the practice of the most vile and sensual rites and worship, in certain of their pagodas. These daughters, often the most beautiful, are separated to the sensual purposes of licentious worship from early years. India witnesses, in these victims, its beautiful flowers corrupted at their earliest buddings. The most revolting sensuality is consecrated by religion, and made part and parcel of its ritual. One needs but to know the world, to believe how truly the Spirit spake three thousand years ago, when he said, "The heart of man is deceitful above all things, and desperately wicked;" but in such cases, let it be remembered, the daughters are the victims, the parents are the criminals. The guilt of the parent is the misfortune of the child; and when the child in such circumstances sins, pity is the emotion we should feel for her, and condemnation and reprobation the sentiment we should entertain for the parents. I believe this practice of India is just one of the old habits of the Canaanites. The Canaanites were the inhabitants of Jericho. It is my conviction, gathered from the character of Rahab, and all that is said of her, and about her, and allowing for the peculiar reserve with which her history is alluded to, that she had been devoted to these infamous rites in some heathen temple from her earliest years, and that she had afterward escaped from it; either from nobler instincts within her obtaining the ascendency, or from a ray of heavenly light creeping into her mind, or from the unextinguished remains of humanity in its loftier phase protesting against a worship so revolting, and regarding what the priests taught as religion to be sheer iniquity and crime. In all probability she escaped, and ran away from their tyranny, and threw herself on the wide world. By so doing she lost the protection of the priest, the patronage of her parents, and she never had the approbation of her country. She was banished from the circles of cultivated life, and insulated from all social intercourse; her house, from necessity and choice, was in a retired part on or under the walls of Jericho; and thus far her escape was a proof of her excellence. Her past life was her sad misfortune; but the world of Jericho, like the world of London, forgot the excellences, redeeming excellences, that illuminated her present, and recollected and retained, and wrote broad, and deep, and legible, the flaw only, which they would not regard as a misfortune, but which God in his mercy and his love saw to be so.

That her existing character was good, and that she had traits in that character which indicated real if recent Christian worth, may be gathered from such facts as those we have alluded to, and from the following. First, the spies intrusted their lives to her. If they did so by a divine command, of which there is no record, then, of course, this part of my argument is worthless; but, if they selected her from her known excellence of character as a repentant and restored and renovated female, then it shows that she must have had reputed excellence to attract their notice, and that there must have been something in her character that caused them to place the deepest confidence in her. It is impossible that men like the spies from the camp of Joshua, full of tact and management, would have intrusted the interests of their country, the victory or defeat of the army of which they were part, and their own lives, to a person notoriously bad. In the next place, there were developed in her conduct traits of real religion that the rest of the Canaanites were strangers to. For instance, she said, "I know that the LORD" (the word "Lord" is in capital letters, showing it to be the translation of "Jehovah,") "hath given you the land, and that your terror is fallen upon us, and that all the inhabitants of the land faint because of you." The Canaanites believed that they would force back the Israelites by stratagem; but she said, "For we have heard"—now, mark the words—"we have heard;" faith comes by hearing, in our case, from the word of God; in her case, by the teaching of others. "For we have heard how the Lord dried up the water of the Red Sea for you when ye came out of Egypt; and what ye did unto the two kings of the Amorites, that were on the other side Jordan, Sihon and Og, whom ye utterly destroyed. And as soon as we had heard these things, our hearts did melt, neither did there remain any more courage in any man, because of you; for the Lord your God, he is God in heaven above, and in earth beneath. Now, therefore, I pray you, swear unto me by the Lord, since I have showed you kindness, that you will also show kindness unto my father's house, and give me a true token; and that you shall save alive my father, and my mother, and my brethren, and my sisters, and all that they have, and deliver our lives from death;" that is her only revenge—her retribution. Surely here are the seeds and elements of real religion; here is a creed most orthodox, a light plain enough to lead her to salvation. Perhaps, by the hearsay of those that she had come in contact with in Jericho, or by some previous ministration of love, of mercy, and of truth, she had learned the knowledge of Jehovah, who is God in heaven and earth, and was thus a Christian in the midst of Jericho.

Another evidence of her worth was her love of the truth of God, and even the preference of that truth, and its obligations, to her apparent duties to her country, and her obligations to her nation; for she gave up all, that she might do what conscience dictated. This was no trivial sacrifice. It is proof that there was in the depths of her heart the power of that divine truth, "He that loveth father or mother more than me is not worthy of me."

In the next place, the entire confidence she reposed in the promise of the spies is another beautiful trait in her character. A bad man is rarely a confiding man. The consciousness of guilt within makes him suspect constantly assault without. Suspicion is one of the strongest instinctive elements of sin: confidence is one of the most beautiful traits of divine grace. Now, this woman's implicit confidence in the simple word of the spies indicates that her character was restored, recast, reformed, sanctified. She entertained true Christians, and so entertained angels unawares; she hides the people of God from persecution; she refuses, at the risk of her life, to betray them; she owns the true God, foresees the fulfilment of his word, and she prays for mercy for herself and her kindred, and all that were near and dear to her. These were traits which a bad character would not have developed, and evidences, to my mind, that, whatever she once was, a Christian she had now become.

But, what was the result and the reward of all this? First, she was the means of safety to herself, her family, and her friends. Secondly, her faith was the means of admission into the commonwealth of Israel, and of incorporation with the church of the living God. Thirdly, God so honored faith in Rahab that she becomes one of the progenitors of Messiah, the light of the Gentiles, the glory of his people Israel. Fourthly, she is distinguished by an apostle as an evidence of what faith can do and dare; and she is recorded by another apostle as a specimen of faith that worketh by love, and purifieth the heart, and overcometh the world; from a child of wrath, she is made a child and a daughter of God; from a citizen of Jericho, a citizen of the heavenly Jerusalem; instead of the doom that fell upon her co-patriots, she obtains the destiny of a place in God's presence, where there is fulness of joy, and where there are pleasures forevermore.

So much, then, for the presumptive good in the character of Rahab. I come now to look at the drawback, and there is a great drawback, in her character. She was guilty of equivocation, or, rather, of what is properly and most honestly called a direct falsehood. It is foolish to attempt to justify her here. I can no more justify this sin in Rahab, than I can condemn the character of Rahab; and I think that the commentators who have attempted to justify it might just as well have defended the policy of Ignatius Loyola, whose great maxim is that the end justifies the means. But, if there be no defence for Rahab's sin, there is much palliation for it. Let us see in what circumstances the sin was committed; and, whilst we do not cease to look upon the sin with reprobation, let us see what can be said for her who was guilty of that sin. Thus God distinguishes—loving the sinner, hating the sin. Thus God accepted Rahab as his own, while he must have forgiven the sin as hers. What are the palliating circumstances? and the palliating circumstances will not make us love the sin, but only feel for the memory of the sinner. First, owing to the guilt of others, she had spent her past life in evil and unrighteous habits. She was seventeen years of age at this time; probably from seven she had lived a stranger to all light, and an alien to the exhibition of the delicacies of ordinary, still more of the delicacies of lofty life. In the second place, such habits become inveterate when they have been long indulged. Who does not know that habit is a second nature? The roots and fibres of a practice long indulged in are not withered in a moment, or extracted in a day; and it is not a disproof of real conversion when man after his conversion still shows some danger of falling into sin. It may be a proof of his failings in former times. In the next place, she had only just come to the knowledge of the truth as it is in Christ Jesus. Obligations she now felt, she never felt before. Duties, responsibilities, she now saw, she never saw before. And, in the next place, she did, what we ask all to do, she acted up to the light that she had; and we believe that he who acts up to the light that he has will never be left in darkness. I have little hope of the quibbling, metaphysical sceptic, who is ever wresting the Bible to find reasons for rejecting Christianity, just because he feels it is only in the sense of its being false that he can have any enjoyment at all; but where I find a man who is not an infidel, yet not a believer, who is honest, sincere, candid, inquiring, honestly and truly so, I believe God will not leave him in darkness. She acted up to the light that she had: and she that hath, to her shall be given, but from her that hath not shall be taken even that that she hath. And, in the next place, she is not set forth as a specimen of what she should be, but simply as an historic character, a personation of how much faith can do; for which we rejoice, whilst we admit and regret that there was something still behind, which faith had not triumphed over, and destroyed.

The Bible is not a record of the lives of angels; it is a record of justified, sanctified persons, with characters frail and infirm. I believe that one of the greatest mischiefs that ever infected the church of Christ was that opinion entertained in the fourth century, that angel life was the great model of human life. Christ is our grand model; and characters that shone in the light of Christ are to be imitated by us just as far as they imitated Christ. How sound is the philosophy contained in that passage where the apostle says, "Be ye followers of us, even as we are of Christ!" When Paul said so, he did not mean them to imitate his persecution of the church. When Peter said so, he did not mean them to imitate his denial of his Master. But, so far as they, being imperfect mirrors, reflected the glories of the perfect Master, so far be thankful and imitate them. Rahab's equivocation the true Christian forgets, in the recollection of Rahab's faith. David's murder, so heinous, those that belong to David's Lord will forget, in the recollection of David's excellence, devotedness, and grace. Peter dissimulated, and Paul, his brother apostle, felt it once his duty to persecute the church. In other words, there is not a character in the Bible that has not some flaw in it. If the sceptic thinks he can take an advantage of it, let him do so. But there is this to be said, that the fact of the noblest characters of the Bible having flaws only shows that there is none perfect but One; and the very circumstance that the historians in the Bible have recorded those flaws shows how honestly they wrote, how truly they portrayed, and that they gave us, not a profile of human nature, but the full face; not an exaggerated, beautiful, and sentimental portrait, but a picture of man as sin has left him, and a picture of man such as, with all his drawbacks and short-comings, grace can make him. There is a shadow where there is the brightest light; there are specks, we have been told, even on the sun's disc. The Holy Scriptures recognize all that is excellent in man as an emanation from God, all that is defective in man as man's own; and they commend the beautiful to our imitation, and set up the sin as a beacon for our avoidance.

Having noticed these traits of this woman's character, let me draw two or three simple lessons from the whole.

First, we see that God honors the very least faith that is developed in a Christian heart. Let us recollect the case of Naaman the Syrian, how little faith there was in him. After he had thought that the rivers of Damascus were as good as Jordan, and after he had been induced to go and do as Elisha bade him, even then the weakness of his faith was shown in this — "Shall there not then, I pray thee, be given to thy servant two mules' burden of earth? for thy servant will henceforth offer neither burnt-offering nor sacrifice unto other gods, but unto the Lord;" forgetting that religion is a thing of the heart, and not a thing of earth, of ceremony, of ritual; yet God honored it, and accepted him in spite of his defects. So of Nicodemus; he came to Jesus by night, ashamed to be seen in his presence by day. He did not even then think it right to put the question that was nearest to his conscience; but, in order that he might edge it in, he spoke thus, "No man can do these miracles that thou doest, except God be with him;" but, nevertheless, Jesus honored that little faith, for we read in the seventh chapter of St. John that Nicodemus became his advocate in peril, and we read afterwards that he took care of the dead body of Jesus; and from coming to Jesus by night, almost a fugitive, we find him ultimately in broad daylight the champion of God, who thus perfects the grace he implants, and implants the grace that he is pleased to perfect. The least atom of real religion in the heart is far more precious than the most splendid and gorgeous ceremonial; God honors the one, he passes by with apathy the other. You may give your body to be burned, you may give all you have to feed the poor, but yet you may not have real religion; but, if you have real religion, it will give a great deal more than this.

Paul writes, "There is neither Jew nor Greek; there is

neither bond nor free; there is neither male nor female; for ye are all one in Christ Jesus." In the Bible, are Christian women, eminent for the piety of their lives, and the devotedness and greatness of their sacrifices for Christ's sake. It is true that female character is not so frequently adduced as an exhibition of the power of the Gospel in the Bible, because it is instinctively less public, and more retiring. We see man's character. He stands upon the stage in noon-day light, visible to all; but woman's Christian character is to be traced, like the silent mountain stream, not by rolling cataracts, but by the green belts of verdure, of blossom, and quiet beauty, that grow all along its margin, indicating alike the purity of the stream and the holy source from which it comes. Christianity is the greatest ornament, as well as the only salvation, of woman. It is from the Bible that all her just excellences have come; it is to the God of the Bible that she ought to give the glory of them. In this country woman occupies so just a position, because the Bible maintains so lofty an ascendency. Let this Bible go down, let the infidel exhaust it, let the priest put his padlock upon it, let confession to man take the place of confession to God, and there is an end of all that sustains, beautifies, and adorns the character of woman.

We learn that one or two Christians in a country bring down many indirect blessings upon those that are there. For instance, Rahab's faith saved her kindred from destruction. And we know that in our own land, and in every country where the Gospel is felt, there is an indirect blessing derived from it. What is it that bathes our nation's forehead as with the first rays of resurrection glory? What is it that runs through all our own land, a ceaseless cement, making all ranks, from the highest to the lowest, cohere, and feel a pervading and a joyous affinity? It is the indirect power of the Gospel of Christ. Thousands have felt its real power, and have become true Christians; tens of thousands live in its twilight, temporally blessed by it, who yet may never be eternally saved by it. Lot in Sodom was the safety of the city; ten righteous men in it would have saved it from complete destruction. And though all in this country at this moment are not true Christians, yet all, I believe, are more or less under the twilight, or the indirect influence, of Christianity. A French pasteur, with whom I recently conversed, was amazed when he saw the lofty reverence for law, the deep sense of order, yet sensitive love of freedom, that pervade English life; every one obeying, each one moving in his proper orbit, without jar, without collision, without disorder, without a wish to have it otherwise. And he said, "I can only account for it by your Bible religion and Bible churches;" and he added, "I can only account fcr the absence of all this in my own country by the want of these." A Frenchman is, at least, no less noble a character than an Englishman. There would not be a finer people in Christendom than the French, if they were only Protestants, and true Christians But, as it is, they are tossed upon the surges of a ceaseless tempest; they feel themselves that they are seated upon a volcano, which will explode again, no man knows how soon; it is more and more obvious that it is real religion alone which will exalt a people, and that, in the absence of it, we may have a republic or a monarchy, we may have what we like, but we shall have neither life nor order. Then, let us thank God for the indirect influence of this faith of ours. The moment any one priest or Pope can say, "Give me your conscience to manage, and your Bible to open and to shut when I please," our national glory is set forever. So long as a people have an open Bible they never can be slaves; whilst a people that have a fast one never can be free. Let us thank God for the Bible; let us hold fast our fathers' birthright, in the best sense of the word; and if God should be pleased to remove the candlestick of our nation's greatness, we shall still retain the light of his countenance.

Let us learn, also, there is mercy and forgiveness in the Bible for the very chiefest of sinners. Rahab is a lasting memorial, inscribed upon which I can read these words: "The blood of Jesus Christ cleanseth from all sin." The woman of Samaria still stands at the well of Jericho, and on her I can read, "He is able to save to the uttermost all that come unto him;" for "Thou hast had seven husbands, and he whom thou now hast is not thy husband." Again, the Gentile woman, who washed his feet with her tears, is another pillar of the truth, and on it I can read, "Her sins, which are many, are forgiven; for she loved much." And all these, from Rahab, one of the earliest, to Paul, the chiefest of sinners, proclaim with growing utterance this essential truth, which is the very core and substance of Christianity, "For God sent not his Son into the world to condemn the world, but that the world through him might be saved." There are no depths of transgression God's great love will not cover; no heights of iniquity God's great mercy will not reach. It has a ransom for every penitent, it is abashed by no guilt; it offers forgiveness to the greatest sinner, and expiation to the greatest sin. Celsus of old objected to Christianity, that it was an asylum and a refuge for the vilest of mankind. The very sneer of the sceptic set forth the very greatest truth of Christianity. Origen well replied, "It is not an asylum, where criminals may flee in order to be kept there; but an hospital, to which the chiefest criminals may come, in order to be healed and cured and made happy there." It is still true that Christ Jesus came into the world to save sinners, even, says the apostle Paul, "the chiefest." The glad news is, that there is instant forgiveness for every man, if he will; there is no reason in the height, there is none in the depth, why every man that hears the Gospel should not be forgiven;

only we must come down from the lofty platform of self-righteousness, and lay aside the grand pretension, and submit to be washed in the same stream with poor Rahab, and to be clothed with the same righteousness with the woman at Jacob's well, and to walk to heaven in the same path that has been beaten smooth by the feet of the chiefest of sinners, as well as by the greatest and the best of saints.

Wherever there is true faith, it is followed by good works. Wherever a man is thus freely forgiven, that man will always be found thus purely to live. To speak of Christian faith without works is perfect nonsense, it is absurdity; it is to speak of the sun shining at noonday without light, and of a fire burning in the grate without heat. If a man be a Christian, he is always good; if he be always bad, he is no Christian at all. Would you not blame me if I were to use such words as "an honest thief, a truthful liar, a sober drunkard"? and with the very same reason, and with equal propriety, a dishonorable, an uncharitable and untrue Christian, are contradictions and nonentities; such a one is no Christian at all. If he be a Christian, notwithstanding many imperfections, drawbacks and defects, he is struggling, striving in the strength of God to bring forth all the fruits of the Spirit of God. But in this matter does not Paul contradict James? We read, in the first, that Rahab was justified by faith; but, on opening the second chapter of the Epistle of James, we find him state, with that quietness that shows that he felt there was no contradiction, "Was not Rahab the harlot justified by works, when she had received the messengers, and had sent them out another way?" Now, the sceptic would seize upon this as a palpable contradiction, and he would say James contradicts Paul. When Paul preached justification by faith in his days, it was liable to perversion; but the very perversion to be guarded against was the evidence, if you will pardon the thought, how evangelically Paul taught.

Do we "make void the law through faith?" says he, "yea, we establish the law." But the very fact that Paul's doctrine was met by that objection, shows that Paul's doctrine was justification by faith, in no degree by works, or law; but when James says that men are justified by works, does he not seem to teach we must get to heaven by works? The man who does not read the Bible as a whole will never learn the truth. The Protestant Bible is the whole Bible, and the Bible alone. If you will read Paul in the light of James, and James in the light of Paul, and both in the light of the Holy Spirit, then you will come to a right conclusion. The obvious explanation is, that Paul speaks to man under the conviction of sin, to whom he says, in answer to his question, "What must I do to be saved?" believe on the Lord Jesus Christ. James speaks to man professing to be justified, and asking what is the evidence of it, to whom he answers, "It is works." I ask Paul, how, being a sinner, can I be justified in the sight of God? and he says, By faith in the Lord Jesus Christ. And I ask James, How shall I show that I am justified? he says, By works. I am justified in my own conscience, by the conscious faith in which I receive the Lord Jesus Christ; and I am justified by works, by showing to the world that true faith is inseparable from lively and from righteous doings: and thus the two apostles perfectly harmonize. To a Christian, such an explanation is not required; in his heart he feels that both are true. We are justified by Christ meritoriously, by faith instrumentally, by works declaratively. Christ is the meritorious title; faith is the instrument that lays hold of it; and works are the fruits that unfold what Christianity is.

We see how salvation may reach the far-distant parts of the earth without all the blessings and the privileges of an open Bible. Whilst it is our duty to send the Bible to all, it is our privilege to know that the least ray of celestial truth, penetrating the heathen pagoda, or the Romish temple, may carry conviction into the intellect and grace into the heart, and reveal the Sun of righteousness, from whom that ray proceeds, to the worshipper. And hence, on the remotest banks of the remotest heathen isle, there may be Christians who have heard the echo of a glorious truth, and live thereby. In the depths of the most degrading section of the Romish population, there may be those who are in Rome, but not of it; some monk carrying a crucifix, but carrying, nevertheless, in his heart, the Christ that was crucified for us; some doing penance bodily, though in their hearts they may have repentance towards God and faith towards our Lord Jesus Christ; and we are the more encouraged to believe so, because God says, "Come out of her, my people, that ye be not partakers of her sins;" indicating that he has a people there, in spite of all that is around them. And how important it is, when we go out into distant lands, that we should drop a truth as we have opportunity, since we never can calculate the effects of a precious truth! God has said, "My word shall not return unto me void." We may be travelling by stage-coach, or in a railway carriage, and yet we may hint a sentence of God's word, and it may return in protracted reverberations of glad music, when our dust is mouldering beneath the green sod, and our spirit will be refreshed by the knowledge of it in the presence of God and of the Lamb. "My word shall not return unto me void," is a promise that cannot be contradicted. Let us ever leave the word wherever we have opportunity.

In places unsuspected by us, there may be the saints and the people of God. Who could have suspected that in the centre of Jericho there should be a holy and pious woman, loving and living for God? And so, amidst the din and noise of our crowded capital, in places we little suspect, from quarters we do not expect, there may be sounding from humble hearts the still, small voice of prayer and thanksgiving; and in the dark nooks of this great city, where the splendid palaces would not shine less splendidly if they did not cast their shadows upon so dark dens and alleys behind them, there may be inhabitants who shall become the heirs of paradise, and in unknown places God may be preparing gems of the purest water for the Redeemer's diadem. Let us not judge where God has not called upon us to do so. Eternity will disclose that there were Christians where we thought, in our exclusiveness, there were none; and it will make manifest the still more painful fact, that many who shone so conspicuously, and talked so eloquently, were not Christians at all. Christianity is not in word, — it is in power. I have listened to what is called the most religious conversation, sometimes, and I have felt that it was utterly destitute of religion throughout; and I have listened to a conversation, in which there was not one word strictly theological, and yet there were evidences of real religion planted in the heart. It is not the word that comes from the lips that is the best exponent of what comes from the heart; but it is the quiet under-tone of Christian life and Christian love, which speaks music to the ear of God, and is, to the discerning mind, the strongest evidence that the grace of God is there.

I learn another lesson from Rahab's history, and it is this: that there never was and there never will be but one way to heaven. Rahab was a Christian, just as truly as we are. There never was but one altar since the fall; there never was but one way to heaven. Rahab, and Paul, and Martin Luther, were all washed in the same blood, clothed in the same righteousness, accepted in the same name. Jew and Gentile, who are truly Christian, are both in one way.

We learn another solemn lesson. The inhabitants of Jericho had the same opportunities for knowing the Gospel as Rahab had, but they neglected them; "they believed not," is the language of the text. And what does this teach us? That it is possible for two persons to hear the Gospel, and one only to receive it. It is not only the clearness of the enunciation of the truth, but the preparedness of the heart, that renders it a savor of life. The unwilling heart will receive the seed as the stony ground, and will rebound, or the birds of the air, as the emissaries of Satan, will snatch it away. Yet it is our duty, as ministers of the Gospel, to sow the seed; it is upon hearers that the responsibility rests of receiving it. The same truth which was the savor of life to Rahab was the savor of death to the rest of the inhabitants of Jericho. Awful truth! that the same sun shining upon one substance melts, and falling upon another hardens it. The rays of the Sun of righteousness in some cases harden the heart, until it becomes like adamant; and in other cases they subdue, until it becomes fit and prepared for God.

In the next place, we see in Rahab a daughter of Abraham, although not in the lineal descent of Abraham. The Jews were his children by descent, and they have been cast out; we are his children by faith, and we are admitted. If the church we belong to could trace its genealogy to an apostle, and, link by link, could substantiate its relationship to Paul, yet it would not be an element of safety, or a guarantee of purity to it and happiness to us. It is not a material connection with even an apostle, but a spiritual connection and communion with the Lord Jesus Christ. It is not Paul's person, nor Paul's cloak, nor Paul's parchment, but it is Paul's Lord and Saviour, that must be ours; and if we hold Paul's doctrine as he taught it, and cleave to Paul's Christ as he clung to him, we need not doubt that we are the children of Abraham and heirs of heaven.

We learn that in the genealogy of Jesus were people of all varieties, and nations, and tribes, and tongues; and, just as in his genealogy were all kinds of persons, so in the purchase of the travail of his soul are all kinds of sinners. Not to Abraham alone was the Gospel preached; not to the Gentile alone, but to the Jew also. It is not our commission to exclude any: it is our privilege to invite all. Rahab, washed in the same blood, is in the presence of the Lamb, and sings unto him who washed me from my sins, and made me a priest unto God for ever and ever. Why should any of us perish? If the worst have been saved, how can we be excluded? Is God unwilling to accept us? If he be so, it is a good excuse; but God is not willing that any should perish. Is Christ unwilling to save you? If he be so, it is a good excuse; but it is not true; he is willing to save you to the uttermost. Is Christ unwilling to assist you? If he be so, it is a good excuse; but it is not true; for he says, "Come unto me, all ye that labor, and are heavy-laden, and I will give you rest." Is heaven too full? If it be so, it is a good excuse; but it is not true; for the record is still, Yet there is room. Are the pleasures and the ambition of the world a sufficient compensation for eternity? If they be so, then it is a good excuse for indulging in them, and never thinking of the future; but they are not so; for he who was able to pronounce the estimate aright has said, "What shall it profit a man, if he gain the whole world, and lose his own soul?"

Are we superior to Rahab in all the elements that build up the Christian character? It is not feasts, nor fasts, nor festivals, that make Christianity; it is not bright and sounding trumpets and gorgeous ceremony that constitute true worship. These are the stalks and the husks, and are, in comparison, worthless in God's sight. The core and the pith of religion is acceptance in the blood of Christ Jesus. When Moses descended from the mount, it was not by words, it was by the glory that shone on his face, that he showed that he had been with God. God's grace is not a sudden explosion of a rocket, making a great noise at the moment, and then passing away; but it is the silent influence of unseen warmth, that makes fertile the soil of many a barren heart, and clothes the life with the verdure and glory of Eden. Let us not be satisfied with Rahab's attainments, having more than Rahab's opportunities and responsibilities; nor let us bė satisfied with the common level: let us rise to loftier heights; let us aspire after nobler Christianity; let us be the best; let us be distinguished in religion, as we are distinguished in the things that are in this world. Cultivate converse with things that are unutterable. Let our glory be, not the wealth we acquire, the wisdom we master, the nations we subjugate, but the victories we win (where victories are noblest) over sin, and Satan, and the world, in the exercise of Rahab's faith, by confidence in Rahab's Lord; and so, with her, inherit the promises; for

"In that fair land shall disappear
The shadows which we follow here,
The mist-wreaths of our atmosphere."

CHAPTER XIII.

BLESSINGS.

Tongues of the dead, not lost,
But, speaking from death's frost,
Like fiery tongues at Pentecost.

"By faith Isaac blessed Jacob and Esau concerning things to come." —HEBREWS 11 : 20.

WE have seen, in rapid succession, some remarkable instances of the power of faith. It is important to study such illustrations. The popular impression is, that faith is a thing always inoperative, and that works are alone precious. The truth is, faith is the root of all that is good and great; it is so in this world; it is eminently so in relation to a higher world. It was not by love, not by patience, not by heroism, not by virtue, but "by faith," the sainted lived and the martyrs died.

Let us examine the faith of Isaac, who had no other foothold than a grave in Canaan. It is said, "By faith Isaac blessed Jacob and Esau concerning things to come." The moral characters of the two were perfect contrasts from the first, and yet both were equally blessed. And does not God do to us as the patriarch Isaac did to his sons? His rains descend upon the evil and the good, upon the just and upon the unjust. The sunbeams and the raindrops alight upon the unproductive clay, as well as upon the fertile soil; upon the rose-tree, and upon the brier and the thorn. God's common blessings are for all his creatures. He opens his hand, and

Jacob and Esau are equally blessed by him. But there are two classes of blessings. There are the blessings of the throne, which the Jacobs only have; and there are the blessings of the footstool, which the Esaus have in common, frequently, with Jacob; there are spiritual blessings, which he gives to his own; there are temporal blessings, which he spreads, in the exercise of infinite beneficence, over all his created family. This teaches us that we are not to infer that God is for us because we suddenly or successively become rich; and that we are not to infer that God is against us because we lose the temporal blessings that we have long or immemorially enjoyed. We are never to infer what the feeling of God's heart is by the sight or the experience of God's hand. Often, when his hand smites sorest, his heart is fullest of love. Often, when the cloud overwhelms and envelops us, the sunshine of his reconciled countenance is nearest to us. We are not to judge what God is by his providential dealings; but we are to judge of his providential dealings by what God is. We are not to argue that God is against us because the world's stream runs counter to us; but we are first to ascertain what God is to us, and what we are to him, and then we are to infer what his dispensations are. Plant your footing on the fatherhood of God, satisfied that he is your father, and that you are his children, and then construe all the dispensations of his providence in the light and sunshine of your father's countenance. A believer does not say, "God is my enemy because I have lost my property;" but he says, first of all, "God is my father; therefore this loss must be friendship. God is my friend; and therefore all that betides me is but the expression of his love, the chastening of his goodness, the evidence of my sonship." Thus Esau and Jacob had common, yet different blessings; but not from this could Esau infer that he was God's child, or Jacob, from the loss of them, that God was his enemy.

It is worthy of notice, as we gather from reading the interesting history which is given in Genesis, that Jacob, the younger, received the principal blessing. This is one illustration of God's sovereignty. How often have we to learn, even now, that grace is not by primogeniture! It is not always the eldest son who is the noblest Christian. It is not always where we would like, and where we should prescribe, that the blessings of grace fall fastest. We need to learn that it is not of flesh, nor of blood, nor of the will of man, but of God. If it were true that a pious man's children were always pious, and that a bad man's children were always bad, then the world would say, original corruption of heart is not true. Virtue and vice, Christianity and the want of it, are the results of education or precedent. God, therefore, interferes in sovereignty, and shows an illustrious saint emerging from a bad man's home, and sometimes a depraved and abandoned prodigal going out from a good man's house; and thus he teaches us, when we use the means with all the vigor with which they ought to be used, that we must ever look above the means, and feel that even the prescription, "Train up a child in the way he should go, and when he is old he will not depart from it," is not enough without the blessing of God. The great law is, Train up a child aright, and he will live a Christian; but even this has its limitation and exception; and such limitation is given in order to illustrate the sovereignty of him who calls whom he will, and has mercy upon whom he will have mercy. Throughout the history of these patriarchs, we have often seen this principle embodied. Abel, the younger, was accepted; Cain was not. Abraham, the youngest in Terah's house, was adopted and chosen of God. So, "Jacob have I loved, and," as it is expressed in the Epistle to the Romans, "Esau have I hated." Yet we must not understand the last expression literally; the word "hate," when contrasted with love, in the Scriptures, is more than once used in the sense of loving less; for instance, "If any man come to me, and hate not his father and mother, and wife and children, and brethren and sisters, yea, and his own life also, he cannot be my disciple." One may not hate his parents; God has said that we must love and honor them; the word is therefore used in the restricted sense of loving less his father and mother than the Lord Jesus Christ. So here, it is said, "Esau have I hated; Jacob have I loved." It does not mean that God hated the one in his sovereignty and loved the other in his sovereignty; but, that he loved the one more than the other. I think it is quite true that God hates nothing but sin; in short, hates nothing that he has made. All that God has made, from the planet in the firmament to the pebble on the sea-shore, from the archangel that is about the throne to the infant that plays by his mother's knee, God does not hate. God hates nothing that he has made. He "so loved the world, that he gave his only-begotten Son;" that none might perish except those that will, "that whosoever believeth on him might not perish, but have eternal life."

There is evidence, from the expression employed in the original record, to which this verse refers, that temporal blessings were not so largely conferred upon Jacob as upon Esau; for, in speaking of his pilgrimage, Jacob was compelled to confess that large temporal blessings were not his lot: "Few and evil have the days of the years of my life been." Esau, however, was chagrined at the blessing, such as it was, pronounced upon Jacob; Esau had temporal blessings promised, but evidently he understood that Jacob had something higher, that is, spiritual. For instance, the blessing upon Jacob was, "God give thee the dew of heaven, and the fatness of the earth, and plenty of corn and wine; let people serve thee, and nations bow down to thee; be lord over thy brethren, and let thy mother's sons bow down to thee: cursed be every one that curseth thee, and blessed be he that blesseth thee. And it came to pass, as soon as Isaac had made an end of blessing Jacob, and Jacob was yet scarce gone out from the presence of Isaac his father, that Esau his brother came in from his hunting." But the blessing that was given to Esau was, "And Isaac his father answered and said unto him, Behold, thy dwelling shall be the fatness of the earth," — this is Esau's, — "and of the dew of heaven from above; and by thy sword shalt thou live, and shalt serve thy brother; and it shall come to pass, when thou shalt have the dominion, that thou shalt break his yoke from off thy neck. And Esau hated Jacob because of the blessing wherewith his father had blessed him." Next we find the blessing, as repeated upon Jacob, to be, "And God Almighty bless thee, and make thee fruitful, and multiply thee, that thou mayest be a multitude of people; and give thee the blessing of Abraham, to thee," — that is, the spiritual blessing, — "and to thy seed with thee; that thou mayest inherit the land wherein thou art a stranger, which God gave unto Abraham." Thus, both had temporal blessings; one only had spiritual. The greatest temporal blessing cannot gladden a sad heart. The least spiritual blessing will be as sunshine in the sorrowful heart. The secret of happiness is grace. The secret of sadness and of misery is the want of it. A true Christian is happy in proportion as he feels that he is a Christian; and, in the absence of Christianity, nothing else can work out or weave within substantial and enduring happiness. There is a moth fretting the richest robe; there is rust upon the purest gold; there is a bitter and aching something in the recesses of royal hearts, which none but he that made them can pluck out.

The blessing that was bestowed by the patriarch, I perhaps ought to have explained at the commencement of my remarks, was a prophetic one. There were two ways of blessing. Aaron blessed the people; but it was the blessing of a priest. The patriarch blessed his son; but it was the blessing of a prophet. We, too, pray for blessings upon ours; but it is as Christians. The special blessing of Jacob was, that he should be connected with that strange and mysterious line, in which were Gentiles and Jews, in which were royal and plebeian ones, out of which the Messiah should come in the fulness of the times. This was the great hope of every mother in ancient Israel, this was the great glory of that remarkable race, that out of them the Messiah was to spring; and to be connected, however remotely, with the great predicted deliverer of our race, was the greatest glory that a Jewish family could possibly hope for or inherit. Now, the special glory of Jacob was, that he should be one of that family out of which the Messiah should come in the fulness of the times. What the ancient Jew rejoiced in, according to the flesh, we may rejoice at in a far higher sense. Then, indeed, to be connected with Jesus according to his descent was the glory of an Israelite; now, to be connected with Jesus by living faith in his blood is the higher glory of a Gentile. The Jew expressed his very innermost feeling, when one came to Jesus, as we are told in the Gospel of Matthew, and said to him, in language which shows the position which the virgin mother of Jesus occupied, "Behold, thy mother and thy brethren stand without, desiring to speak with thee. But he answered and said unto them," — now, here was just nipping in its very bud that which continued, too long and too intensely, the joy and hope of a Jewish parent, — "Who is my mother? and who are my brethren? And he stretched forth his hand toward his disciples, and said," — what extinguished every shade of supposed merit in relationship according to the flesh, and introduced the far higher value of the relationship of faith, — "Behold my mother and my brethren! For whosoever shall do the will of my Father which is in heaven, the same is my brother, and sister, and mother:" he thus showed it was the glory of the virgin Mary, not that she was the mother of Jesus according to the flesh, but that she was a humble worshipper of him who is "a Light to lighten the Gentiles, and the glory of his people Israel." The same idea that the Jews had was expressed in the words, "Blessed is the womb that bare thee, and the paps which thou hast sucked." To which our Lord made the reply, "Yea, rather, blessed are they that hear the word of God, and keep it." How absurd, then, is it to suppose that the virgin Mary's special relation to the Saviour gave her special merit! She was washed, and needed to be washed, in the atoning efficacy of the same blood. Mary is a saint worshipping before the throne; and, if an unspent echo of what is said upon the earth is audible to her holy ear, it must create sorrow, if sorrow can be felt in heaven, that she should be degraded from the place of worshipper before the throne, and made a sort of deity for the reception of the worship of deluded and mistaken men.

Another part of this blessing pronounced specially on Jacob was, that he should be a part of that little band, selected from the midst of the world, that believed and trusted and rejoiced in the blessings of the Gospel. In other words, a special part of the blessing pronounced on Jacob was, that he should be enrolled among the people of God. Esau had everything that man could covet. Jacob had everything that a Christian could hope for, or desire. It was no light privilege to be enrolled among the people of God,—to be taught that he belonged to the seed of Abraham, was a child of God, an expectant of glory. There has always been a church in the world. That word "church" is often grievously misapprehended by us. Some conceive it to be a gigantic hierarchy; others, an immense company of the baptized; and others, a huge material edifice. The church of Christ is not made up of numbers you can count. It will be far greater and more numerous than the exclusive will allow; it will be far more limited than the latitudinarian will admit. The church of Christ is beautifully defined in the words of Quesnel, of the same school as Pascal — both Protestants, yet in Rome. Quesnel wrote some beautiful comments on the New Testament. Pope Clement in 1713 extracted from his writings the choicest sentiments he had uttered, and after each sentiment he added an anathema; the whole is contained in an instrument which has lately been often heard of, named a Bull — that is, a rescript or document of the Pope. Now, one of the most beautiful of the sentiments condemned, and which indicates great Christianity in the writer of it, and great want of Christianity in the condemner of it, is this: "The Church of Christ is the company of God's people, reposing in the bosom of the Father, washed in the blood of the Son, inhabited by the Comforter, looking for the coming of Christ, and for the glory to be revealed." Such is Quesnel's beautiful definition. I hold it to be the truest definition of the church of Christ. Some members of that church are in the Roman church, some in the Greek church, some in the Irish, some in the English, some in the Scotch. Wherever there is a heart that beats with divine grace, there is a member of the church of Christ. Wherever there are two or three such met together, there there is the church of Christ. The normal, the radical idea of the church of Christ, is very briefly defined in the Bible: "Wheresoever two or three are met together in my name, there am I in the midst of them." It is Christ present amid a few that makes that few a church. An architect may raise a stupendous building; ecclesiastics can christen it "a cathedral;" but Christ alone, descending upon those that are within, can make it a church. An orator may collect a crowd to listen to the sentiments he utters; but Christ in the midst of it alone can make it a church. An architect can build a stupendous and beautiful abode, but he cannot make it a palace: whereas the humblest shed, if inhabited by royalty, is constituted, by the presence of royalty, a palace. It is the throne in the house that makes that house a palace; it is Christ in the hearts of a people that makes that people a church. Thus Jacob was added to the church, or to the happy company of them, in the words of the Jansenist, who believe in Jesus, and dwell in the bosom of the Father, and look for the coming of Christ, and for the glory to be revealed. The contrast between the temporal blessing bestowed upon Esau and the spiritual blessing bestowed upon Jacob is explained in the one hundred and forty-fourth Psalm, where the Psalmist prays " that our garners may be full, affording all manner of store: that our sheep may bring forth thousands and ten thousands in our streets: that our oxen may be strong to labor; that there be no breaking in, nor going out; that there be no complaining in our streets:"—Here was Esau's heritage:—and then the Psalmist adds, " Happy is that people that is in such a case;" that is, happy are such people as Esau, who are blessed with such social, political and national blessings. But he also adds, "Yea, happy is that people whose God is the Lord;" that is, the happiness of the first is poor, not to be spoken of, in comparison with the happiness of the second.

Having made these remarks upon the nature of the blessing that was pronounced upon Jacob and Esau, let me observe also that the different benedictions pronounced upon the two were according to the everlasting purpose and sovereignty of God. We read in the twenty-fifth chapter of Genesis, at the twenty-third verse, these words: " And the Lord said unto her, Two nations are in thy womb, and two manner of people shall be separated from thee; and the one people shall be stronger than the other people; and the elder shall serve the younger." This is said to the mother of Jacob and of Esau. And then, the sequel of the twenty-fifth chapter gives the birth of these two, Jacob and Esau. And then, we are told in the ninth chapter of the Epistle to the Romans, at the eleventh verse, "For the children," speaking of Jacob and Esau, "being not yet born, neither having done any good or evil, that the purpose of God according to election might stand, not of works, but of him that calleth; it was said unto her, The elder shall serve the younger. As it is written, Jacob have I loved, but Esau have I hated. What shall we say, then? Is there unrighteousness with God? God forbid. For he saith to Moses, I will have mercy on whom I will have mercy, and I will have compassion on whom I will have compassion. So, then, it is not of him that willeth, nor of him that runneth, but of God that showeth mercy."

We have here, then, the main purpose of God declared before the children were born — that purpose a sovereign one. In this special case, it refers to national, and not to individual election; yet we believe in a personal, as well as in a national election. But in this instance the election was clearly national, and not personal. But it is very remarkable that, while the rejection of Esau was declared beforehand, Esau was not rejected till he himself had rejected God. Esau, I say, was not rejected till he himself had rejected alike his hope and his God; for we read in the same chapter, "Then Jacob gave Esau bread, and went his way: thus Esau despised his birthright." In other words, the sovereignty of God, and the freedom and responsibility of man, are inseparably united. God does not by a mechanical attraction draw man to heaven; and he does not by a mechanical weight, which man cannot oppose, sink him to hell. That is not the language of Scripture. On the contrary, it is true, that wherever man is elected to everlasting life, he is made willing to embrace the truth; and wherever a man is passed by and lost, it is by that person's deliberate rejection of the whole counsel of God. The language is so remarkable in the ninth chapter of the Epistle to the Romans, that it illustrates what I now state. In the twenty-second and twenty-third verses we find this very remarkably brought out. "What if God, willing to show his wrath, and to make his power known, endured with much long-suffering the vessels of wrath fitted to destruction:" — now, many persons have argued as if God made them vessels of wrath, and fitted them for everlasting destruction; this will not appear if we contrast it with the next verse — "and that he might make known the riches of his glory on the vessels of mercy, which he had afore prepared unto glory." Now, it is not said, of the vessels of wrath, that he had fitted them for destruction; they are vessels of wrath fitted by themselves "to destruction;" but when he speaks of the vessels of mercy, it is said, "That he might make known the riches of his glory on the vessels of mercy, which he," that is, God, "had afore prepared unto glory." There is here studied contrast of language. In the case of the lost, it is "fitted," it is not said by whom; in the case of the saved, it is "vessels of mercy, which he," that is, God, "had afore prepared unto glory." And then, the two original words are very distinct. In the one case, it is *κατηρτισμένα εἰς ἀπώλειαν*, that is, "made," or "built up," or "formed by circumstances, and themselves, to destruction." In the other case, it is, *ἃ προητοίμασεν εἰς δόξαν*, "which he had prepared by his grace for glory." In other words, these two verses lead us to conclude that, if Esau lost his everlasting birthright, he lost it because he wilfully and designedly sold it; and that, if Jacob obtained everlasting glory, he got it because God gave it to him, and taught him to seek it by grace. Whatever of sin or of misery is in the creature, by a great law, springs from that creature. Whatever of good, of excellence, of beauty, of glory, is in the creature, is a direct emanation from God. In no sense is God the author of sin. In no sense does he prepare hell for his people. We have in a previous chapter explained that passage in the twentieth chapter of Matthew, which casts great light upon God's purposes to his people. When Jesus addresses the saved, what does he say? "Come, ye blessed of my Father, inherit" — the word "inherit" implies relationship, not merit — "the kingdom prepared for you from the foundation of the world;" that is, enter into that happiness which God has prepared for you from the foundation of the world. But when he speaks to the lost, what does he say? "Depart from me, ye cursed, into everlasting fire, prepared" — for you? no, but — "for the devil and his angels." In other words, the questioning discovery of the lost soul will be, "Why am I here? This place was not made for me, nor was I made for it. I have rushed into everlasting ruin in spite of pressing remonstrances of conscience within, in spite of protesting voices in the providence of God, in spite of warnings from the pulpit, and admonitions from the Scripture. I have rushed into a place that was not made for man at all." So that the most corroding recollection in the hearts of the lost will be, that they are suicides, that they have destroyed themselves. On the other hand, the most thrilling recollection in the hearts of the blessed will be, "By grace, and not by a particle of merit in ourselves." So that heaven will ring with blessings on the God that saved them; and hell will echo with curses on themselves, because they have ruined themselves. We may say, with perfect truth, it costs a man more trouble to get to hell than ever it did to get to heaven. It requires voices to be extinguished, feelings to be crucified, and conscience to be numbed, and stupefied, and kept down; there must be terrible and protracted striving before a man gets to hell. He never lifts up his hand to sin but amid the lightning of protesting truths, and remonstrances from memory, and from the Bible, and God. And, if sinners would only weigh this, they would see how truly blessed is the hope of heaven even now, and how blessed are the people that are in such a case; yea, blessed are the people that have the Lord for their God. To learn the whole lesson from this passage, while Esau's forfeiture of his birthright was his own, which is true, there was in it the purpose of God, no less truly; there was the freedom of the will, and yet the decree of God. He did not say, or was constrained to say, "I thus sinned, and I was impelled to do so by a power that I could not resist." Esau sold his birthright, but he did not feel forced to do so. Does any one ask me how to reconcile an everlasting purpose from the foundation of the world with man's own answerableness to God? I say candidly, I cannot. I am not here to reconcile things that stretch beyond my reason, but to proclaim truths that are written plainly in the sacred volume. I have no doubt that they are reconcilable; and, when we come to that better light, we shall find that the things we do not know now we shall know there, hereafter.

Another fact strikes us here, and it is a mysterious fact,—I think, more perplexing than the one we have just been considering: that God accomplishes his everlasting purposes by the weakness of some, and the wickedness of others. For instance, the blessing that was pronounced on Jacob was pronounced unintentionally by the patriarch. Isaac thought it was Esau, and meant to pronounce the blessing upon Esau, but he pronounced it upon Jacob by mistake. We read also that Jacob, in order to get the blessing from his father, dissembled, lied, played the pretender. You have, then, this striking fact, that God used the misapprehension of the one, and the wickedness of the other, to accomplish his own purposes. Here seems a mystery, and yet it is fact. We trace the same fact in many other things. God is not the author of sin, and yet he may overrule sin to good, and to the accomplishment of his purposes. Perhaps I may address some one whose recollection may remind him that some sin in his past life, instead of descending upon him in retributive vengeance, was overruled to open out some new prospect that led him to some unexpected eminence, and ultimately to his being a better and a happier man; and yet, such is not the direct fruit of sin; it is God interposing by a power mightier than human, and, in the language of the great poet,

"Out of evil still educing good."

So, in the same manner, it was predicted from the foundation of the world that Christ should be crucified. But who crucified him? The Jews. The Jews might have pleaded, when Peter said to them, "Him, being delivered by the determinate counsel and fore-knowledge of God, ye have taken, and by wicked hands have crucified and slain;" and answered Peter, "It was predicted that Christ was to be crucified. We are not to blame." But they did not do so. Why did they not do so? Because their own consciences told them that they did deliberately and freely what they did; and Peter accepted that distinction when he said, "By wicked hands ye crucified the Lord of glory." Now, here is a fact, that God overruled the murder of the Jews to the completion of that atonement on which generations lean, and by which millions in every generation are made happy. So God will overrule the crescent in the East, and the tiara in the West, to great purposes. The weakness of man, and the wickedness of man, he will turn, or he will convert, or he will overrule, to the accomplishment of his own beneficent purposes. The deepest discord shall evolve the richest harmony; and sin shall be proved to be the dark foil by which

God shall show forth the glory of heaven, and the richest grandeur of his vast designs.

We must notice, however, again, how the responsibility of the creature comes into play. When the aged patriarch, who made the mistake, was told of it, did he recall it? No; but, to show how the purposes of God harmonize with our own deliberate doings, when he was told of his mistake, he said, "I have blessed him, and he shall be blessed;" uttering truth by a mysterious instinct, as did Pilate, when he said, "What I have written I have written." How strange are the doings of God! He sketches the outline, and all men step in to fill it up. And how does this humble the great men of the world! When we read of mighty generals, statesmen, geniuses, and patriots, we find that they took the credit to themselves, and said, "We did it." They were not, however, the statuaries. They were the chisels in the statuary's hand. Not the builders, they were but the trowels. They were the humble weapons used by the Great Original. All history, when it is read rightly, will humble man, and exalt God as all and in all. The aged patriarch adhered to what he had done; Esau was bitterly disappointed in his expectations. We are told in the Epistle to the Hebrews, "Looking diligently lest any man fail of the grace of God; lest there be any profane person, as Esau, who for one morsel of meat sold his birthright." You see, the apostle in the Epistle to the Hebrews regards it at once as Esau's sin, and not God's purpose; and then he adds, "that afterward, when he would have inherited the blessing, he was rejected." If you will read the chapter in Genesis, you will see that he comes to his father imploring his blessing, but it could not be reversed. So, he could find "no place of repentance, though he sought it carefully with tears." I have heard some misinformed Christians argue from this passage as if it were possible to ask God for forgiveness on earth, and yet to go away denied it. This is not the meaning; but the repentance that he did not find here was repentance on the part of the patriarch, not on his own part; it is not, he could not obtain a penitent heart for himself, but he could not get his father to alter his mind. It does not mean repentance *quoad* himself, but on the part of his father, "though he sought it carefully with tears."

But it is said, "By faith Isaac blessed Jacob and Esau concerning things to come." How was this faith shown? First, in the most unlikely circumstances he disposes of the land of Canaan amongst his sons, as if he were already in possession of it. Isaac was a stranger and a sojourner, with only a grave in the holy land, which had been bought by Abraham; and yet, long before he enters it, with the improbabilities of ever entering it before him, he distributes it, and assumes the land to be completely his own, when he had nothing but a promise to depend on. Now, this is Christian faith. Faith treats what God promises as being just as real and substantial as if it were the thing itself. So, Isaac here took the promise of God just as if it were the fulfilment of the thing itself. And much occurred in his after life to lead him to doubt whether God would fulfil that promise; and yet his faith never wavered. Esau rose to worldly prosperity; Jacob was oppressed, and a servant to Laban; and yet, the faith that saw all this never faltered, but expected, hoped and felt, that what was promised to him would be fulfilled.

We learn also this, that the blessings which the patriarch promised we may pray for. It is a remarkable fact, set forth throughout the Bible, that the father's piety and the piety and prosperity of the children are in some way connected; so that blessings sought by the one descend and blossom upon the heads and hearts of the others. A child that is the subject of many prayers will never be a castaway. All experience tells us that this is so; and there is a promise stronger than all experience, "I will be a God to thee, and to thy seed after thee." Let us seek such blessings for our own; and, like the patriarch of old, believe that what we ask truly, and what God has promised, he will give faithfully. Heaven and earth may pass away, but God's promises cannot fail. The pillars that sustain the universe may crash, and be reduced to ruin; but the syllables that constitute the promises of God shall endure till all be fulfilled.

The voice of Jacob is not yet spent. It breaks still in the music of growing benedictions. Dead, he speaks; silent, he teaches.

CHAPTER XIV.

THE DYING PATRIARCH.

"As one who, walking in the twilight gloom,
Hears round about him voices as it darkens,
And, seeing not the forms from whence they come,
Pauses from time to time, and turns and hearkens;

"Perhaps on earth I never shall behold
With eye of sense their outward form and semblance,
Therefore to me they never will grow old,
But live forever young in my remembrance —

"Never grow old, nor change, nor pass away;
Their gentle voices will flow on forever,
When life grows bare and tarnished with decay,
As through a leafless landscape flows a river."

"By faith Jacob, when he was a dying, blessed both the sons of Joseph; and worshipped, leaning upon the top of his staff." — HEBREWS 11 : 21.

THE voice that we are now to listen to is that of Jacob; and as there are some beautiful touches in his biography, each of which is instructive, and illustrative of his faith, I will briefly allude to them.

The special instance brought before us is, that "when he was a dying, he blessed both the sons of Joseph; and worshipped, leaning upon the top of his staff." The blessing was a deposit committed to each patriarch to be transmitted to his sons and his heirs; and we shall find that here, after Isaac had blessed Jacob, he repeated it, and bade him "Arise and go to Padan-aram, to the house of Bethuel thy mother's father. And Jacob," it is said, "went out from Beersheba, and went toward Haran. And he lighted upon a certain place, and tarried there all night, because the sun was set; and he took of the stones of that place, and put them for his pillows, and lay down in that place to sleep. And he dreamed, and behold, a ladder set up on the earth, and the top of it reached to heaven; and behold the angels of God ascending and descending on it. And, behold, the Lord stood above it, and said, I am the Lord God of Abraham thy father, and the God of Isaac; the land whereon thou liest, to thee will I give it, and to thy seed; and thy seed shall be as the dust of the earth, and thou shalt spread abroad to the west, and to the east, and to the north, and to the south; and in thee and in thy seed shall all the families of the earth be blessed. And behold I am with thee, and will keep thee in all places whither thou goest, and will bring thee again into this land; for I will not leave thee, until I have done that which I have spoken to thee of. And Jacob awaked out of his sleep, and he said, Surely the Lord is in this place; and I knew it not. And he was afraid, and said, How dreadful is this place! this is none other but the house of God, and this is the gate of heaven. And Jacob rose up early in the morning, and took the stone that he had put for his pillows, and set it up for a pillar, and poured oil upon the top of it. And he called the name of that place Beth-el," that is, the house of God, "but the name of that place was called Luz," or the place of almonds.

As the patriarch pronounced the blessing that preceded the travels of his son, he leaned upon his staff, and worshipped God; that is, he showed that the fountain of the blessing was God, that he himself was but the channel of it; he appealed to God in that act as the author of the blessing, who could make it alight, and be effective; and he himself pronounced it as the mere organ of its utterance, and nothing more. It is so still with the minister of the Gospel. The message is not ours, but God's. Paul may plant; Apollos may water; but unless the God that gives the message is pleased to bless it, all will be ineffective. It shows that the patriarch's outward man was fast dissolving into dust, when he needed the support of that staff with which he had crossed the river, to enable him to raise himself, and bow his head, and pronounce that blessing. The soul suffers not pain with the body; it knows not what dissolution is. Often have I seen, that when the outward tenement was ready to mingle with the dust, the inner soul seemed to catch from afar the splendors of its approaching destiny, and to indicate a vigor and a strength, that tells us that the death of the body is but the emancipation of the soul; that, unshackled, it may unfurl a new and more glorious wing, and only stop where God, the cherubim, and the saints, are. So here the patriarch's body was dissolving rapidly into dust; the outward form was about to mingle with its parent earth; but the inner man was strong, vigorous, rich in faith, replete with hope.

I need not, perhaps, remind the reader that there is in the Bible used by the Roman Catholic Church a very gross mistranslation of the twenty-first verse. The Church of Rome took their translation of the Bible from the Latin Vulgate, translated by Jerome in the fourth century; and it has been translated into English; the New Testament at Douay, and the Old Testament at Rheims. In it the twenty-first verse of this chapter is thus translated: "By faith Jacob, when he was a dying, blessed both the sons of Joseph; and worshipped the top of his staff;" and the note which is attached to it says, that this staff was a sacred rod, or symbol of the Messiah; that this worshipping his staff is a sufficient proof that image-worship is right; and that it is absurd to suppose that God should have mentioned so trifling a thing as leaning upon the top of his staff in so important a statement; and yet this is contradicted in one of their own notes; for, while they thus speak on this passage, yet in one of the apocryphal books, which they hold as divine, a very trifling thing occurs, but, in the note attached to it, it is said, "Here we see that there are jots and tittles in the word of God that seem to us very insignificant, but are nevertheless full of deep and mysterious meaning:" thus showing how complete is the contradiction, and how unfair the commentary that is here given. But any one who refers to the original in the Hebrew will see that the word "staff" may mean "bed;" the patriarch raised himself upon his bed and pronounced this blessing. And if it be "staff," it shows that he was worshipping upon the top of his staff, and not that he worshipped the top of his staff, as they very absurdly allege.

After Jacob received the blessing, he went forth to a distant land, blessed by his father, but knowing not what was before him; and, as far as we can gather from the passage, Jacob went forth with a very heavy heart. One can well sympathize with this. It is not the most pleasant instant in life to leave one's native land; and to those who have left it for the first time, to see the very spires that were familiar to our earliest gaze, and the house, and streets, and buildings, and the roof-tree itself, associated with our earliest joys and sorrows, all fade in distant perspective, while the wave wafts us away to a distant land,— this is not pleasant to any one. The love of country, the love of one's birth-place, is indigenous almost to humanity. And if in that land of ours we have first learned to know how precious is the Bible, how dear a Saviour, how good God has been, it always costs a pang to leave it. If we have heard the glorious Gospel in its pulpits, and God's voice in the rush of its winds and in the chimes of its sea-waves, and felt his providence at every footstep, and his blessing descending on us like the dews of the sky, it is not pleasant to leave all one loves behind, and to brave all one dreads before; and were it not that God is with us, as he promised to the patriarch, wherever we go, it would be a crucifixion of some of the dearest feelings of the human heart. But, in Jacob's case, when he left his native place, there were special reasons for sadness. He had been guilty of sin; he had obtained his birthright by fraud; and this recollection must have pressed heavily on his heart. A sin rankling in the conscience is a far greater impediment to a happy journey than a thorn that has pierced the foot. It is the conscience at peace with God that makes all sounds music, and all sights sunshine. It is the inward peace that makes the elastic step. It is the deep conviction that God is a friend, and all things friendly in God, that makes the roughest places smooth, the steepest hills easy of ascent, and the heaviest burdens comparatively light. If you wish to be brave when called to contend with foes, if you wish to be strong when called to encounter great difficulties, if you wish to be happy in the midst of trials, pray that the sunshine of a Father's face may be upon your heart, and that the peace that comes through the blood of Jesus may keep your hearts and minds continually. Conscience at war with God makes a coward of its possessor. A conscience void of offence both toward God and man has ever made, because, by a great law, it ever makes, a happy man.

It appears that Jacob, then, wearied out with his journey, lay down to sleep, the stone his pillow, the heather his bed, the canopy of heaven his curtain; and all the stars, like the eyes of God's omniscience, gazing down, and watching over him.

He dreamed. Were that said now, we should despise the dream, and smile at the simplicity of the dreamer that believes it. But what would be folly now was loyalty, and wisdom, and Christianity, then: because God speaks not by dreams now. To make a dream regulate any course that you are to pursue, or, because you dream something, to determine therefore to do something, is to forsake God, and to have recourse to idols; it is leaving the only Divine Oracle, which is Scripture, and having recourse to what the oracles of Delphi were, delusions. We are authorized in one single verse to accept a dream then as true, and to reject it now as wrong. "God, who at sundry times and in divers manners" — sometimes by dreams, sometimes by visions, sometimes by signs and symbols — "spake in time past unto the fathers by the prophets, hath in these last days spoken unto us by his Son." In other words, God has now fixed on one method only of conveying his mind to mankind; and, therefore, all the dreams that man ever dreamed are not to weigh one feather against the simple testimony, "Thus saith the Lord." Read your dreams, if you like, in the light of Scripture; but do not read Scripture in the light of your dreams. Take your direction, and your tone, and your impulses, from God's word, in heavenly and in religious things, and from no other source in the height or the depth that man can urge besides. In this dream, — a dream that was to him, and justly, what a text is to us; for, "Thus saith the Lord" was in his dream just as truly as "Thus saith the Lord" is now in our Bible, —he dreamed that he saw a ladder stretching from the earth up to the sky. I do not enter upon details; I merely notice that, in the first place, it may have been designed to suggest to the patriarch a conviction of God's providential presence. He was apt to forget that God governs the world, just as we are. I do not say that many venture to say, theoretically, God has left the world, except it be some wild dreamer among philosophers; or that God gave the world an impulse, and set it a-going, as a man does his watch, and left it. That is not fact. It is just as true that God is, as that God was. The name of the Christian's God is "Jehovah," who was, and is, and is to come; who fills the past, the present and the future; to whom there is no past; in whose sight there is no future; but to whom the past and the future are one wide-spread, illuminated and transparent present. According, therefore, to a Christian's conviction, transactions upon earth are not random phenomena, but rebounds to the touch of God. The least thing that betides a Christian, and the greatest catastrophe that overtakes a nation, are, in a Christian's creed, the acts of God. Angels do, in obedience to his bidding, what the philosophers say second causes do according to the laws and structure of nature. Blessed be God, that there is communion between heaven and earth; that this world of ours, with all its faults, is not a forsaken one; that this race of ours, with all its wickedness, is cast down indeed, but not cast off; it is the prodigal orb, feeding upon husks that the swine do eat, but there is sounding still in its ear, and in its heart, "Arise, and go to thy Father; for there is bread there, and to spare."

But this ladder that Jacob saw may not only be a proof of God's providential government of the world, an evidence that God has not forsaken the world, but it may also have been meant to convey the idea of the mediation of our blessed Lord; for what did Jesus say? "Hereafter ye shall see heaven open, and the angels of God ascending and descending upon the Son of man;" evidently employing the figure of Jacob's dream to set forth his own mediatorial office. This word means a mediation, a bond of connection between man and God. What did sin do? It rent the world from the great continent of heaven; and a deep and dreary and unsounded sea flows between that happy continent and this rent and dislocated orb. "Heaven and earth," in the words of the greatest of poets,

"Stand aloof: the scars remaining,
Like cliffs which have been rent asunder,
A dreary sea now flows between;
But neither heat, nor frost, nor thunder,

Shall wholly do away, I ween,
The marks of that which once had been."

There is enough in our world to show that it belonged to the great continent from which it has suffered a disruption; and enough in it to show that it is not cast off forever. And this glorious Ladder, this divine Mediator, spans the yawning gulf; and now along that archway angels may come to serve us, and our prayers may rise and reach God. Communion is restored; and they that were severed by sin, the separating element, are now united, and made one by Christ, the uniting element, the blood of the covenant, the Mediator between heaven and earth.

When Jacob saw the bright vision, and heard God's beautiful promise, "I am with thee, and will keep thee in all places whither thou goest, and will bring thee again into this land; for I will not leave thee, until I have done that which I have spoken to thee of," he awoke out of his sleep, and said, "Surely the Lord is in this place; and I knew it not." God was there. Then, wherever God is, a church is. What constitutes a church is, not noble architecture, but Christian souls. Wherever a holy heart beats, wherever a group of holy men meets, there God is present; and God thus present in the midst of such constitutes a church, so baptized in the language of heaven, even if it should be excommunicated and persecuted by the uncharitableness of men. It is the Christian mind that sees solemnity wherever it sees God.

"'Neath cloistered boughs each floral bell that swingeth,
And tolls its perfume on the passing air,
Makes Sabbath in the fields, and ever ringeth
A call to prayer.

"Not to those domes whose crumbling arch and column
Attest the feebleness of human hand;
But to that fane, most catholic and solemn,
Which God hath planned;

"To that cathedral, boundless as our wonder,
Whose quenchless lamps the sun and moon supply,
Its choir, wind and waves, — its organ, thunder, —
Its dome, the sky.

"There, as in solitude and shade I wander
Through the green aisles, and stretched upon the sod,
Awed by the silence, reverently I ponder
The ways of God."

But very often we must say of that place, and of every place in which we have sought to worship God, "God was here, and I knew it not." How often have you left the sanctuary, and said, "Such a preacher was there; and I knew it;" and forgot that "God was there; and I knew it not." We are so unmindful and ignorant, not because there is forgetfulness of his promise, "Where two or three are met together in my name, there am I in the midst of them;" but because our unbelief shuts our eyes, the eyes of the inner man, to the perception of God. No external ornaments that man can add to his church will make him have a deep sense of God; whereas, a deep sense of the presence of God will light up the humblest barn with unearthly glory, and make the plainest building beautiful, because arrayed in the beauty of holiness, a beauty that lasts forever. A sense of the Saviour's presence gives consecration to any place; and where there is no sense of that presence, no consecration can make it holy, or other than the place of the dead. He joyfully acknowledged this, "This is none other than the house of God; and this is the gate of heaven." Here, then, is a more strict definition of a church. "This," — a stone pillow, the heather, the blue sky, the lofty hills, the deep valley, — "this," said the patriarch, "is none other than the house of God; and this is the gate of heaven." There was no architectural grandeur, no sky-pointing spire, no fretted roof, no gorgeous ritual, no pompous, or, it may be, impressive ceremony; and yet he said, "It is the house of God: it is the gate of heaven." Let us think of what constitutes a church. Truly, the presence of Christ. And let us not associate with the word "church" the mere decorations of human taste. The glory of the Christian temple is, the presence of the Saviour in the midst of it. The true stones that build a church are not dead ones from the earth's quarry, but living ones laid upon Christ, the Rock of Ages. The name of Jesus builds a church, and the presence of Jesus lends it a consecration that kings and priests cannot give. And wherever, and within whatever walls, God's truth has come home to us with its greatest power, and a sense of a Saviour's presence, mercy and love, has been felt in its strongest effects, men may excommunicate that place, and us with it; but it is the house of God, and it is the gate of heaven.

When he had thus realized this presence of God, it is said that by faith — and every act was by faith — he heard the accents of his God; it was by faith he exclaimed, "How dreadful is this place! this is none other but the house of God, and this is the gate of heaven," and also by faith he set up a pillar, and changed its name. The name before was Luz, that is, the place of almonds; he changed it into a new name, Beth-el, which means, the house of the great God. How often have we felt the temple still to be Luz, a place of almonds! We have brought market thoughts, thoughts of our farms, thoughts of our merchandise, into the house of God, and made it a place of merchandise; whereas, if we bring hearts hungering for living bread, souls seeking to know, to love, and to be refreshed by the presence of the Saviour, then it has been to us, not a market-place, but our Father's house, the house of God, a house of prayer for all people. The catacombs and cellars at Rome were to the early Christians the house of the Lord; the cathedrals that are there in the nineteenth century are but the catacombs of the dead.

The ancient catacombs were the true cathedrals; because Christians loved and worshipped God. The modern cathedrals in Rome are but catacombs; because the spiritually dead, the superstitious and the unbelieving, are there. It is living stones of which a church is built; and the light and the glory that surround and consecrate it are the light of Christ's presence, and of his blessing.

He makes a vow, that if God would go with him, he would fear, worship and serve Him, and dedicate himself, and all his property, to Him. This has been often misconstrued, because it looks like following God for temporal benefits: "If God will be with me, and will keep me in this way that I go, and will give me bread to eat, and raiment to put on." Some have thought it was a sort of mercenary pledge. Some have construed it as if it meant, "If God will give me bread, I will serve him." It is not, however, an argument or bargain with God, but an assurance. It is as if he had said, "If God has promised to give me bread, if God has promised to give me life and length of days, then surely it is the least that I can do to respond to this by dedicating myself and all to Him." And beautifully by faith he consecrates himself, and then all that is his, to the service of God, as it becomes him. Such is a precedent for us, to give ourselves first to the Lord, and then what we have. If we be Christian, — it is not my opinion, but the record of inspiration, — "we are not our own; for we are bought with a price." No man has a right to say that his life is his own; for he cannot guarantee that that heart will beat to-morrow. No man has a right to say that his property is his own; for either he may be taken from it, or it may be taken from him; and, in either case, he cannot control it. But when we see that all we lost in Adam is restored in Christ, and that what we have in providence receives a new consecration when we feel that it is the purchase of the blood of Jesus, then, like Jacob, all we are, and all we have, we shall lay up as treasures in heaven, by consecrating them now to the glory of our blessed Lord, and to the spread and extension of his glorious Gospel. We shall be satisfied with God, in the absence of all; we shall be dissatisfied with all, in the absence of God. Loss will be beautiful, because God remains; gain will be holy, because God sanctifies and consecrates it.

The next sketch that we have in the history of this patriarch, and which also illustrates his faith, occurs in the thirty-second chapter and ninth verse of Genesis. We have seen what occurred to him on his departure from his native land; we shall now see what occurred to him on his return to his native land. At the ninth verse, Jacob says, "O God of my father Abraham, and God of my father Isaac, the Lord which saidst unto me, Return unto thy country, and to thy kindred, and I will deal well with thee:" — that is what he said in the dream, — "I am not worthy," — here is his retrospect, — "of the least of all the mercies, and of all the truth, which thou hast showed unto thy servant; for with my staff I passed over this Jordan, and now I am become two bands." After seven years in the service of Laban for Rachel he was disappointed; after seven years more he was successful; and now he sets his face forward again to the land which he had left in so painful circumstances fourteen years before. He was within sight, at the moment he uttered this thanksgiving, of his native land; its blue hills, its familiar fields, all its cedar-crowned heights, the scenes of his childhood, the fields of his sports in boyhood, all came within his horizon, and presented themselves to the exile's view; and, as he gazes on the grand panorama, he is reminded of all the years that had elapsed between his departure and his return, and exclaims, "I am not worthy of the least of all the mercies, and of all the truth which God has showed unto me." When we, too, take a retrospect, — let it be the retrospect of a few years, or the retrospect of many years, — is there not more to be thankful for than there is to fret at? Do not our blessings outnumber our trials? Have not the mercies we have received exceeded the pangs that we have suffered? Into the cisterns of the poorest soul more blessings have descended than he thinks of. Our road has not been all a dusty one; green paths, made green by the sunshine of the skies, have often been our pathways; goodness and mercy have followed us all the days of our life. But here is the difference between a worldly man and a Christian looking backwards. The worldly man takes a retrospect at the end of a year, or at the end of a protracted cycle; he studies all the gains he has reaped, the good fortune, as he calls it, which he has experienced, the manifold suns of prosperity which have shone upon him; and he thanks his own skill, good luck, or stronger and earlier efforts; and gives all the glory to the gods of his own hands. But when a Christian takes a retrospect of all the way that he has been led, like the patriarch of old, he sees God's hand in every turn, God's presence in every blessing, God's direction whenever he had lost the way, and needed to be shown how to walk. Here is just the difference. Atheism sees God in nothing; Christianity sees God orbed in the tiniest dew-drop, as well as in the great and all-encompassing sea. The true Christian sees God's presence and God's providential goodness in all the little currents of individual and domestic life, in all the roaring cataracts and gigantic streams of public and of social life. A Christian feels God breathe upon him in the earliest winds of the morning, fold him in his fatherly embrace in the shades of descending night, and speak confidingly to him as to a son, in benedictions that descend upon him like the dews of heaven; and he has a happy, because he has in him a confiding and a trustful, heart. "Thou God, seest me," is not, with a Christian, a barren dogma; "Whom have I in heaven but thee? and there is none upon earth that I desire beside thee," is not with a Christian a distant poetical dream; but both are the convictions of his heart, and the happy experience of his life.

When Jacob notices God, like the Christian still he singles out first mercy, "all the mercies" he had experienced. Everything we have is the fruit of mercy. We need to be humbled first in the dust to feel this. We have forfeited all; and whatever we have is the fruit of God's mercy in Christ. It is mercy that shines in every dispensation, that speaks in every event, that beats in every pulse, that gives us the bread and the cup of cold water. Wherever we look, every blessing that we have will be felt and seen to be the flower and the fruit that grows and blossoms on sovereign and unmerited mercy. We associate mercy with the forgiveness of our sins, and truly so; but we ought to associate it also with the bread that we eat day by day; for that crumb of bread, that cup of water, are just as truly the purchase of the blood of Jesus, and the gift of the mercy of God, as the forgiveness of our sins, and the salvation of our souls. One difference between a worldling and a Christian is, that the worldling grasps the bread as his right, where the Christian accepts the bread from the hand of sovereign mercy and undeserved goodness.

But the patriarch commemorates, not only mercy, but truth, — "And of all the truth." We too may feel thankful for God's truth. But in what respect can truth make us thankful? Jacob believed the promise, found the promise to be true, and gave God the glory of it. Have we never embarked upon a promise, and felt it waft us safely to success? Have we never made the experiment of trusting God's promises; and, if we have, has any one of them ever failed? Never yet did a dying Christian admit that one single promise on which he laid the stress of his happiness or his hopes has given way. Whatever God has promised in his word is stronger than what man has performed in fact. You may rest upon a promise of God, and feel that the very pillars of the universe may collapse and crash, heaven and earth may pass away, but one jot or one tittle of God's promises shall not pass away till all be fulfilled. We are not more thankful, just because we are so proud. We have a latent surmise that we deserve much more than God has given us, and therefore we feel dissatisfaction with what he *has* given. But when we feel that we have forfeited all, and have no right to the light of day and the happiness of life, then, like Jacob, we shall lift up our hearts to God, and we shall say, "We are not worthy of the least of all the mercies, and of all the truth, which thou hast showed unto thy servants."

The last scene that I will briefly notice in the patriarch's history was that mysterious one, not so mysterious to us as to him, when he wrestled with the angel until daybreak, as recorded in the thirty-second chapter of Genesis, at the twenty-fourth verse. "And Jacob was left alone; and there wrestled a man with him until the breaking of the day. And he said, Let me go, for the day breaketh. And he said, I will not let thee go, except thou bless me. And he said unto him, What is thy name? And he said, Jacob. And he said, Thy name shall be called no more Jacob, but Israel: for as a prince hast thou power with God and with men, and hast prevailed. And Jacob asked him, and said, Tell me, I pray thee, thy name. And he said, Wherefore is it that thou dost ask after my name? And he blessed him there. And Jacob called the name of the place Peniel:" — that is, the face of God, — "for I have seen God face to face, and my life is preserved." Who was this mysterious being that wrestled with the patriarch? The answer is, it was unquestionably the Lord Jesus Christ, and no one else less. You will recollect that, in the blessing of the patriarch upon the sons of Joseph, he said, "God, before whom my fathers Abraham and Isaac did walk, the God which fed me all my life long unto this day, the angel which redeemed me from all evil, bless the lads." That text has been quoted as if the angel there were a created being, and as if angel-worship were practised by the patriarch. But any one who will read the passage will find that "the angel" is but the expletive of the Being in the previous verse, "God which fed me," "The angel which redeemed me." "Redeemed" is in the singular number; and, therefore, "angel" is but the expletive of "God." And "angel," literally translated, is, "the sent one." Now, that this angel was none other than God is evident from the twelfth chapter of Hosea, at the fourth verse, where it is said, "Jacob had power over the angel, and prevailed; he wept, and made supplication unto him; he found him in Bethel, and there he spake with us;" now, what does he add? — "even the Lord God of hosts; the Lord is his memorial;" that is, Hosea tells us that the angel's name was Jehovah. In other words, that it was Christ, or God in our nature. And there is no doubt that that divine Being who spake from the bush, who appeared to Manoah, who wrestled with Jacob, who spake by the prophets, was no less than the Lord Jesus Christ, visiting the family of man before his incarnation, set up before the foundation of the world, "the Lamb slain from the foundation of the world."

But the lesson we gather from this instance is, that earnestness in prayer is the evidence of Christian faith. Jacob wrestled, in the language of Scripture, with the angel, and would not let him go; because he felt the need, and, therefore, earnestly he asked for the blessing. You may depend upon it that we shall pray earnestly for that which we feel deeply. The reason of formal prayers is not because they are written, or because they are the reverse, but because below them there are insensible and formal hearts. Whenever the soul is deeply convinced of its want, because it feels it, and thoroughly satisfied that there is but one that can remove it, that soul will not be put easily away; it will not let the Saviour go until he bless it. If, therefore, we are without the blessedness of him whose sins are forgiven, if our hearts are without that blessedness which alone makes happy hearts, the reason is, that we have not asked, that we have not persistently and earnestly asked, not ceasing to pray until the possession of the blessing suggests the duty of transposing prayer into praise, and thanking him who has heard our petitions. It is a terrible thought, but a very real one, that the reason that men are not Christians is, that they do not pray; and the reason that they do not pray is, that they do not feel the need of the blessings of the Gospel. Were it with spiritual things as with temporal things, all men would pray. When one needs bread, a sensation implanted in his nature urges him to seek it; but, the more that one needs living bread, the less he feels his need. Hence, the man, the woman, who feels most humbled by a sense of sin, most in need, most destitute of that which is the Gospel, are just the very persons that give the strongest evidence of the work of grace upon their hearts. Persons, on the other hand, who think they are rich, and increased in goods, and have need of nothing; who do not feel the necessity of prayer; who do not practise prayer, or only as a form, and not as the expression and the exponent of their inner life, and their deep wants and their earnest desires; who feel all is smooth and right, and just as they would wish it, —give the least sign of the work of God's grace upon their hearts. Let us pray, not only for blessings, but that we may feel our need of them; not only for forgiveness, but for a sense of the indispensable necessity of possessing that forgiveness.

Because Jacob wrestled, and had success, he received a new name, Israel. Do you think that God accepts not prayer? Do you think that he is unwilling to hear you? Men's natural conception of God is, that he is a Being that watches and waits to destroy them; but the true idea of God is, that he longs for you, and that he waits to welcome you; and that, before you speak, he hears the beating of the heart, and judges of your wants, not by what the lips say, but by what the heart beats. True prayer is that which men cannot hear; and such prayer is often lifted up on the exchange, amidst the collisions and stir of party dispute, on the highway, in the crowded thoroughfare. Many a prayer rises from a meek and humble heart, and ascends faster than an angel's wing can clip, and higher than an archangel's wing can soar; and comes down in responsive benedictions, grace and glory, and life that shall never end. Do we, then, pray by faith? The patriarch prayed as Jacob, by faith; the patriarch returned to his home as Israel, the man that had power with God, and prevailed.

Thus we have seen that life in the retrospect of which the patriarch leaned upon the top of his rod, and worshipped God. All the storms he had passed, all the dangers he had seen, all the crosses he had met with, all the losses he had sustained, did not conceal from him God's good hand guiding him; and, therefore, his last words became the song of victory, somewhat like Simeon's, "Now, Lord, lettest thou thy servant depart in peace; for mine eyes have seen thy salvation." By faith, the patriarch saw God in all the dispensations of his providence, — in all his wanderings, his losses, his crosses, his joys, and his sufferings. One of the truest evidences of a heart right with God is, that in all things that heart sees God. With a Christian, the idea of God is not a dead dogma, petrified in his creed; but a living, plastic power, ever present in his heart. With him, to know God, and to see God, and to recognize God, needs no syllogism, nor demonstration, nor argument. As truly as the outward ear hears the song of birds, and the outward eyes see the sun in the firmament, the inward ear of faith hears God's great voice, and the inward eye of faith sees the shadow of God's presence sweep along the world. Hence he acknowledges and leans on God. The Christian realizes God's presence in the concave of the sky, and on the bosom of the earth; and, when the worldling can hear nothing but the clamor of the world's tongues, the strifes and collisions of the world's disputants, and the noise of the ceaselessly revolving wheels of Mammon, a Christian's ear can hear that word "God" reflected from every object, and, like a voice uttered amid the mountain gorges, reverberating in multiplied repetitions, till the whole world sounds one word, "God," and all the universe is lightened with the glory of one Being, God. In his least and loftiest engagements, a Christian recognizes God. "Thou, God, seest me." "My Father." "My God."

We learn, from these sketches in the patriarch's biography, that praise and prayer are the expressions of Christian life. Expiration and inspiration are not more necessary to our natural life than prayer and praise are to our Christian life. And, therefore, in the Christian's experience, what he suffers and what he enjoys equally lead him to God. James says, "Is any among you afflicted?"—What is he to do? To commit suicide? No.—"Let him pray."—"Is any merry?"—What is he to do? To launch into all sorts of wild excesses? No.—"Let him sing psalms." A Christian's joys bring him to God in praise; a Christian's sorrows bring him to God in prayer; in every phase of his experience, it leads him to God in adoring praise, or in humble and earnest prayer.

Do you, dear reader, believe, not simply the facts we have read from the biography of an ancient patriarch, but the lessons some of which we have noticed in the course of these remarks? Do you feel that holy men of old spake as they were moved by the Holy Ghost; and that these things are written for our profit? The facts vary, but the truths are the same yesterday, to-day, and forever. Do you believe in him, by whose blood Jacob was forgiven, by whose righteousness he was justified, in whose name the patriarch is now enrolled in the registers of the blessed, and beside whose throne, with the crown upon his head, and the palm in his hand, he praises and worships continually? Are you, let me ask, a Christian? It is the most momentous question that can be put; and it is a question that demands, not an answer next year, but an answer to-day. Either Christianity is true, and the instant reception of it is the instant duty of every human being; or it is a fable, and ought to be abjured, and repudiated, and despised. There is no such thing as moderate Christianity. You must be a Christian with the whole heart, or you must be a worldling with the whole heart. There are but two successions in the sight of God—the succession of saints by grace in one line, and the succession of sinners by nature in the other; and these two lines will meet at the judgment-seat, one to take its exodus to everlasting joy, the other to take its departure to the place it has prepared for itself, everlasting misery. To which do you belong? Am I a child of God, or am I not? It is not subscribing a creed, it is not repeating a prayer, it is not belonging to a church or chapel, that constitutes Christianity; but it is having the heart so changed that divine things shall be felt to be the most important; it is having the thoughts so sanctified that they shall rest upon none short of God; and it is having the life so characterized, so elevated, its tone so altered, that, whether we eat or drink, we shall do all to the glory of God. Accept the blessings that are offered by the Lord, by being Christians. When the poor hear of gold to be gathered upon the shores of the distant Pacific, how many thousands rush there in order to be rich! When the sick man hears of a clime whose air is balm, whose sunbeams are health, he leaves home and friends, and goes to that clime to get health. If you are convinced that you are poor, because destitute of those riches that constitute the currency of heaven,—if you feel that you are dying, soul, and body, and spirit, and that none but Christ can save you, — then this day will not close, and to-morrow's sun will not rise upon you, without your exclaiming, with the whole heart, "Lord, I believe; help mine unbelief. To thee I come; to whom can I go but unto thee? Thou hast the words of eternal life."

CHAPTER XV.

A PILGRIM'S FOOTPRINTS.

> "Hast thou not glimpses, in the twilight hour,
> Of mountains where immortal morn prevails ?
> Comes there not through the silence to thine ear
> A gentle rustling of the morning gale,
> A murmur, wafted from that glorious shore,
> Of streams that water banks forever fair,
> And voices of the loved ones gone before,
> More musical in that celestial air ?"

"By faith, Joseph, when he died, made mention of the departing of the children of Israel ; and gave commandment concerning his bones." HEBREWS 11 : 22.

It would take too much time to review all the circumstances in the history of Joseph. I assume that most readers are acquainted with that most interesting history, far more beautiful than any romance; for real history is ever much more beautiful than romance. The few points which we shall select for instruction will not be unfamiliar to most. I will draw lessons, rather than quote passages.

The first feature that strikes us, in the history of this patriarch, varied and checkered as ever history was, is, that he was rich, of great power, occupying a lofty position, — the very loftiest in the realm of Pharaoh; and yet that he remained, from first to last, triumphantly a Christian. We know how much more easy — if one may make a comparison — it is to be a Christian where there is no pressure of trials, than it is where one is surrounded by a thousand points in — if I may use the expression — a negative state, ever ready to draw off every Christian principle, feeling and sympathy, from our souls. It is difficult to be great, and yet to remain steadfast. Few are able to hold perfectly balanced a full cup, and few are willing to take or to hold an empty cup. Very few can bear great prosperity; very few like to accept great poverty. Yet, wherever there is Christian faith planted in the heart by the Spirit of God, there is a divine faith that can live in all latitudes, under all circumstances, and prove itself, in poverty and riches, the victory that overcometh the world. We often find, in the history of the church of Christ, instances of men retaining their Christianity uncompromised in the very highest, most seductive and perilous of circumstances. There were Christians in Cæsar's household. We read, too, in the Acts of the Apostles, that there was a Christian chief minister in Candace's Ethiopian court. *Vixere fortes ante Agamemnona.* There were heroes before Agamemnon, only there was not a Homer to sing them. There have been Christians since the days of the apostles, heroes and martyrs; but there has been no inspired pen to record them; more, perhaps, in high places than we are disposed to admit, and still more in low places than sometimes we dream of. But surely, if it be beautiful, if it be delightful, to see a Christian battling with the waves of poverty, affliction and distress, and unsubdued, — often bowed, but never vanquished, — it is no less delightful to see those beautiful flowers, Daniel, Joseph and others, amid the rank grass of great prosperity and splendid circumstance. The loyalty that is rendered to the earthly master or sovereign, in such circumstances, becomes still more luminous by being inspired by the loyalty and the love that we owe to our heavenly one; and it will always be found that the most effective subject of an earthly monarch is the most elevated son of our Father who is in heaven.

In Joseph we have an instance of the value, the practical effects and permanence, of early Christian education. Joseph was taught, when he was young, the truths of the Gospel,—for Abraham, Isaac and Jacob, were Christians,—and when he was old he did not forsake them. The Jewish religion—if we may so call ancient Christianity—was most explicit on our duties to the young. "Thou shalt teach them to thy children;" that is, the doctrines and words of the Bible; "Thou shalt teach them to thy children, when thou risest up and when thou liest down;" and it is said of Abraham, who lived by faith, "I know," says God, "that he will command his household after him." In fact, Christianity, just in proportion to its purity, has been the patroness of the earliest possible Christian education of the young; and what makes this more remarkable, if we go beyond the Bible, no other religion is found to be so. It is a fact that Christians should know, that, if you go outside the Bible, the education of the very young has always been treated with more or less contempt, or total disregard. For instance, in Athens, they had schools for young men, but they had none for children, and the idea of schools for infants was never dreamed of. In Sparta, they had garrison schools for making first-rate soldiers, but none for anything besides. And in Rome, such a mean idea had the *domini rerum*—the lords of the world—of education, that the lowest of Greek slaves were employed to be the teachers of the children of the patricians and senators of Rome. And during the crusades, when the Roman church was in its culminating glory, even then their schools were miserable huts, or commonly monks' cells, whilst the churches were cathedrals, and the priests were the princes and the kings of the earth. What a testimony, too, is here against that church, thus unfaithful to its primary and noblest function! A large school attached to a church is a much greater ornament than a lofty spire, glittering in rising and setting suns. A great number of children, educated through the liberality of a Christian congregation, is a glory it must not be proud of, but it may indeed well be thankful for; for, if there be one blessing that is the demand of the age, — if there be one great blessing and want which needs to be secured in the age, — it is the Christian, earliest Christian, not merely teaching, but training of the young; the promise not being, "Teach a child the way he should go, and when he is old he will not depart from it," but, "Train up a child in the way he should go, and when he is old he will not depart from it." We do not teach the vines on the wall to grow up southward or northward, but we train them. We are not merely to tell children what they are to do, and what they are to know, but we are to try to train, develop, regulate, guide them. The Christian teacher is one of the noblest characters; and I have as much respect for a Christian teacher, any day, as I have for the greatest archbishop. The function of that teacher is a precious, a noble, a responsible one. It is, I admit, a most laborious one, and it is, in our country, although this cannot be said so much now as formerly, a very ill-paid one; but it is a very important one; and better that you should make the furniture of your drawing-room less splendid, than, in order to save some ten or twenty pounds a year, that you should take an inferior governess or teacher into your family. Get the most efficient, practical, finished teaching for your children, and you do more for the next generation than anything you can attempt. The true Christian teacher reminds me of the fresco-painter, applying his colors to the wet plaster, and as often as they fade renewing them, until at last they become fixed and permanent as the very material itself. We have in Joseph an instance of early Christian education, showing itself in after consistent life.

We learn from the history of Joseph a lesson no less valuable, — a man may be a Christian, and yet in the world; that it is not inconsistent with the Christian character to take office, to wield power, or to take up reins, delicate and most responsible, if providentially put in his hand. Joseph was a Christian, and yet we find him the right hand, the prime minister, of Pharaoh. I know that some Christians, personally excellent men, some of whom I have met, commonly called "Plymouth Brethren," say, that it is utterly improper that a man should wear the honors he inherits with his estates, or enter upon any responsibility, such as that of a member of Parliament, a commander in the navy, or officer in the army; that it is perfectly incompatible with Christian principle to take such an office. I do not know where they find this; and, were I addressing such, I would ask them, how it occurs to them that society is to be worked, if every man, the moment he becomes a Christian, is to abandon it? It must also occur to them that Joseph accepted office — responsible office — in the court, not of a Christian king, but of a heathen and idolatrous king. It might, too, be remembered by them that it is the scriptural distinction, to be *in* the world, but not to be *of* the world. God has placed us by his providence in the world; God has raised us by his grace above the world. His grace and his providence do not come into collision; I remain in the world, where his providence has placed me; I will try to live above the world, as his grace alone can enable me. And do we not praise God when we hear of good men, great men, raised to great power? Are we not thankful, instinctively so, — and there are instincts in the Christian heart better than all logic, — when we hear that great power has been lodged in the hands of Christian principle? And, moreover, let me add, is not this abjuration,

— not of the evil, but of the occupations and of the functions of the world, — very like monasticism, and therefore very like the system from which monasticism springs — Popery? For what is the principle of that creed? That in the world, at the post of duty, it is impossible to be a Christian; and therefore we must escape out of the world, as they call it, though not really so, and live in a convent, in order to be a Christian. Is not this very like the unbelief that doubts God's word, and like the cowardice that runs from the post where the great Captain of the faith has placed us? And, were convents and monasteries lawful, does history show that there has been less of the world in them, when these have been unroofed, than there has been in courts and palaces? I venture to assert broadly, and from the knowledge of the rapacity, the violence, the wickedness, the crimes, that have been perpetrated in these "dove-cots," that the last place to flee to, in order to get out of the world, is to go into a convent or a nunnery. Is it true that hoods and cowls are greater defences against the world than crowns and coronets? Is it true that there is more purity, more unworldliness, in the society of a monk, than in the society of a prince? The whole thing is a misconception on the part of some, a decided deception on the part of others. The truth is, heaven is in a Christian's heart; and wherever a Christian goes, and whatever he puts on, and whatever he calls himself, the sunshine of his Christianity plays around him: and the world is in the worldling's heart; and wherever that worldling goes, or whatever he puts on, and whether he wears a hood or a crown, whether he goes into a convent or a palace, he carries the world with him, and the world is still in him. It is not the place we are in that will make us Christians, but it is being Christians by grace that will keep us so, whether, like Joseph, we be at the monarch's right hand, or, like the poorest of the land, dwell in an unknown and unpenetrated circle. Joseph was a Christian in power, and he sanctified that power to good and holy purposes.

We hear another voice here: Joseph not only acted in power as Christian principle must have dictated, but, elevated to the very loftiest condition, he never forgot his people. There was always found in his heart a resounding echo to their groans, their sorrows, and their prayers. This is a rare thing; perhaps one ought not to say it is rare, but rather it is a difficult thing. In proscription his Christianity stood, in persecution by his brethren it still stood, in temptation in the palace it endured, at Pharaoh's right hand it failed not; it was a Christianity that weathered all sorts of storm and sunshine, and was more resplendent at the last than, if possible, it was at the first. We well know that when one has been elevated, in the providence of God, to an exalted condition, he is very apt to try not to think of, not to see, or to have intercourse with, those he has left in the valley below. He thinks — human nature is prone to think — that the shadow of those he has left would darken the splendor he has been raised to; whereas, in truth, the contrast between that shadow and the splendor would make the splendor only more beautiful. Joseph, if he did not know this, at least felt this: and in Pharaoh's palace his heart was warmed to Israel's claims, and his hand was liberal to their wants, their necessities, and their trials.

Joseph, in other words, carried his religion, as we should carry ours, into the home, into the ship, into the field, into the parliament, into the cabinet, into the palace. Wherever man can go, there his Christianity should go with him. The grace of God is not an aromatic perfume, to be put in a glass bottle, corked, stopped, and laid aside for special occasions; but it is that which should overflow, and give tone, and fragrance, and ornament, to all that man is. Wherever man is, and whatever power he wields, he is always, if a Christian, to recollect that he is responsible to God for its use, and by grace he will act under a sense of that responsibility.

Whatever man is made in God's providence, he is so made, not for himself, but for others. No man lives for himself, whether he think it or not; and no man ought or will, if a Christian, live for himself. Why was Solomon made wiser than the rest of mankind? Not for himself, but that others might be enlightened by his wisdom. Why was Samson made stronger than other men? Not for himself, but that others might be defended by his strength. And hence it comes to pass, that the loftiest power and the largest generosity should always be like twin sisters, never separated. Do you think that the ten thousand palaces of London would be less splendid were they to cast down their shadows upon a less amount of misery? Do you not think that, wherever there is largeness of wealth and magnificence of expenditure, there there ought to be generosity of heart and munificence of charity? Wherever there is one element that makes us superior to others, that element is not a property that we may do with as we like, but a trust of which we are the trustees, and for which we are answerable to God. When we take a retrospect of life, the only property of any real good or satisfaction in that moment, which we shall look back upon and delight in, will be that which we have sent before us into heaven, that which we have invested in the noblest and most beneficial of purposes, for the noblest and most beneficent of ends. You are not your own; ye are bought with a price, the precious blood of a Lamb without spot and without blemish.

If Christianity should thus shine in a palace, as it did in the case of Joseph, we must not forget that it must equally shine in the case of the humblest possessor of the humblest power. We are not responsible to God for the place that we occupy in society, but for the use that we make of that place in society. God makes the man that had ten talents responsible for these; the man that had five, not responsible for ten, but only for five; and the man that had one, responsible for one only. And so we, wherever we are placed, are responsible for the use that we make of that amount of influence that God has given us. If, therefore, we are in business, it is possible to be a religious man. I have heard men in business say, it is scarcely possible. I surely must doubt this, that in the business of this great commercial capital a man cannot be a Christian. Are there no instances of religious men becoming prosperous men in business? Is it true that only villains prosper on the exchange, and in the mart, and at the wharfs? Is it true that business is so utterly denuded of Christian principle that one must cheat, and lie, and deceive, in order to get bread? I will not believe it; I will not think so badly of the world, bad as the world is. There are Christian men, acting upon Christian principles, in the every-day business of this life; and, to my mind, nobly do those foreheads, pale, it may be, with toil, shine forth amidst the dust of the shop and the noise of the commercial thoroughfare, — more nobly, in my judgment, than the fronts of warriors amid the smoke and the din of battle; for the first, too, are occupying the high and perilous places of the field, and doing their duty like good soldiers of the Lord Jesus Christ. Should we suffer by being honest in business, true to our colors, then it may be that we shall have our names in the martyrology of heaven, if we have it not on earth. Martyrdoms are not for adhering to a great religious truth, but for carrying out that great religious truth in its most difficult place of development, — the every-day life, and every-day conduct. At all events, if the worst come to the worst, what a beautiful epitaph would this be, "Here lies the man who lost his all, because he would not cheat or lie! Here lies the man that embraced poverty like a bride, in order that he might maintain his principles uncompromised, and his duty to his conscience loyal to the last!" It is, therefore, possible, wherever man may be placed in the providence of God, to be the Christian, to act the Christian; and if we do not, the cause is not any lack of proffered grace on God's part, but because we do not ask it, or do not look for it.

The next voice we hear is from the death-bed of Joseph: it is recorded, "When he died he made mention of the departing of the children of Israel." I have heard that a thoughtless man was once impressed, if not converted, by reading the melancholy record in an early chapter of Genesis, "And he died." The most illustrious and sainted of humanity must lie down and die. This sentence no power can divert, no appeal can escape from, no wisdom can repel, "In the day thou eatest thereof thou shalt surely die."

> "Art is long and time is fleeting,
> And our hearts, though stout and brave,
> Still, like muffled drums, are beating
> Funeral marches to the grave."

"And he died," closes every biography. Every gray hair on the head is symptomatic of going down to the grave; every ache in the heart is a premonition of decay; every beat of the heart, like every swing of the pendulum, carries the life nearer to its termination. But, whilst it is true that we die as Joseph died, it is no less true it is only the body that dies, — the soul does not. "Dust thou art, and to dust returnest," was never written of the soul; in the case of the saved, and in the case of the lost, it endures. Time has dominion over years, months, days, minutes; it has none over the soul. Saved by grace, or lost forever by its own suicidal conduct, it must appear just as death finds it, and stand before God just as nature left it, or grace consecrated and made it. And, in the case of a Christian, death is not dying at all. I often realize this thought; I think it is worth dwelling on, that what we call death, in a Christian's experience, is merely change; it is the soul laying aside its trammels, laying down the tent in which it has sojourned, laying aside the ashen robe that it wore, and leaving that worn-out robe in the grave, to rise a bridal raiment, a resurrection garment. And the instant that the soul is severed from the body — without even a suspension or an interruption of the continuity of consciousness, of life, or feeling of joy, or of peace — it passes from the gray twilight of this life into the noonday splendor of that better world; the moment of an aged Christian's death is the evening twilight of time meeting and mingling with the morning twilight of eternity — so that death, the night between, is scarcely perceptible at all. So a Christian can die, and so Joseph did die; and so, by God's grace, we will live, and we shall die, as Joseph did. And when he departed, what was the result? what followed? Joseph, like Abel, speaks; as it is said, in a previous verse, "being dead he yet speaketh." When a Christian dies, he enters on two immortalities. He leaves one immortality in the world, and he carries another immortality into the presence of God. A Christian, to those who knew him really and truly, never dies on earth. Is there not in every man's home a certain place that is a shrine of beautiful recollections? Is there not in every man's calendar one day that is a holy and solemn anniversary? Is it not true that there are moments when, in the coldest shadows of the present, and in the brightest lights of the future, you hear voices that the world hears not, and see forms that the world sees not, and there is really communion with the pious dead, which nothing upon earth can suspend, destroy, or take away? We leave behind us an influence that walks the world, pleading for whatsoever things are pure, just, and beautiful; or, if unrenewed, we leave behind us an influence that walks the world the advocate of Satan, and contributing to the ruin of souls. It is this consciousness that being dead we speak, that we leave an influence behind us when we leave this world, that makes life itself more solemn even than dying. Let us, then, pray that what influence we leave may be like that of those who are recorded in the eleventh chapter of the Hebrews. There we read that Abel, being dead, speaks for his Lord; Enoch, being dead, still sounds forth the beauty and the safety of a walk with God; Noah, being dead, tells us still of his acceptance of God's word, his stormy going, his happy landing on Ararat; and Abraham, being dead, yet tells us how by faith he went out, not knowing whither, in obedience to God's command; we hear the tones still of Isaac's blessing; we listen to the words of Joseph's mention of the departure of his brethren, and his giving commandment concerning his bones. In this blessed book, we have a compendium of the most lasting, beneficent, and sanctifying influences, so that we hear in it the first hope that religion breathed, and the last sigh that faithfulness to it expired. Joseph left behind him an influence that did not die; and, in order to be a ruling recollection of that influence, it is said, he made mention of this exodus, and gave commandment concerning his bones. How is it that by faith he made mention of this going forth of the children of Israel? Why should he mention the departing, or, as it is called in the second book of the Bible, the exodus of the children of Israel? The way in which faith was exercised in this was simply that his own brethren had become so dead, under the impression of a cruel and undeserved tyranny, that they had even let go the bright hopes of an exodus from Egypt, and an entrance into the promised land. Joseph retained this bright hope, regarded the fulfilment of the promise as certain: he did not ask, how should it be performed? he counted neither possibilities nor probabilities; he seized the promise, because it was the promise of his God; and he made mention, long before it took place, of their exodus from Egypt, as a thing just as certain as if it had actually taken place. This is faith in the promises of God, to believe that whatever God has promised is just as certain, and as worthy of committing our soul to, as if the thing were already absolutely accomplished; this is faith.

We learn also, from this fact, that God's true church never can be destroyed in the worst, nor yet be wholly corrupted in the best, circumstances. There was a church in the midst of Egypt; the only church upon earth was amid the thraldom and the furnaces of Egypt; it survived its persecution, emerged in Canaan, and laid the foundations of the whole church of Christ. The bush may blaze upon Horeb, but it shall not be utterly consumed, for God is in the bush. The ship, like Paul's, may be dashed to pieces on the rocks, but not one of the crew shall perish. The earthen vessel may be shivered like a potter's vessel, but the precious perfume it contains shall only spread the wider over all the earth.

And when Joseph thus made mention of the departure of the children of Israel from Egypt, he showed them that his heart was not there, and that, of course, their heart ought not to be there also. Now, this is a very beautiful trait. With everything to keep the heart in Egypt, that heart, like a captive bird in its cage, beat against the wires, and longed for the pure air and bright light of its own native sky. In spite of Egypt, and in spite of Egypt's splendor, the patriarch's heart, like the needle to the pole, still vibrated toward Canaan — Jerusalem. And is not this the very type, the very model, of what a Christian should be? The gifts of God's providence should never satisfy us, without the grace of God's Holy Spirit. The flowers that grow about our feet, profusely scattered by a good God, are only designed to make us long and thirst for that better land, where these flowers are in their native soil, and where they bloom never to wither.

What God gives us, in his providence, makes us only responsible; it does not make us Christians. Gifts of God's providence commend God to us, but they do not commend us to God. The greater the prodigality of his gifts, the less should we be satisfied with them. What a sad evidence of deterioration is it, that man becomes so benumbed with God's gift, that, instead of its being a prompter to God the giver, it becomes a blind that obscures and conceals him! What a sad necessity is there seen in that fact for the removal of the gift at times, for a darkening of the sunshine with a cloud, and for some piercing memento, "This is not your rest; arise, and seek a better!" All the splendors of Egypt could not make Joseph happy without his beloved Canaan. All the riches, and the honors, and the power, that you may have in this world, ought never, and will never, if our hearts be right, make us satisfied, until we reach our home that is beyond the stars. Happiness is not a thing that grows on, before, around us, or that is to be collected from beneath us; it is an inspiration from God's grace. Wherever there is a heart made happy, there the desert will become beautiful; and wherever the heart is heavy with sorrow, there the brightest scene will be barren and unprepossessing. Paradise begins in the individual heart, spreads out its green margin over all the earth, until he that has paradise in his heart sees paradise reflected from all the world besides. It is our union and communion with God that gives us happiness; and, in the absence of God, all the wealth and splendor that Joseph had could not make him happy; on the contrary, — still in the midst of it unsatisfied, as man's great heart must ever be, — he made mention; it is the language of repeated mention, as if his morning and his evening allusions in the midst of Egypt, — when he rose up and when he lay down, when he came in and when he went out, — were still "Canaan, Canaan." "Set your affections, not upon things that are beneath, but upon things that are above, where Christ is at the right hand of God."

It is said, he gave commandment, when dying, concerning his bones. What evidence is here of the distinction that subsists between the soul and the body is worth noticing as we pass. I think there is no one thing that more strongly and pointedly shows that man is not to be numbered with the brutes that perish than this,—that, with the full consciousness of dying, which no other creature has, with the full consciousness that he is dying, he can give direction, clear, explicit, about the disposing of the tent that he is to cast off, or the bones that he is to lay down. This alone stamps man as a creature possessed of a soul that can never die; for the last act, the very will that you make, is the evidence that you feel that you are leaving only the stricken tent in which you can sojourn no longer, and are about to soar to a house eternal in the heavens, not to cease to be.

"And he gave commandment concerning his bones." But this faith was also shown in this one fact, that when he did so he showed the certainty of going into Canaan. When he gave commandment concerning his bones, it was to be an expressive exhibition to his countrymen that they, in due time, should be marched into Canaan.

He himself was about to die; his bones now rest under the shadow of Carmel, or beneath the deep foundations of the towers of Jerusalem, or, it may be, beneath the mosque of Omar; but the day comes when the trumpet shall sound, and the patriarch's bones shall come bone to bone, in the language of Ezekiel, and he shall rise, and possess the land of which he made mention; for in that land was the grave of Jesus that was opened, and because it was opened our graves shall not continue shut forever.

By faith, too, he made mention of the carrying his bones into Canaan in order to teach them this: If he, the patriarch, would not so much as leave his dust in Egypt, how much less ought they to leave their hearts in Egypt! It was to be to every Israelite a memento that the patriarch had so little sympathy with that land, so little of the earthliness and worldliness that might glue him to that land, that he wished to be rid of its idols, not even a bone to be left in it, that it might be felt by them, and felt more vividly, that his heart was where his treasure and his hope were.

Let us, in the world, not be *of* it. Let us rejoice in the prospect of admission to a holier and a happier, into the true rest that remaineth for the people of God. Let us pray for that faith which shall enable us to detach our hearts from this world, and to fix those hearts on a better world; and, above all, which will show the way that leads from the outer court, which this world is, into the grand temple, which that world will be; that way, Jesus Christ, the way, the truth and the life. Let us hear the voice of the departed patriarch, as it comes down from his spirit beside the throne, or rises from his bones resting in Palestine: "Set your affection on things above, not on things on the earth."

CHAPTER XVI.

THE CLOUD OF WITNESSES.

"The glorious company of the apostles : praise thee.
The goodly fellowship of the prophets : praise thee.
The noble army of martyrs : praise thee.
The holy church throughout all the world : doth acknowledge thee ;
The Father of an Infinite Majesty."

"Wherefore seeing we are also compassed about with so great a cloud of witnesses, let us lay aside every weight, and the sin which doth so easily beset us, and let us run with patience the race that is set before us, looking unto Jesus the author and finisher of our faith ; who for the joy that was set before him endured the cross, despising the shame, and is set down at the right hand of the throne of God." — HEBREWS 12 : 1, 2.

How practical is every truth of Christianity! The bright catalogue of saints who, being dead, yet speak, which the apostle has given, is not like the catalogue of the ships in Homer, a mere amusing description, or in the oration of Demosthenes, a mere flourish; it is followed by a close, personal and practical purpose: "Wherefore," he says, "because we are compassed about with so great a cloud of witnesses, let us lay aside every weight."

How thoroughly in earnest is every writer of the New Testament! There is not the least hint of a sentiment or expression that would indicate that the apostolic mind was not charged with the intensest and the deepest earnestness. They contemplate a world in ruins, souls perishing, a God of mercy, instant forgiveness for the greatest sin, instant acceptance for the chiefest of sinners; and with an urgency, and an eloquence, simple but intensely earnest, they bid all flee for refuge to the hope set before them in the Gospel. At the conclusion of the bright roll, full of the richest poetry, charged with the most vivid and beautiful illustrations, is the practical corollary: "Wherefore seeing we also are compassed about with so great a cloud of witnesses, let us lay aside every weight, and the sin which doth so easily beset us." Being dead, they all speak.

Whatever incidents are recorded in the Old Testament, in the Patriarchal, in the Levitical, or in the New Testament, that is, in the Christian dispensation, are not put there as dead facts, mere characteristics of the ages, and instructive to those that were the subjects of them; but they were written aforetime for our learning; these names are teachers to us alike by lip and life; these are voices which are still sounding along the corridors of centuries, and reasoning, in the midst of the nineteenth century, with a force that grows, and an eloquence that becomes weightier as the world rolls on, — of righteousness, and of temperance, and of judgment; and, so far, every character who adorned the history of the past lived, not for himself, but for us. I have often thought of the great and striking fact, that every man's life is, in its measure, vicarious; that every man lives, whether he like it or not, not for himself, but for others. If he will not give his life a holy offering for the benefit of others, God will exact it from him as a reluctant sacrifice for the benefit of others. It is true of every man, — the worst and the best, the saint and the sinner, — "Being dead, they yet speak," and their life lives after them. I have said, every one has two immortalities: one that shoots beyond the stars, and finds its enjoyment in the presence of God and of the Lamb; another immortality, as if the shadow of it, walks the world, the accustomed haunts in which he lived, the society with which he mingled, and there acts, if that of a holy man, for the good of souls, their happiness and progress. Those saints in the eleventh chapter of the Epistle to the Hebrews lived that we might live; they labored that we might enter into their labors; they died that we might hear them still. The race-course on which we are to run (to employ the figure used by the apostle) has been beaten smooth by the countless feet that trod it on their course to glory; and now these men stand around us like lights to illuminate our course to bliss; like stars overhead, shining splendidly upon us; like pillars of fire by night, and pillars of cloud by day; each one emitting a directive voice, "This is the way: walk ye in it."

What renders these witnesses, with whose cloud we are surrounded, so precious to us, is the variety of their experience. Are we, like Abel, associated with depraved and wicked brothers? Then, like Abel, we must serve God, whether others will join or will resist. Are we, like Enoch, alone in the midst of the world? And this is often the case when a single person becomes a Christian in the higher walks of life, and he must walk with God and against those that are about him, and in spite of those that love him, and often amid the satire, and the sneers, and the scorn, of those who ought to know better. If we are alone, like Enoch, we must walk with God alone. If, like Abraham, we are summoned to leave our own country, we must do it, going we know not whither. If, like Moses, we are covered with reproach, let it be the reproach of Christ, and it will be resplendent with honor. Do you think that one single witness, in this sparkling catalogue, repents of what he did, or of what he suffered? Not one. In a very few years (for the old must soon die, and the youngest may soon die), all in the world that shines, captivates, ensnares, will be of no more value than a transient sunbeam that has passed away, or the echoes of the wind that has swept through a broken archway. Then to know that we chose the better part, that we embraced the Saviour, that we held fast, and counted all but loss for him, will make the future so bright and so happy, and the past so memorable in our retrospect of it!

The expression employed to denote the number of the witnesses is "a cloud." I do not think, with many of the commentators whose sentiments I have consulted on the passage, — but I speak as to reasonable men; judge ye, — that the word "cloud" refers at all to the pillar of cloud that guided the Israelites in their journey through the wilderness. I think it is employed just in the sense in which it is used by heathen writers. Every schoolboy knows that, in his Homer, the words νέφος Τρωῶν mean, literally, "a cloud of Trojans," and also νέφος πεζῶν, literally, "a cloud, or number, of foot-soldiers." "A cloud of witnesses" means "a vast collection," "a great multitude." And just as the cloud in the sky is the collection of a countless multitude of drops that are exhaled from the earth, and, in the form of vapor, float past us, or envelop and cover us, so we have, on each side and over us, a great multitude, a "great cloud" of witnesses. And, perhaps, it is not forcing the figure when I say, that just as the globules of water that compose the cloud are exhaled from the earth, and are borne sky-ward by the beams of rising and setting suns, so the origin of these believers was of the earth earthy; they were sufferers like us; every trial that we have they had; every pain that we feel they felt; but, as the cloud, when it has risen from the earth, is fringed and sometimes gilded with the golden glories of rising and of setting suns, and shines with a splendor that is not its own, but borrowed from that sun by whose beams it exhaled from the earth, so the mighty company of them that have washed their robes and made them white in the blood of the Lamb will shine in a splendor not their own, but borrowed from the Sun of righteousness, unto whom alone they give the glory, the praise, the thanksgiving, and the honor. Whatever was in their original state was from beneath; whatever is in their present glory and beauty is from above.

But they are not only a cloud, but a "cloud of witnesses." They witness to something; and, therefore, they are called witnesses. They witness to the preciousness of truth, to the importance of real religion, to the happiness of loving, and fearing, and serving God. They illustrated their testimony with their lives, and they surrendered those lives freely when it was needed, to illustrate their testimony by their death. They are witnesses, a cloud of witnesses, for us. Just as the cloud descends in showers and waters the earth, or wards off the too hot sunbeams from us that are below, so these witnesses float as a cloud before us, not for themselves, but for us. Never was a witness' testimony committed to the air, or a martyr's blood shed upon the earth, that has not its aim, its end, its object, that does not still cry, — the blood from the earth, and the testimony from heaven, — "Be ye steadfast, unmovable, always abounding in the work of the Lord."

But there is not only "a cloud of witnesses," but it is said to be a cloud of witnesses encompassing us. In other words, we are here represented as moving in the midst of a shining throng. The image of the apostle is, that we are running on a race-course; a race-course is of a continuous length, and of a certain breadth; and he supposes standing upon each side of the race-course these illustrious witnesses, from Abel down to Rahab, each witness standing with his deposition in his hand, inscribed with his testimony, his struggles, his victory, each casting light upon the course in order to guide us; each a voice upon the right hand and upon the left, saying, "This is the way: walk ye in it." The apostle supposes that we are running a course that may, in some way, interest the saints in glory; and that we are surrounded, while we run, with these testimonies for God, for truth, for duty, which they have bequeathed to us as our blessed and their glorious heritage.

But, whilst it seems the apostle's idea that the cloud of witnesses is near to us, it may be true, though it is not so explicitly revealed, that these witnesses may still be spectators of the saints that are striving and struggling upon earth. The cloud in which they are may carry them from heaven to earth. We know not, we see not, their presence; but we derive encouragement from the knowledge that, though we see not them, yet they may see us. Those we loved on earth may be spectators at this moment of those they left behind them. The partition-wall that separates time from eternity may be so thin that those on the other side may hear the voice of praise and prayer lifted up to God from those that are on this side; and the eye of saints in glory may have that penetrating power that it can see through the partition, and witness the countless races that are on their course to immortality and glory. But, if so, they are neither media between us and God, nor are they intercessors for us with God. They neither pray for us, nor are they to be prayed to; at least, there is no evidence of it. Their only function is, witnesses of the conflict, deeply, intently interested in its issue. Thus, around and over us may stand and watch, like stars and sentinels of the sky, the mother that taught us in our infancy, the father that toiled for our well-being, the faithful minister that preached to us the everlasting Gospel, the friends with whom we took sweet counsel as we walked together to the house of God. And, if it were not for the din and noise of the ceaseless wheels of this world's machinery, we might hear, ringing clear and beautiful as Heaven's own tones, the voices, the familiar voices, of those that we once loved, saying to us, "We are witnesses of your cares; we are spectators of your conflict. My children, my friends, my relatives, my father, my mother, be faithful, be steadfast, run the race that is set before you, looking not to us, but looking unto Jesus. The race is rough, but it is short; the strife may be sharp, but it will be soon over. Hasten onward; we pant for your presence; we have washed our robes, and made them white in the blood of the Lamb, and we wait to be perfectly happy only for the completion of the body of Christ, and the entrance into our rest of those who are racers in the course we ran and completed." It is an interesting and a pleasing thought; it is not an unscriptural one; it may be perverted, but so may every truth; for the deepest truths lie always nearest to the deadliest heresies, as the greatest lights ever have beside them the deepest and the darkest shadows. We know not where the dead are. We speak of "up" and "down," but "up" at twelve o'clock at noon is "down" at twelve o'clock at night. It may be that those who have preceded us to glory are far nearer to us at this moment than our friends in Scotland, or our relatives in India, or our brethren on the continent; and that they may know far more what is done upon earth than we suppose. But, whatever they may know, — again I guard myself, — there is no reason for our praying to them, or for our concluding that they pray for us. Their function to earth is to be witnesses, and no more, of our race to glory.

And from this passage, that there is "so great a cloud of witnesses," and that all have met together, of all nations, all kindreds, and all people, we gather this very important lesson, that there is but one place in which all the people of God, of all ages, are gathered. This cloud is all composed of one united fellowship and company. Some parts of the cloud may be nearer to the sun than other parts; and, therefore, fringed with a greater glory; but all the witnesses that compose the cloud are in the same bright sphere, and enjoy the same happy rest. It is a blessed thought, there are not different nooks of the universe for different generations of the saints of God; but that you and I, dear reader, if we are faithful, and steadfast, and true, shall meet in that happy rest, and mingle with Abraham, and Isaac, and Jacob, the world's gray patriarchs. The goodly fellowship of the prophets, the noble army of martyrs, all that have lived holily, all that have died faithfully, we shall meet, and mingle and commune with. There is but one bright place, — "Abraham's bosom," "the rest that remaineth," "presence with Christ," — into which all God's people are gathered, and made unspeakably happy.

We learn, also, that there is but one way to that place. If there were different roads, then what would be the use of relating the experience of a saint on one road as at all useful to a saint on another road? There never was but one way to heaven since Adam fell: and in that way Abel, Enoch, Noah, Abraham, and all the saints, have walked, and entered into their rest. The way may not be always on its surface the same. It may sometimes be covered with grass, sometimes with gravel, sometimes paved with stones. It may in one part be smooth, in another rough. The storm and the thunder may be heard here, the still small voice of goodness and of peace may be heard there. But it is the one road that leads to heaven. In it only must we move; and it matters not how near we walk to it, if we walk not in it, we are not in the way to heaven. If I were to say, the way to heaven is only through the Scotch church, that would be bigotry of the most intense kind; or, if you were to say, only through the Church of England, that would only match it; but it is not bigotry to say, that the way to heaven is through Christ; and that, whether it be in a barn or under the fretted roof of a grand cathedral, wherever two or three hearts cluster round him and beat responsive to his touch, there is a road to heaven that neither Pope nor prince can shut up, free — without money and without price. There is but one way to heaven, and that way they all walked in. Abraham was a Christian as truly as Martin Luther. Enoch was a Protestant as really as John Knox or Calvin. The truth of God is old as creation; it was first, it shall be last; it will be all and in all. And these witnesses are pointed out to us to show what their experience was. If they did not fall when they met with rough places, if they were not frowned out of the way, nor shamed out of the way, nor discouraged in the way, nor suffered to offend in the way, then, let the road still be as rough as it can be, and let the storm pelt as hard as it may, we, too, derive courage from them, and we, too, may reach the end. In the beautiful words of the finest of living poets, I mean Longfellow, who seems in them to have caught the spirit of the text:

> "Lives of good men" (the cloud of witnesses)
> "all remind us
> We can make our lives sublime,
> And, departing, leave behind us
> Footprints on the sands of time :
>
> "Footprints that perhaps another,
> Sailing o'er life's solemn main, —
> A forlorn and shipwrecked brother, —
> Seeing, may take heart again.
>
> "Let us, then, be up and doing,
> With a heart for any fate ;
> Still achieving, still pursuing,
> Learn to labor and to wait."

Or, translated into its original, "seeing we are compassed about with so great a cloud of witnesses, let us lay aside every weight, and the sin which doth so easily beset us, and let us run with patience the race that is set before us."

Having thus tried to illustrate the peculiar allusions contained in the grand motive applied and urged by the apostle, let me endeavor to explain some of the phraseology, descriptive of the Christian life, which is also employed by him.

He says, "Run with patience the race that is set before us." The expression "run," as soon as mentioned, calls up the idea of exertion, labor, effort. Many Christians think that, the moment they are saved by grace, they will be wafted, on unruffled waters, as it were, in a boat into which they have been unconsciously laid, and in which they are borne on until they appear before God in happiness and glory. Nothing good upon earth is attainable without labor. I do not believe that one man has a vastly greater genius than another, but that men's minds, like men's heights, differ but slightly, and that drudgery and labor are the great secrets of distinction and of difference. Nothing on earth is attainable without labor. And, if this be so in the things of time, nothing can be gained, except by renouncing indolence and apathy, in our aspirations after eternity. Rest is yonder, labor is here. The goal, the prize, and the Giver of it, are in the future; running, resisting, striving, is here. Grace does not supersede effort; it only stimulates and stirs it. God saves us as rational and responsible men; not as clods, or dead and inanimate stones. Grace is not an exemption from running, but an introduction to the race-course, and strength and sufficiency to keep us in it, and to make us successful on it. Wherever there is great genius, it has been as remarkable for its capacity for great labor as for its own inherent energies: and wherever there is richly the grace of God, it has been found stimulating to duty and sustaining in duty. That man has not the grace of God who depends upon his laboring, running, striving, as his right to heaven; and that man has not the grace of God who thinks he will get to heaven without running and striving. Christ's promise is, "My grace is sufficient for you;" not, "My grace is a substitute for you." Many persons read that promise as if Christ said, "My grace is a substitute for you;" but the words are, "My grace is sufficient for you:" and the apostle says, it teaches us, as its instinctive tendency, "to deny ungodliness and worldly lusts, and to live soberly, and righteously, and godly, in this present world, looking for that blessed hope, even the glorious appearing of Jesus Christ, our great God and Saviour."

Let us notice, next, the individualism or personality in this race. Each is to run, to labor, to strive, just as if there were no one else on the race-course with him. I believe that one of the most mischievous facts, if one may call a fact so, is that in our congregations every one listens as one of a vast multitude, and listens as much for his neighbors as for himself. People seem to do congregationally what porters do mechanically, so distribute the load that a fraction only reaches the conscience of each that listens. Each must try to hear just as if the preacher were speaking to him alone. We must die alone, we must stand before Christ alone, we must answer alone, each for himself: none, none, none besides, neither priest, nor prelate, nor any one else, can answer for his brother. Insulation and loneliness of soul is a sublime, a solemn and a pressing duty; and the man who has never tried to be alone knows very little yet what it is to be a Christian. Let us live, not conventionally, always in a crowd, but a good deal alone. Our great concern is, less with our fellow-racers, and more with ourselves. And when we approach the Lord's table, let us avoid that great defect that creeps over and escapes in words from so many, "I wonder what business such a one has at this table. I wonder what right such a one has at this table." We are to go there each alone; and to feel alone with God, as if no eye were upon us but his. Sufficient for your brother is his own responsibility. Each of us must give an account, says the apostle, for himself: each man must bear his own burden: we have enough to do to bear our own; we cannot take charge of our brother's. Very probably we shall find that the true way to do a brother good is to think less about him and to elevate ourselves more. Were each a thorough reformer of himself, all society would be thoroughly reformed. I believe that he who labors by the grace of God to elevate his own character to the highest possible pitch of moral significance and grandeur, will exercise upon the sphere in which he moves and lives the highest and the most happily transforming influence. Let us ever remember that whilst there are many in the race-course, — and so far the remembrance is encouragement, — that each man must run as if all depended upon himself.

Let us now notice the race-course. "Let us run," says the apostle, "the race that is before us." What fact does this teach? It is not left for us to select the race-course: it is "set before us;" — set before us in the promises, in the prophecies, in every page and passage of the word of God; and set before us by the footprints that are on it of those that have preceded us. It is a beaten way, and it is so plain, that, while the great theologian, or the carping intellectualist, or the mere critic, may mistake it, the wayfaring man will not miss it; "the wayfaring man shall not err therein." It is as wayfaring men we keep in it. If we object to be wayfaring men, we shall stumble. And here lies the reason why many learned men mistake it, and many plain men find it, that the former set about to pick up and analyze the minerals and flowers that are scattered over it, or to admire the actions and the grace and the symmetry of the racers that are on it; whereas the wayfaring man goes on to it in this capacity alone — to mind nothing except one thing, to run the race that is set before him; and so he keeps the way.

This race-course on which we are to run may vary very much in its outward aspects, but still it is the race that God has set before us. It runs through every variety of social existence; through every winding and by-path and public road of human life; through the shop, the counting-house, the pulpit, the parliament, the bench. We may pick up a flower upon it, but we must not stop a minute to do so; we may drink of the brook by the way, but we must do it like the philosopher of old, with the hollow of the hand, rapidly. This race-course runs at times through patches of sunshine so beautiful, but, alas, so brief! at other times through valleys, and stony deserts, and barren heaths, and up hills; Sodom blazing behind, but Jerusalem shining before; at other times it runs through sick beds, and where we must lie down and die, or between the graves that contain the early dead; and at other times over the wrecks of fortune, the loss of name; and sometimes through martyrdom and death itself. Let us run, notwithstanding; it is the race that God has set before us. We are not responsible for the direction the race-course takes, or the stones and pits on it; we are only responsible for running the race that is set before us. Our responsibility lies in running on the race-course,—we have nothing to do with making it; it is God's prerogative to set the race-course,—it is our privilege and our duty to run on it as set before us.

We are to run this race set before us, however rough, however smooth, however crooked, however perplexing, "with patience;" that patience which is so easily said, and so rarely exhibited in all its beauty, and in all its power. If you want to see patience, look at it as it sat, like a golden diadem, upon the brow of Jesus, when he answered nothing, and stood the judge of all, at the bar of Pilate. It is preëminently a Christian grace. Insensibility is want of humanity, apathy is stoicism,—patience is part of Christianity. One would think that it would be, "Run the race with courage;" and yet it is not so. Courage is more admired by man, it is less approved of God. Courage, wherever it exists,—and far be it from me to question in the least the heroic courage of our brave men and our heroes, who have fought and fallen for our sakes,—seeks to be seen, to be admired, to be applauded; it needs the outward props and stimuli of outward recognition; whereas, patience sits silent, lonely, beautiful, emitting no trumpet-sound, satisfied to live under the eye of Jesus, and to behold the face of our Father who is in heaven. Thus, then, patience is eminently the Christian grace; and with this patience we are to run the race that is set before us. We shall find much in the race that will make that true in your case which is said in the word of God, "Ye have need of patience." We shall find, not only how often you need patience, but how very seldom we have exhibited it. When we come to places of sickness and of suffering, and see all God's billows roll over us; when all things shake and rock, and nothing seems secure; when we are placed under clouds that will be dissipated only by the light of the resurrection morning, or amid pains and anxieties which will only be scattered when we are placed in Abraham's bosom; when our trials seem so heavy that we are ready to be crushed under them,—patience, nestling in the heart, will begin its quiet under-song, and will sing, it may be in a plaintive minor, "Father, not as I will, but as thou wilt;" and patience will whisper to you what she hears from the Heavenly Father, "Be of good cheer; I will never leave thee, nor forsake thee." Its practical effects upon our own spirit we cannot exaggerate; for sometimes we shall find in the race-course that the hill is so steep, and the streams we have to cross are so broad, and the enemies we have to meet so many, and the principalities and the wickedness in high places so powerful, that we shall almost say, like the Israelites, "Better had we died in Egypt;" but patience will teach what she has learned, "Stand still and see the salvation of our God." And when all seems impassable before you, and mountains rise that seem insurmountable, patience will whisper to you "Be still, and know that I am God," and will remind you, "Seeing we are compassed about with so great a cloud of witnesses," who had the same trials, the same difficulties, the same perplexities, "let us run with patience the race that is set before us." To put it on a lower ground, I say nothing is so unprofitable as impatience, nothing is so pleasant and so useful as patience. A fretting, discontented spirit eats out the soul's happiness, and destroys it; whereas, a patient spirit bows beneath the storm as it passes, and waits and hopes for and enjoys the sunshine that follows. Run, then, with patience, the race that is set before you.

And, adds the apostle, "lay aside every weight;" and lastly, on which I make very few remarks, "the sin which doth so easily beset us." The first I regard as laying aside the excessive love of things that are in themselves innocent; and the second, as the crucifying whatever is our besetting sin.

The first is, "lay aside every weight." Just as in the race the racer laid aside every encumbering piece of raiment that might cling too close around him, or prevent the free action of his limbs, so we are to lay aside every weight. And this reminds me of a solemn fact, that more men lose their souls by the excessive love of what is perfectly innocent, than by the unlawful love of what is positively forbidden. I believe it is not so much flagrant sin that sinks so many, as the excessive love of that which is in itself, in its place and in its proper proportion, scriptural, innocent, and good. For instance, when certain persons were invited to the marriage feast,—in other words, when they were invited to run the race set before them,—what prevented them from entering on that race-course? One said, "I have bought some oxen." That was perfectly right; the distinction of property, the possession and the duty of property, all are right; but he so loved it, and gave it so vast and disproportionate an importance, that, for the sake of trying his oxen, he refused to run the race set before him. Another said, "I have purchased a farm, and must go and see it:" and in his case it was a weight that he would not lay aside. And the third said, "I have married a wife, and therefore I cannot come;" thereby making that a reason for not entering on the race which ought to have been a stimulus and an excitement to him to do so. And thus, by our excessive, unscriptural and sinful love of things that are positively lawful, we retain weights that press us down to the earth, and prevent our running the race set before us. Literature is one of the most elegant studies of the human mind, and wherever Christianity has attained its loftiest influence literature has risen to its highest possible development; but, if our love of literature should prevent our cultivation of the heart, then we are to lay aside that weight, which prevents our running the race set before us. Politics is a duty and a study for statesmen, and ought to be so; but, if their excessive attention to the state prevent their due attention to the welfare of their souls, they must, however painful, however unpopular, lay aside that weight which prevents their running the race set before them. A right hand must be cut off, father and mother and sister and brother must be abjured, if they prevent our running that race, or act as dead weights that may bring us down to the earth, instead of assisting us in pursuing the course that is set before us. The greatest pleasure and the greatest profit must alike be surrendered for Christ's sake.

There are some things in this race we must subordinate: these are what I have now mentioned. There are other things we must sacrifice, and these are what I now add,—"the sin which doth so easily beset us." Now, every man has some predominating passion, tendency, disposition, desire, sympathy, vanity, which always strives and struggles to come uppermost, and to take the lead, and to sit upon the throne of his heart, and to dictate law to him, and guide his course through the world. I do not know what it is, because I cannot read men's hearts; but, whatever be that sin with which you are most troubled, whatever be the passion you are most liable to, and whatever that temper may be which is your trial, whatever that tendency may be which is leading you, and trying to lead you, from God, that is your great foe: do not only fight with the devil, but also with that which is worse to you, — the sin that doth most easily beset you. Each man knows his own heart, and, therefore, each should seek to ascertain what sin is mightiest there, and bring it to the blood of Jesus, that its guilt may be expiated; bring it to the Spirit of Jesus, that its roots may be extirpated; and, thus forgiven the sin, and thus made master over it as a predominating force, you will run the more easily the race that is set before you. The fact that you are conscious of it, and that you hate it, and struggle against it, is evidence of grace. Was it not an apostle who said, "I find a law in my members warring against the law of my mind, and bringing me into captivity to the law of sin which is in my members"? It was indeed the "chiefest of sinners," indeed "the least of saints," "not worthy to be called an apostle," but, compared with us, the greatest of all saints and teachers, — the apostle Paul. If, therefore, you have light to see the sin that doth most easily beset you, then bring to bear upon that sin the appliances that God has given you in the Gospel, — pray for his grace, beg his Holy Spirit, pray for divine strength to be made perfect in weakness; and thus run the race set before you.

Meantime, I would say to you who have entered on this race, Be patient, be prayerful. While your eye is upon the crown and your feet upon the race-course, let the heart often beat, if the lips are dumb, "Lord, I believe: help mine unbelief!" O, blessed thought, that God needs not to hear the lips speaking; he can hear what the heart beats, he can see the heart's polarity, he can appreciate those cries, and groans, and yearnings, and aspirations, which eloquent language cannot embody, and which lips cannot utter: and he that sees in secret, and hears in silence, will give you grace and glory, and every good thing. Run that race, make every effort in God's strength to reach the goal. He that placed you on it will help you in it. Just notice, as a single illustration of this, the man who has made up his mind most fatally to be rich. He divests himself of every obstruction, denies himself every comfort; even the richest luxury upon earth — the luxury of doing good — he denies himself; and he sets out with his whole heart, and strength, and mind, to be rich; — watches the price of stocks: his first inquiry in the morning is the market, his last thought at night is the market; his Bible is his ledger, his sanctuary is his counting-house; and, if he stumbles into God's house, he brings his body only, but not his mind, for it is traversing his ledger, or counting over his merchandise. The man is wholly in his pursuit: his whole soul and strength are concentrated in it. And if a man can thus live for so much trash as may be grasped thus, shall not we run with concentrated energy the race that is set before us, seeking what we are sure we shall obtain, — unsearchable riches, a crown of glory that fadeth not away?

And if these words meet the eyes of any who have never thought of this race, who know that they are not running the race, — my dear reader, angels pity you, the cloud of witnesses, if there be weeping among the blessed, must weep at the sight of you; and if their voices could become audible, yet being dead they would speak, — O, with what piercing eloquence! — if they could prevail upon you to enter that race, which is an arduous one, but a happy one; for the heaviest labor becomes light when the heart is made happy by the grace of God. Are you in that course? It is easy to know. Either you are floating with the stream, or you are going against it. Men are never drifted to heaven: they must always strive, struggle. If you are drifting, it is on the currents and the eddies of this world, which are carrying you onward and downward. There is, in such a case, no doubt where you are. No man ever goes to hell at all ignorant of the fact; no man ever finds himself in heaven without knowing long before, predetermining, preärranging, running, laboring, striving. I believe it costs more effort, more drudgery, and, surely, far more misery, to get to hell, than it costs toil or trouble to get to heaven. No man toils so hard as he who digs cisterns and then finds them broken; and he labors little, in labor's worst sense, who goes to the fountain of living waters, and drinks without money and without price. If you are not in this course, arise and go to your Father. To be happy is the end of life; and the grand prescription, the only panacea, is in the Gospel of the Son of God. There is no happiness in this world in sin, and there is no happiness in the world to come without Christ; and, glorious fact! there is not a soul that hears and reads these things that may not be instantly happy by laying aside the weight that clogs him, and the sin that besets him, and starting, at God's bidding, and in Christ's name, and in the Spirit's strength, upon the race set before him in the Gospel.

CHAPTER XVII.

LOOKING TO JESUS.

O Lord, thou seest, from yon starry height,
Centred in one the future and the past.
Fashioned in thine own image, see how fast
The world obscures in me what once was bright.
Eternal Sun! the warmth which thou hast given
To cheer life's flowery April fast decays;
Yet, in the hoary winter of my days,
Forever green shall be my trust in heaven.
Celestial King! O, let thy presence pass
Before my spirit, and an image fair
Shall meet that look of mercy from on high,
As the reflected image in a glass
Doth meet the look of him who seeks it there,
And owes its being to the gazer's eye.

"Wherefore seeing we are compassed about with so great a cloud of witnesses, let us lay aside every weight, and the sin which doth so easily beset us, and let us run with patience the race that is set before us, looking unto Jesus, the author and finisher of our faith; who for the joy that was set before him endured the cross, despising the shame, and is set down at the right hand of the throne of God." — HEBREWS 12: 1, 2.

I HAVE endeavored to explain the nature of the cloud of witnesses here described as constantly enveloping us. I have showed that those who are enumerated in that bright catalogue, the eleventh chapter of the Epistle to the Hebrews, beginning with Abel, and ending with all that were stoned and sawn in sunder, and sealed their testimony with their blood, are the leading witnesses alluded to by the apostle.

These witnesses are said to be formed into a cloud. A cloud is the water drawn from the seas, the rivers and the earth, floating in innumerable drops in the form of a cloud, — minute drops, indeed, but still drops: their origin is from the earth, but the splendor with which the cloud is gilded often amid setting suns, the golden and the gorgeous hues which these clouds frequently assume, are all derived from that sun by whose beams the component particles of the cloud were extracted or exhausted from the earth. Our origin is from the earth, but our splendor is from the sun — the Sun of righteousness. All that we have as men is of the first Adam, — the earth, earthy: all our moral beauty and splendor as believers is from the transforming touch of the rays of that unsetting Sun who has risen with healing under his wings. I have unfolded the idea of the apostle, that of a race-course which we are to run; on each side of which there is a long line of martyr-witnesses beholding us in our struggles, our toils, our temptations, our trials, constantly witnessing, constantly looking on, anxious, if anxious they can be, about the issue, and waiting and panting till it be accomplished. I said, these may be, not simply the witnesses here named, with their depositions in their hands, showing how holily they lived, how faithfully they died; but it may be actually and truly the sainted dead, nay, not the dead, but the spirits of just men made perfect, who may see us, though we cannot see them, and hear our groans and sorrows, and prayers and praises, though we cannot hear them: for those that are gone before may be nearer those that are left behind than those that have crossed the channel are to us that are upon this side of it. But I added, as guarding it, that if it be so, — if Abraham, and Isaac, and Jacob, may see us, — if fathers and mothers, and sisters and brothers, and relatives in glory, may be witnesses of our struggle and our race, — they are not media between God and us, they are neither to be assumed as praying for us, nor we to suppose that we are warranted to pray to them. If they hear at all, they hear simply as witnesses, having nothing to do with us, and we having nothing to do with them, except under the consciousness that so splendid an array is around us, the spectators of what we are doing, to acquit ourselves as men, to fight the good fight, and finish the course, and enter on the joy that is set before us.

I next stated that the race is "set before us." Thank God that it is so! We cannot select it: it is set before us. There is but one way, one race-course, that leads to the goal, that leads to the *βϱαβευτης*, as he was called, the One that holds the prize in his hand, the One that we are to look at; and if we do not run on that race-course, we never can reach the prize. The Bible is the map that describes it, the chart on which we see it clearly and distinctly before us. It may run through many a winding,—through trade, through merchandise, through traffic, through parliament, through the palace. It may have smooth parts and rough parts, and clouds and shadows. In other places it may have steep hills, it may have innumerable difficulties. But onward is our course: we are not responsible for the smoothness or the roughness of the road—God settles that; we are only responsible for the enjoyment of the privilege and the discharge of the duty of running on it, our eyes upon the prize, our hearts with the Saviour, our hope to the end. I have showed how we are to run it, "with patience." I have showed that courage was the mission of the few; patience is the duty of us all. While impatience, like a moth, frets the fair robe of contentment and of peace, patience keeps our minds in quiet, and is the equilibrium and the balance of the human affections and the human faculties. And, in the next place, I showed that we are to lay aside every weight. Weights, I showed, were incumbrances, not sinful in themselves, but obstructions to our progress. There is no more sin in being rich, than virtue in being poor. It is a most miserable estimate of Christianity to think that a man with five thousand pounds a year cannot be as good as a man with a hundred pounds a year. Avarice is not in the amount we have, but in the grasp we take of it. The man who is truly large-hearted will be so, if he have a hundred pounds a year or a hundred thousand pounds a year; just as a man will be temperate whether he drink from a bottle or a cask. It is what a man is that determines the use that will be made of what he has. So here, the weights that hang upon us may be in themselves innocent, but when we hold them so fast that, though we see them standing in our way, we will not let them go; that, though we feel that we have to run at our utmost speed, and must lay aside every weight that would prevent us doing so; if we cannot do this, we retain the weights, and we may lose the race. I have also remarked that, besides these weights, there is "the sin which doth so easily beset us." Now, that must be cast away, because it is in itself evil. The former we subordinate, the latter we sacrifice. Sin must be expiated through Christ's blood, extirpated by Christ's Spirit, or it will utterly obstruct our course to glory.

I shall notice, in this closing chapter, a subject very large, but on which I can offer a very few thoughts — "looking unto Jesus." This expression is very remarkable. It means 'looking off to Jesus." This shows how purely Protestant, how truly evangelical, is the New Testament. It seems absurd to say so, it almost requires an apology for saying so; yet one must see how guarded the sacred penmen are, that every one shall be taught to look at nothing on earth but One who is the great path to glory, the great title to heaven, the only Saviour of sinners. As if Paul had said, "I have laid before you a splendid catalogue, and reviewed the whole of that moral galaxy, sparkling and illustrious, like ten thousand stars; but amid all this splendor you must not be dazzled with it. You must not look at Abel, nor at Enoch, nor at Moses, nor at the best that ever lived, or the most sainted that ever were admitted into glory, although they are all splendid; but, when you run the race, you must look off from them all, and concentrate your first look and your last look, your first hope and your last hope, upon Jesus. Seeing we are compassed about with so great a cloud of witnesses, let us lay aside every weight, and the sin which doth so easily beset us, and let us run with patience the race that is set before us, looking — not to the witnesses — but unto Jesus." What a fine parallel to this is that passage in the first chapter of John, where it is said of the apostle Andrew, and one of John's disciples, that they "heard John speak, and they followed Jesus," — not John. We perceive how we are to see the witnesses sparkle, but are yet to look, not at the witnesses, but at Jesus. It seems as if Paul had caught the last and the first words of the Baptist, "Behold the Lamb of God," and had echoed those words again: "Run the race set before you, looking, not at the sides of the race-course, lest the stars that sparkle there dazzle you; not looking downward at the fairest flowers that bloom in amaranthine beauty under your feet, lest you stumble; looking, not behind, but forgetting the things that are behind, lest you be drawn back again; and looking forward and upward at Jesus; and, as you look at him, you will run with safety, with certainty, with speed, the race that is set before you in the Gospel."

Now, then, since looking at Jesus implies that we are to look to him for what will enable us to run that race, we are led naturally to inquire, what shall we look to Jesus for as strengthening and sustaining us in the race? First, we are to look to Jesus as the only atonement for our sins. Abel's blood — that first and illustrious witness — was shed, but that blood does not cleanse from any sin. We are to look to Jesus as the only atonement in heaven, on earth, or given among men, by which our sins can be blotted out. We need to look at this atonement every moment. The Israelite had his morning lamb as his morning sacrifice, and his evening lamb as his evening sacrifice; because every day had its sins needing to be forgiven. So must it be in this race. We need to look every minute to Jesus. We have a constant, daily sense of sin, fresh sin; and we cannot run the race with the burden, the conscious burden, of unforgiven sin. If we make the experiment, we shall stumble and fall; and, therefore, to run this race with safety, comfort, and hope of success, we must keep looking every moment, at every step, to that blood that cleanseth from all sin. It is true at every stage of our journey, "If we say we have no sin, we deceive ourselves;" but it is our consolation and our strength, at every step of the race, that, "If any man sin, we have an advocate with the Father," and, "If we confess our sins, he is faithful and just to forgive us our sins, and to cleanse us from all unrighteousness." Never let us forego that great truth — the atonement of Christ Jesus. Never let us forget the precious thought, that there, and there alone, we have — what at every stage, and every moment, we need — cleansing, forgiveness, pardon, through his blood.

In the second place, we are to look to Jesus, not only as the atonement, but as all our righteousness, and our only title to heaven. Some, perhaps, think that this is a distinction without a difference; because, it is argued, if our sins be forgiven, what else do we need? But, there are two things in man's fall: he not only deserves utter ruin by his sin, but he has forfeited the happiness that he once had. And before man can be restored, he needs his sin forgiven, that he may escape hell, and next, the title restored, that he may enter into heaven. Now, we must look to Jesus, not only as the atonement by which we have forgiveness, but as the righteousness which alone is our title to heaven. He suffered all that we deserve as sinners; he earned for us all that we have lost as creatures; by his blood we are delivered from condemnation; by his righteousness, imputed to us, and received by faith, we are entitled to heaven. He was delivered for our sins; he was raised for our justification: so that while I run that race, I look to Christ, and to no other on the right or on the left, behind or before, for the forgiveness of my sin, and for the title that, presented at the judgment-seat, will secure for me an admission into the realms of glory. Thus, we run the race, looking unto Jesus. Shut your eyes, or withdraw the eye, and look to something else for pardon and for righteousness, and that instant you fall, and, it may be, forever; but, if you keep your eyes fixed upon him, as the mariner keeps his upon the pole-star, your course will be clear, your path will be straight and onward, like the arrow to its mark.

We are to look at Christ in this race in another capacity; that of our great High Priest and Intercessor at God's right hand. Whilst Joshua was warring in the valley below, Moses was interceding and pleading on the mount. Whilst the disciples were tugging and toiling at the oar in the storm, Jesus was praying for them upon the hill-side. Surely it must be to the racer on this Christian course a most sustaining and strengthening thought, that he runs, labors, strives, but not in his own strength; for "Simon, Satan hath desired to have you, that he may sift you as wheat; but I have prayed for you that your faith fail not." To know, whilst we run, that we have sympathy in the skies, — that, whilst we are toiling, we have One interested in us, able, willing, mighty to save to the uttermost, — makes the roughest parts of the race-course become smooth, its darkest places shine in his light, the most desponding heart draw courage, and the weakest feel divine strength made perfect in its weakness. Does Satan accuse us? Christ has answered every accusation. Does a violated law proclaim its penalties? Christ has magnified it, and made it honorable. Does the law say, Do and live? Christ says, I have done it, and thou shalt live. Does Satan say of every racer on the course, Cut him down? Christ says, Spare him yet another year, if peradventure he may finish his course with joy. Do we fear we shall fall? Christ says, I will never leave thee; I will never forsake thee. Thus, while we run this race, let us look to Jesus as the only atonement, as the only righteousness; turn not to Abel, or to Enoch, or to Abraham, as our intercessor, but unto Jesus as ever living to make intercession for us.

Whilst we run this race, we are to look to Jesus as our king. He is not only our priest, but also our king. When we believe on Jesus, we believe on him just as he is set forth in the Gospel. Christ has two great offices united in him, never united in one before. The house of David had the royalty; the house of Aaron had the priesthood; but Christ combines in his person the royalty of David and the priesthood of Aaron. The house of Aaron and the house of David, the priest and the king, are both in Christ Jesus; and we cannot have a Saviour who is only a priest, nor can we have a Saviour who is only a king; we must have him in both capacities. As a priest, he expiates our guilt; as a priest, he extirpates our guilt; as a priest, he pardons sin; as a king, he governs the sinner. His priestly office relates to God; his kingly office relates to us. As a priest, he makes it possible for God to forgive us; as a king, he makes us long to accept forgiveness from God. As a priest, he restores us to the divine favor; as a king, he imprints on us the divine image. He makes us his property by his blood, for he is our priest; he keeps us his property by his sceptre, for he is our king. And thus Christ, as priest and king, — the priest-king, who sits and rules upon his throne, — is to be looked to by every Christian racer on the Christian race-course.

But we are to look to Jesus also as our prophet. We need not only expiation for our sins, and purification from their pollution; but we need here and there a little, line upon line and precept upon precept; and he is not only the way and the life, but the truth; he is not only our priest and our king, but our prophet; and in this character we look to him when we hear him speak to us in his promises, in his doctrines, in his holy word; we are to hear him as our great and infallible teacher, — not the opinions of divines, nor the decisions of synods, nor the voice of the church, nor the decision of the priest, — at least, if we hear these, we are to try them all by what Christ says. We are not to test Christ's word by man's, but man's word by Christ's. We are not to care what man says, but what Christ says. Our rule of faith must not be what the best men say, or what the most men say, or what the wisest men say; but what Christ, the prophet, speaks to his church. And "God, who at sundry times and in divers manners spake in time past unto the fathers by the prophets, hath in these last days spoken unto us by his Son;" and if again we were placed on the Mount of Transfiguration, and if Moses and Elijah were to appear in the splendors of that mount, the voice that would be emitted from it would still be, "Hear not Moses, hear not Elijah; this is my beloved Son; hear ye him." We are to run the race set before us, therefore, looking unto Jesus as our great prophet and teacher.

We are to run this race, looking unto Jesus as our great example also. Perhaps this is the great idea that is specially before us, looking to him as the model witness, as the great specimen of victory, of trial, affliction, and death. And I am satisfied of this, that, in Jesus, we shall find an example, perfect and complete, of all we wish to know, and of all we wish to see. Do I wish to know what his example teaches in reference to his own holy word? I think not the least precious part of the example of Christ, at least, the most striking, is his constant reference to his own word. I have often thought the most wonderful testimony to the greatness and perfection of this holy book, the Bible, is, that the Inspirer of it always referred to it when he was asked a question. When they asked him to solve a difficulty, he might have said, "I tell you, because I am the wisdom of God;" but he did not do so; he said, "How readest thou? What say the Scriptures? Have ye not read? Search the Scriptures; for these are they that testify of me." In other words, the Living Original referred the inquirer back to the infallible copy. What a testimony, then, to that blessed book, the Bible! We have not high enough opinions of it: we have skimmed its surface, and have talked of it; we have not descended into its depths, and fetched up the pure gold that lies embedded below the surface. And, what is not less striking is, that his own experience was always expressed in it. Some think the Psalms are not fit for Christian worship. I like many of Dr. Watts' hymns extremely; I like still more those of James Montgomery; and many of Newton's and Cowper's are very beautiful; but I would not give the Psalms for all the hymns that were ever written. I cannot conceive that these Psalms are unfit for our own worship, when the Son of God expressed his innermost experience in the words of the Psalms of David, "My God, why hast thou forsaken me?" and almost every fulfilment of a prophecy was the echo of a sentiment in the Psalms of David. When we run this race, let us look to Jesus, as an example for instruction and imitation in this, that he constantly referred to his own word.

Look to him also as an example of intercourse with the world. Jesus was in it, and not of it. When he went to the publican's table, it was not as a convivial guest, but as a missionary.

Look to Jesus, as an example, in his joys. His joy was nothing that this world can give; it was no flower that blooms upon any of this world's stalks. The joy set before him was seeing the travail of his soul, the salvation of sinners, the glory of God.

And his example in sorrow is beautiful. Jesus is never said to have smiled, but he is said very often to have wept; truly he was the Man of sorrows. We are not called to weep as he wept. He bore our burden; our curse was upon him; and a long and a heavy way was his; and he suffered that we might rejoice. But still his human sorrow was not from what he suffered, but it was from seeing what sin had done. When he gazed upon Jerusalem, and wept over it, it was because Jerusalem had not known in this her day the things that pertained to her peace.

Let us study the whole character of Jesus as an example; and I think this alone must be sufficient to convince the sceptic. It would be supposing a miracle to imagine that Christ was the production of the age that he lived in; it requires very simple faith to allow that he was a divine being. Even sceptics have admitted that the example of Christ was the most perfect thing that was ever presented. We have all heard of Rousseau, the greatest sceptic of his day. Now, what does he say? "I will confess to you," — this is a man who had no faith in Christianity at all, — "I will confess to you that the majesty of the Scriptures strikes me with admiration, as the purity of the Gospel hath its influence on my heart. Peruse the works of our philosophers, with all their pomp of diction; how mean, how contemptible are they, compared with the Scriptures! Is it possible that a book at once so simple and sublime should be merely the work of man? Is it possible that the sacred personage, whose history it contains, should be himself a mere man? Do we find that he assumed the tone of an enthusiast, or ambitious sectary? What sweetness, what purity, in his manner! What an affecting gracefulness in his delivery! What sublimity in his maxims! What profound wisdom in his discourses! What presence of mind, what subtlety, what truth, in his replies! How great the command over his passions! Where is the man, where the philosopher, who could so live, and so die, without weakness and without ostentation? When Plato describes his imaginary good man, loaded with all the punishments of guilt, yet meriting the highest rewards of virtue, he describes exactly the character of Jesus Christ; the resemblance was so striking that all the fathers perceived it. What prepossession, what blindness must it be, to compare the son of Sophroniscus to the Son of Mary! What an infinite disproportion there is between them! Socrates, dying without pain or ignominy, easily supported his character to the last; and if his death, however easy, had not crowned his life, it might have been doubted whether Socrates, with all his wisdom, was anything more than a mere sophist. He invented, it is said, the theory of morals. Others, however, had before put them in practice; he had only to say, therefore, what they had done, and to reduce their examples to precepts. Aristides had been just before Socrates defined justice; Leonidas had given up his life for his country before Socrates declared patriotism to be a duty; the Spartans were a sober people before Socrates recommended sobriety; before he had even defined virtue, Greece abounded in virtuous men. But where could Jesus learn, among his contemporaries, that pure and sublime morality of which he only hath given us both precept and example? The greatest wisdom was made known amongst the most bigoted fanaticism, and simplicity of the most heroic virtues did honor to the vilest people on earth. The death of Socrates, peaceably philosophizing with his friends, appears the most agreeable that could be wished for; that of Jesus, expiring in the midst of agonizing pains, abused, insulted, and accused by a whole nation, is the most horrible that could be feared. Socrates, in receiving the cup of poison, blessed, indeed, the weeping executioner who administered it; but Jesus, in the midst of excruciating tortures, prayed for his merciless tormentors. Yes, if the life and death of Socrates were those of a sage, the life and death of Jesus are those of a God." What an admission from a sceptic! "Shall we suppose the evangelical history a mere fiction? Indeed, my friend, it bears not the marks of fiction; on the contrary, the history of Socrates, which nobody presumes to doubt, is not so well attested as that of Jesus Christ. Such a supposition, in fact, only shifts the difficulty, without obviating it; it is more inconceivable that a number of persons should agree to write such a history than that one should furnish the subject of it. The Jewish authors were incapable of the diction, and strangers to the morality, contained in the Gospel; the marks of whose truth are so striking and inimitable, that the inventor would be a more astonishing character than the hero." And yet, after all this, the man died, as he had lived, an unbeliever! But such a testimony, from such lips, emanating from such a heart, must be the extracted acknowledgment of a deep and an irrepressible conviction, let forth to be of use to us as a testimony in other ages. Thus we are to run the race set before us, looking unto this perfect example of Jesus.

But especially are we to look to him as "the author and finisher of our faith." Here is Christ having all the glory of the issue of this course. He is the author of our faith. The first seed of grace is dropped into the heart by his hand; the heart is prepared by his Holy Spirit to receive that grace. He sets us in the course; he keeps us in the course; he guides us to the end of the course; he gives us the first movement; he crowns us at the last moment. Jesus calls us before we answer, inspires us before we move. We do not spontaneously go to him first; he, in his sovereign love, touches us first. We love him, because he loves us; we follow, because he draws; we obey, because he commands; we answer, because he invites. In other words, he is the author of our faith. Christianity, embodied in the character of man, is a response to the summons of Jesus. But he is not only the author, he is also described here as "the finisher of our faith." He finishes what he begins; he begins what he finishes. He takes to himself the glory; he gives to us the prize, the honor, and the issue of it. He laid the foundation of our faith in his blood; he keeps the faith in us, and us in the faith, by his Spirit; and he develops that faith into full fruition when the race is run, and the course is finished, and the journey is over.

This will brighten life's dark spots, and sweeten and sanctify its bright spots. Afflictions will become beautiful in the light of his countenance; and the rays of his glory, stricken through the sorest trial, will make us sing in the midst of it, and say, before it is finished, "It is good for me that I have been afflicted." When we see death approach to undo the silver cord, to break the golden bowl at its fountain, the invader will present a very different aspect, seen in the light of the countenance of Jesus, from what he does as seen by strangers to the cross; he will come a consecrated servant from Christ the master, to relieve us from running, doing, laboring, and to introduce us into that rest where there is fulness of joy.

In all time of our tribulation, in all time of our wealth, in the hour of death, and in the day of judgment, let us look to Jesus. When the human heart grows faint, and the human arm grows weary, and the strong men bow themselves, and the grasshopper is felt to be a burden, still look to Jesus. When the last pulse quivers at the wrist, and the last beat hesitates and trembles in the heart, — when skill has no more resources, and life has no more stages,— look exclusively to one, and that one — Jesus!

www.ingramcontent.com/pod-product-compliance
Lightning Source LLC
LaVergne TN
LVHW010212110826
845151LV00004B/1062

* 9 7 8 1 4 2 5 5 2 9 3 6 9 *